The North American Fourth Edition

Cambridge Latin Course

Unit 2

REVISION TEAM

Stephanie Pope, Chair
Norfolk Academy, Norfolk, Virginia

Patricia E. Bell
Centennial Collegiate and Vocational Institute, Guelph, Ontario

Stan Farrow
Formerly of the David and Mary Thomson Collegiate Institute,
Scarborough, Ontario

Richard M. Popeck
Stuarts Draft High School, Stuarts Draft, Virginia

Anne Shaw
Lawrence High School and Lawrence Free State High School,
Lawrence, Kansas

CAMBRIDGE
UNIVERSITY PRESS

CAMBRIDGE UNIVERSITY PRESS
Cambridge, New York, Melbourne, Madrid, Cape Town, Singapore, São Paulo, Delhi

Cambridge University Press
32 Avenue of the Americas, New York NY 10013-2473, USA

www.cambridge.org
Information on this title: www.cambridge.org/9780521779951

The *Cambridge Latin Course* is an outcome of work jointly commissioned by the Schools Council before its closure and the Cambridge School Classics Project, and is published under the aegis of the University of Cambridge School Classics Project in the UK and the North American Cambridge Classics Project.

First published 1970
Fourth edition 2001; course updated by addition of DVDs 2009

Printed in the United States of America

Library of Congress Cataloging-in-Publication Data
Cambridge Latin course. Unit 2 / revision team, Stephanie Pope ... [et al.]. -- North American 4th ed., updated 2009
    p. cm.
    Includes index.
    ISBN 978-0-521-76999-0 (hardcover) -- ISBN 978-0-521-77995-1 (softcover)
    1. Latin language--Grammar--Problems, exercises, etc.   2. Latin language--Readers.
I. Pope, Stephanie M.

    PA2087.5.C33 2009
    478.82'421--dc22

                                                                                    2009001077

ISBN 978-0-521-76999-0 hardback
ISBN 978-0-521-77995-1 paperback

ACKNOWLEDGMENTS
Layout by Newton Harris Design Partnership
Cover photographs: *front* "Gayer-Anderson" cat © The Trustees of the British Museum, mosaic from Fishbourne Roman Palace, photograph by Roger Dalladay; *back* mosaic of a merchant ship, photograph by Roger Dalladay
Maps and plans by Robert Calow / Eikon
Illustrations by Peter Kesteven, Joy Mellor, and Leslie Jones

Contents

IN MEMORIAM

Ed Phinney

1935–1996

IN BRITANNIA

Stage 13

1 hic vir est Gāius Salvius Līberālis.
  Salvius in vīllā magnificā habitat.
  vīlla est in Britanniā.
  Salvius multōs servōs habet.

2 uxor est Rūfilla.
  Rūfilla multās ancillās habet.
  ancillae in vīllā labōrant.

3 hic servus est Vārica.
  Vārica est vīlicus.
  vīllam et servōs cūrat.

4 hic servus est Philus.
   Philus callidus est.
   Philus numerāre potest.

5 hic servus est Volūbilis.
   Volūbilis coquus optimus est.
   Volūbilis cēnam optimam
   coquere potest.

6 hic servus est Bregāns.
   Bregāns nōn callidus est.
   Bregāns numerāre nōn potest.
   Bregāns fessus est.
   Bregāns dormīre vult.

7 hic servus est Loquāx.
   Loquāx vōcem suāvem habet.
   Loquāx suāviter cantāre potest.

8 hic servus est Anti-Loquāx.
   Anti-Loquāx agilis est.
   Anti-Loquāx optimē saltāre potest.
   Loquāx et Anti-Loquāx sunt geminī.

9 Salvius multōs servōs habet.
   servī labōrant.
   servī ignāvī et fessī sunt.
   servī labōrāre nōlunt.

trēs servī

trēs servī in vīllā labōrant. haec vīlla est in Britanniā. servī dīligenter labōrant, quod dominum exspectant. servī vītam dūram dēplōrant.

Philus:	*(pecūniam numerat.)* iterum pluit! semper pluit! nōs sōlem numquam vidēmus. ego ad Ītaliam redīre volō. ego sōlem vidēre volō. *5*
Volūbilis:	*(cēnam in culīnā parat.)* ubi est vīnum? nūllum vīnum videō. quis hausit? ego aquam bibere nōn possum! aqua est foeda!
Bregāns:	*(pavīmentum lavat.)* ego labōrāre nōlō! fessus sum. multum vīnum bibī. ego dormīre volō. *10*
	(Vārica subitō vīllam intrat. Vārica est vīlicus.)
Vārica:	servī! dominus noster īrātus advenit! apud Cantiacōs servī coniūrātiōnem fēcērunt. dominus est vulnerātus.
Bregāns:	nōs dē hāc coniūrātiōne audīre volumus. rem nārrā! *15*

Britanniā:		**lavat: lavāre**	*wash*
Britannia	*Britain*	**labōrāre nōlō**	*I do not want to work*
dūram: dūrus	*harsh, hard*		
dēplōrant:		**fessus**	*tired*
dēplōrāre	*complain about*	**advenit: advenīre**	*arrive*
pluit	*it is raining*	**apud Cantiacōs**	*among the Cantiaci*
sōlem: sōl	*sun*		*(a British tribe)*
Ītaliam: Ītalia	*Italy*	**coniūrātiōnem:**	
redīre volō	*I want to return*	**coniūrātiō**	*plot*
aquam: aqua	*water*	**vulnerātus**	*wounded*
bibere nōn			
possum	*I cannot drink*		
foeda	*foul, horrible*		
pavīmentum	*floor*		

Slave chains.

A neck-chain being worn by volunteers.

Clues to a Roman Mine

Salvius had visited the Cantiaci to inspect an iron mine. The site of one of these mines has been found in southern Britain.

Quantities of slag (waste from extracting the iron) have been found at the site. In the 19th century 225,000 tons (100,000 tonnes) of it were removed from the site and used for road building.

Rusty water at the site shows that there is iron in the ground.

The stamp on a tile shows that the mine was run by the Roman fleet (CLBR stands for classis Britannica).

coniūrātiō

Vārica rem nārrāvit:

"nōs apud Cantiacōs erāmus, quod Salvius metallum novum vīsitābat. hospes noster erat Pompēius Optātus, vir benignus. in metallō labōrābant multī servī. quamquam servī multum ferrum ē terrā effodiēbant, Salvius nōn erat contentus. Salvius servōs ad sē 5 vocāvit et īnspexit. ūnus servus aeger erat. Salvius servum aegrum ex ōrdinibus trāxit et clāmāvit,

"'servus aeger est inūtilis. ego servōs inūtilēs retinēre nōlō.'

"postquam hoc dīxit, Salvius carnificibus servum trādidit. carnificēs eum statim interfēcērunt. 10

"hic servus tamen fīlium habēbat; nōmen erat Alātor. Alātor patrem suum vindicāre voluit. itaque, ubi cēterī dormiēbant, Alātor pugiōnem cēpit. postquam custōdēs ēlūsit, cubiculum intrāvit. in hōc cubiculō Salvius dormiēbat. tum Alātor dominum nostrum petīvit et vulnerāvit. dominus noster erat perterritus; 15 manūs ad servum extendit et veniam petīvit. custōdēs tamen sonōs audīvērunt. in cubiculum ruērunt et Alātōrem audācem interfēcērunt.

metallum	a mine
hospes	host
quamquam	although
ferrum	iron
effodiēbant: effodere	dig
ad sē	to him
ex ōrdinibus	from the rows
inūtilis	useless
carnificibus: carnifex	executioner
nōmen	name
vindicāre voluit	wanted to avenge
itaque	and so
ubi	when
cēterī	the others
pugiōnem: pugiō	dagger
custōdēs: custōs	guard
ēlūsit: ēlūdere	slip past
manūs ... extendit	stretched out his hands
veniam petīvit	begged for mercy
audācem: audāx	daring, bold

"tum Salvius saeviēbat. statim hospitem, Pompēium, excitāvit et īrātus clāmāvit,   *20*

"'servus mē vulnerāvit! coniūrātiō est! omnēs servī sunt cōnsciī. ego omnibus supplicium poscō!'

"Pompēius, postquam hoc audīvit, erat attonitus.

"'ego omnēs servōs interficere nōn possum. ūnus tē vulnerāvit. ūnus igitur est nocēns, cēterī innocentēs.'   *25*

"'custōdēs nōn sunt innocentēs,' inquit Salvius. 'cum Alātōre coniūrābant.'

"Pompēius invītus cōnsēnsit et carnificibus omnēs custōdēs trādidit."

saeviēbat: saevīre	*be in a rage*
cōnsciī: cōnscius	*accomplice*
supplicium	*death penalty*
poscō: poscere	*demand*
nocēns	*guilty*
innocentēs: innocēns	*innocent*
coniūrābant: coniūrāre	*plot*
invītus	*unwilling, reluctant*

Bregāns

When you have read this story, answer the questions on page 10.

tum Vārica, postquam hanc rem nārrāvit, clāmāvit,

"Loquāx! Anti-Loquāx! dominus advenit. vocāte servōs in āream! ego eōs īnspicere volō."

servī ad āream celeriter cucurrērunt, quod Salvium timēbant. servī in ōrdinēs longōs sē īnstrūxērunt. vīlicus per ōrdinēs   *5* ambulābat; servōs īnspiciēbat et numerābat. subitō exclāmāvit,

"ubi sunt ancillae? nūllās ancillās videō."

"ancillae dominō nostrō cubiculum parant," respondit Loquāx.

"ubi est coquus noster?" inquit Vārica. "ego Volūbilem vidēre nōn possum."   *10*

"Volūbilis venīre nōn potest, quod cēnam parat," respondit Anti-Loquāx.

Bregāns mediīs in servīs stābat; canem ingentem sēcum habēbat.

"ecce, Vārica! rēx Cogidubnus dominō nostrō hunc canem   *15* mīsit," inquit Bregāns. "canis ferōcissimus est; bēstiās optimē agitāre potest."

subitō vīgintī equitēs āream intrāvērunt. prīmus erat Salvius. postquam ex equō dēscendit, Vāricam salūtāvit.

"servōs īnspicere volō," inquit Salvius. tum Salvius et Vārica per ōrdinēs ambulābant. *20*

puerī puellaeque in prīmō ōrdine stābant et dominum suum salūtābant. cum puerīs stābant geminī.

"salvē, domine!" inquit Loquāx.

"salvē, domine!" inquit Anti-Loquāx. *25*

Bregāns, simulac Salvium vīdit, "domine! domine!" clāmāvit. Salvius servō nihil respondit. Bregāns iterum clāmāvit, "Salvī! Salvī! spectā canem!"

Salvius saeviēbat, quod servus erat īnsolēns.

"servus īnsolentissimus es," inquit Salvius. Bregantem ferōciter *30* pulsāvit. Bregāns ad terram dēcidit. canis statim ex ōrdine ērūpit et Salvium petīvit. nōnnūllī servī ex ōrdinibus ērūpērunt et canem retraxērunt. Salvius, postquam sē recēpit, gladium dēstrīnxit.

"istum canem interficere volō," inquit Salvius.

"hoc difficile est," inquit Bregāns. "rēx Cogidubnus, amīcus *35* tuus, tibi canem dedit."

"ita vērō, difficile est," respondit Salvius. "sed ego tē pūnīre possum. illud facile est, quod servus meus es."

in āream	*into the courtyard*
sē īnstrūxērunt: sē īnstruere	*draw oneself up*
per ōrdinēs	*along the rows*
sēcum	*with him*
rēx	*king*
Cogidubnus	*Cogidubnus (British ally of the Romans, appointed king under Emperor Claudius)*
equitēs: eques	*horseman*
equō: equus	*horse*
puerī puellaeque	*the boys and girls*
geminī	*twins*
simulac	*as soon as*
īnsolēns	*rude, insolent*
ērūpit: ērumpere	*break away*
nōnnūllī	*some, several*
retraxērunt: retrahere	*drag back*
sē recēpit: sē recipere	*recover*
pūnīre	*punish*
illud	*that*
facile	*easy*

Questions

1 Why did Varica want to inspect the slaves? What did he tell the twins to do (lines 2–3)?
2 In line 4 which two Latin words show that the slaves were in a hurry? Why did they hurry?
3 In lines 8–11 why were the slave-girls and Volubilis missing from the inspection?
4 **canem ingentem sēcum habēbat** (lines 13–14). What did Bregans say about this dog (lines 15–17)?
5 Salvius was an important Roman official. How do lines 18–19 show this? Give two details.
6 How did Salvius react in lines 28 and 29 when Bregans called out to him? Why do you think Salvius called Bregans **insolentissimus** (line 30)?
7 What happened to Bregans after Salvius hit him?
8 How did the dog nearly cause a disaster (lines 31–32)?
9 Who saved the situation? What did they do?
10 **Salvius ... gladium dēstrīnxit** (line 33). What did Salvius want to do? Why did he change his mind?
11 **ego tē pūnīre possum** (lines 37–38). Why do you think Salvius is or is not likely to carry out this threat?
12 What impression of Bregans do you get from this story and why?

British hunting dogs were prized all over the world. One is shown here on a Romano-British cup.

Mosaic of a hunting dog.

About the Language I: Infinitives

A Study the following pairs of sentences:

Loquāx cantat.
Loquax is singing.

Loquāx **cantāre** vult.
*Loquax wants **to sing**.*

servī dominum vident.
The slaves see the master.

servī dominum **vidēre** nōlunt.
*The slaves do not want **to see** the master.*

puerī currunt.
The boys are running.

puerī celeriter **currere** possunt.
*The boys are able **to run** quickly.*

Salvius Bregantem pūnit.
Salvius punishes Bregans.

Salvius Bregantem **pūnīre** potest.
*Salvius is able **to punish** Bregans.*

The form of the verb in boldface is known as the **infinitive**. It usually ends in **-re**.

B Translate the following examples and write down the Latin infinitive in each sentence:

1 Anti-Loquāx currit. Anti-Loquāx currere potest.
2 Bregāns labōrat. Bregāns labōrāre nōn vult.
3 geminī fābulam audīre volunt.
4 puerī festīnāre nōn possunt.

C Verbs, like nouns, belong to families. Verb families are called **conjugations**. The vowel that precedes the **-re** of the infinitive determines the conjugation to which the verb belongs.

For example:
First Conjugation   cantāre
Second Conjugation   vidēre
Third Conjugation   currere
Fourth Conjugation   pūnīre

To which conjugation do the following verbs belong?

1 dūcere   5 festīnāre
2 dormīre   6 manēre
3 postulāre   7 audīre
4 habēre   8 facere

D The verbs **volō**, **nōlō**, and **possum** are often used with an infinitive. Each forms its present tense as follows:

(ego)	volō	*I want*	(ego)	nōlō	*I do not want*
(tū)	vīs	*you (s.) want*	(tū)	nōn vīs	*you (s.) do not want*
	vult	*s/he wants*		nōn vult	*s/he does not want*
(nōs)	volumus	*we want*	(nōs)	nōlumus	*we do not want*
(vōs)	vultis	*you (pl.) want*	(vōs)	nōn vultis	*you (pl.) do not want*
	volunt	*they want*		nōlunt	*they do not want*

(ego)	possum	*I am able*
(tū)	potes	*you (s.) are able*
	potest	*s/he is able*
(nōs)	possumus	*we are able*
(vōs)	potestis	*you (pl.) are able*
	possunt	*they are able*

E **possum**, **potes**, etc. can also be translated as "I can," "you can," etc.:

nōs dormīre nōn possumus.   *We are not able to sleep or We cannot sleep.*

ego leōnem interficere possum.   *I am able to kill the lion or I can kill the lion.*

F Further examples:

1 ego pugnāre possum.
2 nōs effugere nōn possumus.
3 tū labōrāre nōn vīs.
4 coquus cēnam optimam parāre potest.
5 celeriter currere potestis.
6 in vīllā manēre nōlō.
7 labōrāre nōlunt.
8 vīnum bibere volumus.

Salvius fundum īnspicit

postrīdiē Salvius fundum īnspicere voluit. Vārica igitur eum per fundum dūxit. vīlicus dominō agrōs et segetem ostendit.

"seges est optima, domine," inquit Vārica. "servī multum frūmentum in horreum iam intulērunt."

Salvius, postquam agrōs circumspectāvit, Vāricae dīxit,   5

"ubi sunt arātōrēs et magister? nōnne Cervīx arātōribus praeest?"

"ita vērō, domine!" respondit Vārica. "sed arātōrēs hodiē nōn labōrant, quod Cervīx abest. aeger est."

Salvius eī respondit, "quid dīxistī? aeger est? ego servum   10
aegrum retinēre nōlō."

"sed Cervīx perītissimus est," exclāmāvit vīlicus. "Cervīx sōlus rem rūsticam cūrāre potest."

"tacē!" inquit Salvius. "eum vēndere volō."

simulatque hoc dīxit, duōs servōs vīdit. servī ad horreum   15
festīnābant.

"quid faciunt hī servī?" rogāvit Salvius.

"hī servī arātōribus cibum ferunt, domine. placetne tibi?" respondit Vārica.

agrōs: ager	*field*
segetem: seges	*crop, harvest*
frūmentum	*grain*
horreum	*barn, granary*
intulērunt: īnferre	*bring in*
arātōrēs: arātor	*plowman*
magister	*foreman*
nōnne	*surely*
praeest: praeesse	*be in charge of*
eī	*to him*
perītissimus: perītus	*skillful*
sōlus	*alone, only*
rem rūsticam: res rūstica	*the farming*
cūrāre	*look after, supervise*
simulatque	*as soon as*
hī	*these*
ferunt: ferre	*bring*

"mihi nōn placet!" inquit Salvius. "ego servīs ignāvīs nūllum   *20*
cibum dō."

tum dominus et vīlicus ad horreum prōcessērunt. Salvius tamen
duo aedificia vīdit. ūnum aedificium erat sēmirutum.

"quid est hoc aedificium?" inquit Salvius.

"horreum novum est, domine!" respondit vīlicus. "alterum ·   *25*
horreum iam plēnum est. ego igitur horreum novum aedificāre
voluī."

"sed cūr sēmirutum est?" inquit Salvius.

Vārica respondit, "ubi servī horreum aedificābant, domine, rēs
dīra accidit. taurus, animal ferōx, impetum in hoc aedificium fēcit.   *30*
mūrōs dēlēvit et servōs terruit."

"quis taurum dūcēbat?" inquit Salvius. "quis fuit neglegēns?"
"Bregāns!"

"ēheu!" inquit Salvius. "ego Britannīs nōn crēdō. omnēs
Britannī sunt stultī, sed iste Bregāns est stultior quam cēterī!"   *35*

ignāvīs: ignāvus	*lazy*	**impetum: impetus**	*attack*
aedificia: aedificium	*building*	**fuit**	*has been*
dīra ·	*dreadful, awful*	**neglegēns**	*careless*
taurus	*bull*	**Britannīs: Britannī**	*Britons*
animal	*animal*		

About the Language II: -que

A In this Stage, you have met a new way of saying "and" in Latin:

puerī puellae**que**   *boys and girls*

Note that -**que** is added on to the end of the second word.

B -**que** can also be used to link sentences together:

dominus ex equō dēscendit vīllam**que** intrāvit.
The master got off his horse and went into the house.

Further examples:

1 Vārica servōs ancillāsque īnspexit.
2 Bregāns canisque in ōrdine stābant.
3 Salvius āream intrāvit Vāricamque salūtāvit.

Practicing the Language

A Complete each sentence of this exercise with the most suitable infinitive from the box below. Then translate the whole sentence. Do not use any infinitive more than once.

> īnspicere   numerāre
> manēre   dormīre
> labōrāre   bibere

1 Philus est callidus. Philus pecūniam . . . . . potest.
2 Loquāx et Anti-Loquāx sunt fessī. puerī . . . . . volunt.
3 Salvius est dominus. Salvius servōs et fundum . . . . . vult.
4 Cervīx est aeger. Cervīx . . . . . nōn potest.
5 Volūbilis laetus nōn est. Volūbilis aquam . . . . . nōn vult.
6 servī contentī nōn sunt. servī in vīllā . . . . . nōlunt.

B Complete each sentence with the correct form of the noun. Then translate each sentence.

1 (agricola, agricolae) in fundō labōrābat.
2 (custōs, custōdēs) fūrem nōn vīdērunt.
3 (servus, servī) epistulās longās scrībēbant.
4 cūr (canis, canēs) prope iānuam lātrābat?
5 (senex, senēs), quod multam pecūniam habēbat, vīllam magnificam aedificāvit.
6 (amīcus, amīcī), postquam in forō convēnērunt, ad tabernam contendērunt.

C Fill in the gaps in this story with the most suitable verb from the box below, and then translate the whole story. Do not use any word more than once.

cōnspexī	pulsāvī	vituperāvī	obdormīvī	fūgī
cōnspexistī	pulsāvistī	vituperāvistī	obdormīvistī	fūgistī
cōnspexit	pulsāvit	vituperāvit	obdormīvit	fūgit

servus in cubiculō labōrābat. servus, quod erat fessus, in cubiculō . . . . . . Salvius, postquam cubiculum intrāvit, servum . . . . . . ; statim fūstem cēpit et servum . . . . . .

Rūfilla, quod clāmōrēs audīvit, in cubiculum ruit.

Rūfilla: tū es dominus dūrus! cūr tū servum . . . . . ?
Salvius: ego servum . . . . . , quod in cubiculō dormiēbat.
Rūfilla: heri, tū ancillam meam . . . . . , quod neglegēns erat. ancilla perterrita erat, et ē vīllā . . . . . .
Salvius: in vīllā meā ego sum dominus. ego ancillam . . . . . , quod ignāva erat.

D Copy the following exercise onto your own paper. For each number you will need to cross out the words in the given case, and then translate the resulting sentence. For example, if "dative singular" is listed after the number, then you will cross out every word in the dative singular.

1 **accusative singular**: ignāvum custōdem custōdēs innocentēs mē arātōrem innocentem eam nūllum interficere aedificium nōlumus
2 **dative singular**: Salviō servō Salvius servum neglegentī ignāvō coniūrātiōnī neglegentem mihi tibi pūnīre potest
3 **accusative plural**: arātōrī cēterōs vōs aegrō ferōcēs vītās cibum custōdēs dare novōs nōs nōlunt
4 **dative plural**: fessīs hospitibus Bregāns vōbīs dominīs canibus novīs canem arātōribus ostendere aegrīs vult
5 **accusative singular and dative plural**: vīlicus vīlicum vōbīs servōs cēterīs servīs servum ferrum nōbīs eum geminīs īnspiciēbat
6 **dative singular and accusative plural**: vōs servī tibi segetēs ferrum novō aedificiō ē terrā omnēs effodere vītās possunt

Britannia

... the spine-chilling sea and the Britons at the very
end of the earth.

Catullus

The population of the island is countless. Houses
rather like those in Gaul are to be seen everywhere
and there are enormous numbers of cattle. They use
either bronze or gold coinage.

Julius Caesar

Although the Romans thought of Britannia as a strange and distant land
at the very edge of the known world, the island had its own highly
developed civilization before the Romans arrived. We know from
archaeological evidence that the Britons or Celts were very good
metalworkers, carpenters, weavers, and farmers. They exported grain,
cattle, gold, silver, iron, hides, hunting dogs, and slaves. The Roman
concept of civilization was essentially urban-centered. The Celts were
tribal, agricultural peoples and Britannia primarily a rural province.
Therefore Romans, writing about the Britons, did not usually recognize
the Celtic achievements.

Celtic bronze hand mirror.

*The discovery of coins
everywhere indicates that this
was no longer a barter economy.*

*Bronze and enamel
ornament from a horse
harness, showing the
artistry of British
craftsmen.*

The Romans who conquered: Julius Caesar (left) and the Emperor Claudius (right).

The British Tribes

When the Romans invaded Britain, they had to fight against many separate Celtic tribes. These tribes had certain things in common. They all spoke the Celtic language (the basis of Welsh, Irish, and Gaelic today); they used weapons of iron; they were ruled by kings or queens advised by a council of warriors. A chieftain was a wealthy landowner who controlled a small area and owed his loyalty to a king or queen. Most chieftains maintained a band of warriors who practiced their fighting skills by hunting wild animals and raiding settlements belonging to other tribes.

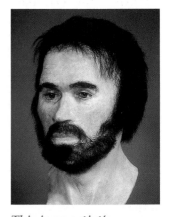

This is an artist's reconstruction of the head of a man whose body was found preserved in a peat bog.

Celtic art was characterized by abstract rhythmic patterns, spiral curves, and stylized imaginary animals. Most Celtic art has been found decorating everyday objects made of pottery and various metals.

Celtic religion was in the hands of the Druids. These were powerful priests who acted as judges in disputes, kept the oral traditions and knowledge of the tribe, and worshiped the gods in sacred woodlands with ceremonies that sometimes included human sacrifice. They encouraged fierce British resistance to the Roman invasion.

The Roman Conquest

The first Roman general to lead his soldiers into Britain was Julius Caesar, in 55 B.C. Caesar wrote an account of his visit to Britain, in which he described the inhabitants as fierce warriors, living on good agricultural or pasture land, in a country rich in timber and minerals. Their skills included not only farming but also making pottery and working with iron and bronze.

Caesar wanted to find out whether the wealth of Britain was worth the trouble of occupying it with Roman troops. But after another short visit in 54 B.C., he did not explore any further. His attention was diverted to wars elsewhere, first against the Gauls and then against his own Roman government. Ten years later, he was assassinated.

Caesar's great-nephew, Augustus, became the first Roman emperor. He and his immediate successors did not consider Britain to be worth the trouble of conquering. But in A.D. 43 the Emperor Claudius decided to invade. Perhaps he had received fresh information about British wealth; more probably he needed some military success for his own prestige. Claudius did not lead the invasion force himself, but he followed it, spending sixteen days in Britain, watching his army's assault on Camulodunum (Colchester) and giving official approval to the actions of his commander, Aulus Plautius.

Eleven British kings surrendered after this campaign, and Britain was declared a Roman province, with Aulus Plautius as its first governor. This meant that the Romans were taking over the country as part of their

Claudius built a triumphal arch at Rome to celebrate the capture of Britain. Part of the inscription survives.

Aulus Plautius' men dug these ditches to defend their camp at Richborough. The fortifications were added later, in the third century A.D.

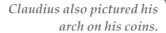

Claudius also pictured his arch on his coins.

The Romans set up cities in Britain, with forums and temples. This is a model of the temple of the deified Emperor Claudius at Camulodunum.

empire. From then on, Roman officials would enforce Roman law and collect Roman taxes. Romans would be able to buy land in Britain and use it for agriculture or mining. The Roman army, fed by an annual tribute in grain and hogs, would be present to keep the peace in the province, firmly and sometimes brutally.

The stories in Stages 13 to 16 are set in the time of Britain's most famous governor, Gnaeus Julius Agricola. Agricola stayed in the province for seven years (A.D. 78–85). He led his army into the Scottish highlands where he built a number of forts, some of which are still being discovered by aerial photography. He effectively put an end to Scottish resistance in A.D. 84 at the battle of Mons Graupius in Scotland.

Romanization

Agricola's mission in Britain was not just military victory. Agricola also stopped civic corruption and abuses in tax collection. In addition, according to his son-in-law, the historian Tacitus, Agricola "wanted to accustom the Britons to a life of peace, by providing them with the comforts of civilization. He gave personal encouragement and official aid to the building of temples, forums, and houses. He educated the sons of the chiefs … so that instead of hating the Latin language, they were eager to speak it well."

In Stage 14 we will see how some British farmers began to build country villas in the Roman style. Towns, too, built or rebuilt on the

Roman road (Watling Street) still in use in Britain.

Roman grid system, were centered about a forum, with its town hall and law court, and included other public buildings such as public baths, temples, theaters, and amphitheaters. The Romans were remarkably tolerant of religions differing from their own and many Celtic gods were given classical clothing and symbols and assimilated into the Roman pantheon: Apollo-Maponus, Mars-Cocidius, Sulis-Minerva.

Latin became the vehicle of all official business, of law, and of commerce. Gradually, a network of new roads spread across the province. The roads were originally built for the use of Roman soldiers, but before long they were being extensively used by merchants as well. Trade between Britain and the continent of Europe increased rapidly. British pottery works began to imitate Roman bronzeware and earthenware. Roman peace and security promoted the interchange of ideas, material wealth, and new elegance and comfort.

Some Britons became very wealthy from trade and welcomed the Romans enthusiastically; many of the leading families responded to Agricola's encouragement to adopt a Roman lifestyle. Other Britons suffered severely from the arrival of the Romans; others again were hardly affected at all. Many no doubt had mixed feelings about becoming part of the Roman empire. It gave them a share in Roman prosperity and the Roman way of life, but it also meant Roman taxes and a Roman governor backed by Roman troops. However, whether welcome or unwelcome, the Romans were to remain in Britain for nearly four hundred years.

Britain in the first century A.D.

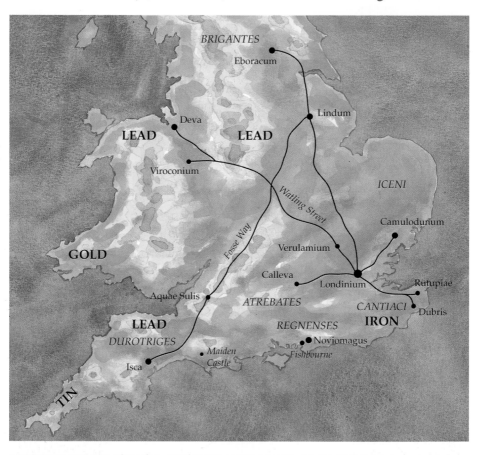

BRIGANTES
Eboracum
Lindum
Deva
LEAD   **LEAD**
Viroconium
ICENI
Camulodunum
Watling Street
Fosse Way
Verulamium
GOLD
Calleva
Londinium
Rutupiae
Aquae Sulis
ATREBATES
CANTIACI
Dubris
LEAD
REGNENSES
IRON
DUROTRIGES
Noviomagus
Maiden
Castle
Fishbourne
Isca
TIN

Imports and Exports

Among the items exported from Britain in Roman times were grain, hunting dogs, and metals: iron, gold, tin, and lead. In return, Britain imported wine, oil, and other goods from Rome and the rest of the empire.

A lead miner.

Jars of imported wine buried with a wealthy Briton who lived before the Roman conquest.

Important Events and Dates

Emperor	Year	Event
	B.C.	
	55–54	Julius Caesar's expeditions to Britain.
	44	*Caesar assassinated.*
Augustus	27	*The first emperor.*
	A.D.	
Tiberius	14	
Gaius (Caligula)	37	
Claudius	41	
	43	Invasion of Britain under Aulus Plautius. Claudius enters Colchester in triumph. Vespasian's expedition against the Durotriges. Britain becomes a Roman province.
	51	Defeat of Caratacus in Wales.
Nero	54	
	60/61	Revolt of Boudica in East Anglia.
Vespasian	69	*Civil war in Italy.*
	75	The building of Fishbourne palace begins.
	78	Agricola comes to Britain as Governor.
Titus	79	*Eruption of Vesuvius.*
	80	Agricola's Scottish campaigns begin.
Domitian	81	Salvius is sent to Britain.
	84	Battle of Mons Graupius.
Honorius		
	410	Romans cease to defend Britain.

Salvius

Gaius Salvius Liberalis was born in central Italy but, like many ambitious and clever young men, he soon moved to Rome, where he gained a reputation for speaking his mind. After becoming a successful lawyer, he was made a Roman senator, probably by the Emperor Vespasian. In A.D. 78, at a very early age, he was chosen as one of the Arval brotherhood, a group of twelve distinguished men who met to perform religious ceremonies and in particular to pray for the emperor and his family. Salvius was also put in command of a legion; not only was this a great honor, but it also could lead to further honors in the future. Not long afterwards (that is, about 40 years after the Roman occupation), in about A.D. 81, Salvius was sent to help Agricola, the Roman governor of the province of Britain.

Salvius' main task was probably to supervise the law courts and look after the southern part of the province while Agricola was away fighting in the north. He would have traveled around the country acting as a judge; he may also have arranged for some of the money raised by farming and mining in Britain to be sent regularly to the emperor in Rome. Our stories imagine Salvius and his wife Rufilla living in an impressive villa not far from Noviomagus (Chichester) on the south-east coast of Britain.

Our knowledge of Salvius comes mainly from the details on a gravestone discovered in central Italy and an inscription found in a wood near Rome. He is also mentioned by two Roman writers, Pliny and Suetonius. Another gravestone has been found dedicated by his son:

Gaius Salvius Vitellianus set this up in his lifetime to Vitellia Rufilla, daughter of Gaius, wife of Gaius Salvius Liberalis the consul, priestess of the Welfare of the Emperor, best of mothers.

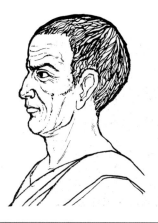

An artist's impression of Salvius. How closely does it fit your idea of his character?

Word Study

A Give a derivative from the Vocabulary Checklist to match each definition. Use the underlined word as a clue.

1. a large <u>building</u>
2. able to be <u>wounded</u>
3. a person <u>new</u> to an activity
4. to render of <u>no</u> value
5. to <u>keep</u> in one's possession

B Give derivatives of **dīcō** suggested in the phrases below.

1. to assert the opposite   _ _ _ _ _ _ d i c t
2. to foretell   _ _ _ d i c t
3. an official order/proclamation   _ d i c t
4. farewell speaker at a graduation   _ _ _ _ d i c t _ _ _ _ _
5. a blessing   _ _ _ _ d i c t _ _ _
6. legal power to hear cases   _ _ _ _ _ d i c t _ _ _

C Match the definitions to the derivatives of **cantō**.

1. recant   **a** a rooster
2. incantation   **b** singer of solos in a church/synagogue
3. disenchant   **c** to withdraw beliefs formerly held
4. canticle   **d** hymn words taken directly from the Bible
5. cantata   **e** to set free from illusion
6. chanticleer   **f** singing a magical spell
7. cantor   **g** a musical composition sung, not acted

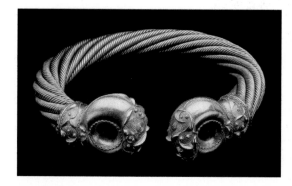

This spectacular gold torque (neck-ornament) was made about 70 B.C., presumably for a British chieftain.

Stage 13
Vocabulary Checklist

Verbs are now listed by their principal parts.
For further explanation see page 216, paragraph G.

adveniō, advenīre, advēnī	*arrive*
aedificium	*building*
aeger: aegrum	*sick, ill*
alter: alterum	*the other, the second*
cantō, cantāre, cantāvī	*sing*
cēterī	*the others, the rest*
coniūrātiō: coniūrātiōnem	*plot*
custōs: custōdem	*guard*
dēcidō, dēcidere, dēcidī	*fall down*
dīcō, dīcere, dīxī	*say*
excitō, excitāre, excitāvī	*arouse, wake up*
fessus	*tired*
horreum	*barn, granary*
interficiō, interficere, interfēcī	*kill*
ita vērō	*yes*
nōlō, nōlle, nōluī	*do not want, refuse*
novus	*new*
nūllus	*not any, no*
numerō, numerāre, numerāvī	*count*
ōrdō: ōrdinem	*row*
possum, posse, potuī	*can, be able*
retineō, retinēre, retinuī	*keep*
ruō, ruere, ruī	*rush*
sē	*himself, herself, themselves*
sum, esse, fuī	*be*
trahō, trahere, trāxī	*drag*
vīta	*life*
volō, velle, voluī	*want*
vulnerō, vulnerāre, vulnerāvī	*wound*

APUD SALVIUM

Stage 14

1

multae amphorae sunt in plaustrō.

Vārica: Phile! portā hanc amphoram in vīllam!
Philus: amphora magna est. difficile est mihi magnam amphoram
portāre.
Vārica: cūr?
Philus: quod ego sum senex.

2

Vārica geminōs in āreā cōnspicit.

Vārica: Loquāx! Anti-Loquāx! portāte hanc amphoram in vīllam!
Loquāx: amphora gravis est. difficile est nōbīs amphoram gravem
portāre.
Vārica: cūr?
Loquāx: quod nōs sumus puerī.

3

	Bregāns prō amphorīs stat.
Vārica:	Bregāns! portā hās amphorās in vīllam!
Bregāns:	amphorae gravēs sunt. difficile est mihi amphorās gravēs portāre.
Vārica:	sed necesse est!
Bregāns:	cūr?
Vārica:	necesse est tibi amphorās portāre quod Philus est senex, quod Loquāx et frāter sunt puerī, et …
Bregāns:	quod tū es vīlicus!

Rūfilla

Rūfilla in cubiculō sedet. duae ōrnātrīcēs prope eam stant et crīnēs compōnunt.
Salvius intrat. Rūfilla, simulatque eum cōnspexit, ōrnātrīcēs ē cubiculō dīmittit.

Rūfilla: Salvī! vir crūdēlis es. ego ad hanc vīllam venīre
           nōlēbam. in urbe Londiniō manēre volēbam.
           Londinium est urbs pulcherrima, ubi multās amīcās   5
           habeō. difficile est mihi amīcās relinquere. nōn
           decōrum est mātrōnae Rōmānae sine amīcīs habitāre.

Salvius: Rūfilla! quam levis es! ubi in urbe Londiniō
           habitābāmus, cotīdiē ad mē veniēbās. cotīdiē mihi ita
           dīcēbās, "Semprōnia, amīca mea, est fortūnātior quam   10
           ego. marītum optimum habet. marītus eī rēs pretiōsās
           semper dat. vīllam rūsticam eī prōmīsit. ego quoque
           vīllam rūsticam habēre volō, sed tū mihi nihil dās."
           tandem vīllam rūsticam tibi dedī, sed etiam nunc nōn
           es contenta.   15

Rūfilla: sed ego prope urbem habitāre volēbam. haec vīlla ab
           urbe longē abest.

Salvius: tū ipsa hanc vīllam ēlēgistī. ego, quamquam pretium
           magnum erat, eam libenter ēmī. nōnne haec vīlla est
           ēlegāns? nōnne etiam magnifica?   20

Rūfilla: sed hiems iam appropinquat. amīcae meae semper in
           urbe hiemant. nōn commodum est mihi in vīllā
           hiemāre. decōrum est mihi cum amīcīs hiemāre.
           mātrōna Rōmāna sum. amīcās meās vīsitāre nōn
           possum. in hōc locō sōla sum.   25

Salvius: quid dīxistī? sōla es? decem ancillās habēs, novem
           servōs, duās ōrnātrīcēs, coquum Aegyptium ...

Rūfilla: et marītum dūrum et crūdēlem. nihil intellegis! nihil
           cūrās!
           (exit lacrimāns.)   30

ōrnātrīcēs:		**vīllam rūsticam:**	
ōrnātrīx	*hairdresser*	vīlla rūstica	*a country house*
dīmittit:	*send away,*	**etiam**	*even*
dīmittere	*dismiss*	**ab urbe**	*from the city*
crūdēlis	*cruel*	**tū ipsa**	*you yourself*
Londiniō:		**pretium**	*price*
Londinium	*London*	**libenter**	*gladly*
amīcās: amīca	*friend*	**ēlegāns**	*tasteful, elegant*
relinquere	*leave*	**hiems**	*winter*
decōrum: decōrus	*right, proper*	**appropinquat:**	
mātrōnae: mātrōna	*lady*	appropinquāre	*approach*
sine	*without*	**hiemant: hiemāre**	*spend the winter*
levis	*changeable,*	**commodum:**	
	inconsistent	commodus	*convenient*
fortūnātior:		**novem**	*nine*
fortūnātus	*lucky*	**lacrimāns**	*crying, weeping*

A lady with four ōrnātrīcēs.

Domitilla cubiculum parat

I

"Domitilla! Domitilla! ubi es?" clāmāvit Marcia. Marcia anus erat.
  "in hortō sum, Marcia. quid vīs?" respondit Domitilla.
  "necesse est nōbīs cubiculum parāre," inquit Marcia. "domina familiārem ad vīllam invītāvit."
  "ēheu!" inquit Domitilla. "fessa sum, quod diū labōrāvī."   5
  "puella ignāvissima es," inquit Marcia. "domina ipsa mē ad tē mīsit. necesse est tibi cubiculum verrere. necesse est mihi pavīmentum lavāre. curre ad culīnam! quaere scōpās!"
  Domitilla ad culīnam lentē ambulābat. īrāta erat, quod cubiculum verrere nōlēbat.   10
  "ego ōrnātrīx sum," inquit. "nōn decōrum est ōrnātrīcibus cubiculum verrere."
  subitō Domitilla cōnsilium cēpit et ad culīnam quam celerrimē festīnāvit. simulac culīnam intrāvit, lacrimīs sē trādidit.
  Volūbilis attonitus, "mea columba," inquit, "cūr lacrimās?"   15
  "lacrimō quod miserrima sum," ancilla coquō respondit. "tōtum diem labōrāvī. quam fessa sum! nunc necesse est mihi cubiculum parāre. nōn diūtius labōrāre possum."
  "mea columba, nōlī lacrimāre!" inquit Volūbilis. "ego tibi cubiculum parāre possum."   20
  "Volūbilis! quam benignus es!" susurrāvit ancilla.
  coquus cum ancillā ad cubiculum revēnit. dīligenter labōrāvit et cubiculum fēcit pūrum. ancilla laeta
  "meum mel!" inquit, "meae dēliciae!" et coquō ōsculum dedit.
  coquus ērubēscēns ad culīnam rediit.   25

anus	old woman	miserrima	very miserable, very sad
necesse	necessary		
familiārem: familiāris	relation, relative	diūtius	any longer
diū	for a long time	nōlī lacrimāre	do not cry
domina ipsa	the mistress herself	pūrum: pūrus	clean, spotless
verrere	sweep	mel	honey
scōpās: scōpae	broom	ōsculum	kiss
lentē	slowly	ērubēscēns	blushing
lacrimīs sē trādidit	burst into tears		

II

tum Marcia cubiculum intrāvit. anus vix prōcēdere poterat, quod urnam gravem portābat. Domitilla, ubi Marciam cōnspexit, clāmāvit,

"ecce! dīligenter labōrāvī. cubiculum fēcī pūrum. nunc necesse est tibi pavīmentum lavāre." 5

Marcia, quamquam erat attonita, Domitillae nihil dīxit. sōla pavīmentum lavābat. tandem rem cōnfēcit.

Domitilla statim ad Rūfillam festīnāvit.

"domina," inquit, "cubiculum tibi parāvimus, et pavīmentum fēcimus nitidum." 10

Rūfilla cubiculum cum Domitillā intrāvit et circumspectāvit.

"bene labōrāvistis, ancillae," inquit. "sed, quamquam nitidum est pavīmentum, nōn decōrum est familiārī meō in hōc cubiculō dormīre. nam cubiculum est inēlegāns. necesse est nōbīs id ōrnāre." 15

"tablīnum est ēlegāns," inquit Domitilla. "in tablīnō, ubi dominus labōrat, sunt multae rēs pretiōsae."

"ita vērō," inquit Rūfilla, "in tablīnō est armārium ēlegantissimum. in tablīnō sunt sella aēnea et candēlābrum aureum. age! Domitilla, necesse est nōbīs ad tablīnum īre." 20

vix	hardly, scarcely	ōrnāre	decorate
urnam: urna	jar, jug	armārium	chest, cupboard
sōla	alone, on her own	aēnea	made of bronze
nitidum: nitidus	gleaming, brilliant	candēlābrum	lamp-stand,
bene	well		candelabrum
nam	for	aureum: aureus	golden, made of gold
inēlegāns	unattractive	age!	come on!
id	it	īre	go

A comb and manicure set from Roman London.

About the Language I: Adjectives

A Study the following sentences:

> servus **īrātus** nōn labōrābat.
> *The **angry** slave was not working.*

> dominus servō **fessō** praemium dedit.
> *The master gave a reward to the **tired** slave.*

> agricola servum **ignāvum** pūnīvit.
> *The farmer punished the **lazy** slave.*

The words in boldface are adjectives. They are used to describe nouns. In each of these examples, the adjective is describing the slave.

B Adjectives change their endings to match the *case* of the noun they describe.

In the first sentence above, **īrātus** is nominative because it describes a nominative noun (**servus**).
In the second sentence, **fessō** is dative because it describes a dative noun (**servō**).
In the third sentence, **ignāvum** is accusative, because it describes an accusative noun (**servum**).

C Translate the following examples:

1 ancilla perterrita ad culīnam contendit.
2 coquus ancillam perterritam salūtāvit.
3 cīvēs mercātōrem fortem laudāvērunt.
4 cīvēs mercātōrī fortī praemium dedērunt.
5 senex fīlium bonum habēbat.
6 senex fīliō bonō vīllam ēmit.

Write down the Latin noun and adjective pair in each sentence and state whether it is nominative, dative, or accusative.

D Adjectives also change their endings to match the *number* (i.e. singular or plural) of the nouns they describe. Compare the following examples with those in section **A**:

> servī **īrātī** nōn labōrābant.
> *The angry slaves were not working.*

> dominus servīs **fessīs** praemium dedit.
> *The master gave a reward to the tired slaves.*

> agricola servōs **ignāvōs** pūnīvit.
> *The farmer punished the lazy slaves.*

E Translate the following examples:

1 fēminae laetae per viās ambulābant.
2 fēmina laeta per viās ambulābat.
3 gladiātor leōnēs ferōcēs necāvit.
4 coquus servīs aegrīs cibum parāvit.
5 pictūra pulchra erat in ātriō.
6 Volūbilis ōrnātrīcem trīstem cōnspexit.

Write down the Latin noun and adjective pair in each sentence and state whether the pair is singular or plural.

F When an adjective changes its ending in this way it is said to *agree*, in case and number, with the noun it describes.

G Adjectives like **magnus**, **parvus**, and **multī**, which indicate *size* or *quantity*, usually come before the noun they describe; other adjectives usually come after the noun.

Translate the following:

1 Bregāns magnum taurum dūcēbat.
2 coquus amīcīs parvam cēnam parāvit.
3 multī Britannī erant servī.
4 fūrēs ingentem serpentem timēbant.
5 Rūfilla duās ancillās in cubiculō vīdit.

in tablīnō

When you have read this story, answer the questions.

postrīdiē Salvius et Philus in tablīnō sunt. intrat Rūfilla.

Rūfilla:	mī Salvī!
Salvius:	occupātus sum! necesse est mihi hās epistulās dictāre.
	ego rem celeriter cōnficere volō. ubi est sella mea?
	(*Salvius sellam frūstrā quaerit.*) 5
	heus! ubi est ista sella?
Rūfilla:	mī cārissime! aliquid tibi dīcere volō.
Salvius:	tē nunc audīre nōn possum. dē hīs epistulīs Philō
	dīcere volō. ecce! servus meus parātus adest. stilī et
	cērae adsunt – heus! ubi est armārium meum? quis 10
	cēpit?
Rūfilla:	Salvī! audī!
	(*tandem Salvius uxōrī cēdit et Philum dīmittit.*)
Salvius:	ēheu! abī, Phile! nōn commodum est mihi epistulās
	dictāre. 15
Rūfilla:	bene! nunc aliquid tibi dīcere possum. ubi in urbe
	Londiniō nūper eram, familiārem convēnī.
Salvius:	tot familiārēs habēs! eōs numerāre nōn possum.
Rūfilla:	sed hic familiāris est Quīntus Caecilius Iūcundus. ubi
	mōns Vesuvius urbem Pompēiōs dēlēvit, Quīntus ex 20
	urbe effūgit. quam cōmis est! quam urbānus!
Salvius:	hercle! ego Pompēiānīs nōn crēdō. paucī probī sunt,
	cēterī mendācēs. ubi in Campāniā mīlitābam, multōs
	Pompēiānōs cognōscēbam. mercātōrēs Pompēiānī nōs
	mīlitēs semper dēcipiēbant. dē mercātōribus 25
	Pompēiānīs audīre nōlō.
Rūfilla:	stultissimus es! familiāris meus nōn est mercātor.
	Quīntus vir nōbilis est. eum ad vīllam nostram invītāvī.
Salvius:	quid dīxistī? Pompēiānum invītāvistī? ad vīllam
	nostram? 30
Rūfilla:	decōrum est mihi familiārem meum hūc invītāre.
	ancillae familiārī meō cubiculum parāvērunt. ancillae,
	quod cubiculum inēlegāns erat, sellam armāriumque
	tuum in eō posuērunt.
Salvius:	īnsāna es, uxor! Pompēiānī mendāciōrēs sunt quam 35
	Britannī. num tū sellam et armārium ē tablīnō
	extrāxistī?

Rūfilla:	et candēlābrum.
Salvius:	prō dī immortālēs! ō candēlābrum meum! ō mē miserum!

40

mī Salvī!	*my dear Salvius!*
heus!	*hey!*
cārissime	*dearest*
aliquid	*something*
cēdit: cēdere	*give in, give way*
bene!	*good!*
nūper	*recently*
convēnī: convenīre	*meet*
tot	*so many*
cōmis	*courteous, friendly*
urbānus	*smart, fashionable*
paucī	*a few*
mīlitābam: mīlitāre	*be a soldier*
cognōscēbam: cognōscere	*get to know*
mīlitēs: mīles	*soldier*
in eō	*in it*
num tū … extrāxistī?	*surely you did not take?*
prō dī immortālēs!	*heavens above!*
ō mē miserum!	*oh wretched me! oh dear!*

Questions

1 Why has Rufilla come to see Salvius?
2 Why does she address him as **mī Salvī** and **mī cārissime**?
3 What does Salvius want to do? Why can he not do this? (Give two reasons from lines 4–11.)
4 Whom has Rufilla met in London? What information does she give about this person in lines 19–21?
5 Why does this news not please Salvius? (lines 22–26)
6 Explain why he becomes angrier in lines 29-30 … and even more upset in lines 35–37.

A wax tablet with a government stamp on the back. Salvius, as a Roman administrator, may have used official tablets like this one.

About the Language II: Adjectives (cont.)

A In the first language note in this Stage you met sentences like this:

> cīvis servum **bonum** laudāvit.
> *The citizen praised the good slave.*

The adjective **bonum** agrees with the noun **servum** in case (accusative) and number (singular). The endings of both words look the same.

B Now study this sentence:

> cīvis servum **fortem** laudāvit.
> *The citizen praised the brave slave.*

The adjective **fortem** agrees with the noun **servum** in case (accusative) and number (singular) as in the previous example. The endings, however, do not look the same. This is because they belong to different declensions, and have different ways of forming their cases. **fortis** belongs to the third declension and **servus** belongs to the second declension.

C Translate the following examples:

1 Quīntus fābulam mīrābilem nārrāvit.
2 in vīllā habitābat senex stultus.
3 gladiātor bēstiās ferōcēs agitābat.
4 dominus amīcō fidēlī dēnāriōs trādidit.
5 multī mercātōrēs vīnum bibēbant.
6 agricola omnibus puerīs pecūniam dedit.

Write down the Latin noun and adjective pair in each sentence and state whether the pair is nominative, dative, or accusative, singular or plural.

Oyster shells are common finds on Roman sites in Britain.

Quīntus advenit

Quīntus ad vīllam advēnit. Salvius ē vīllā contendit et eum salūtāvit.

"mī Quīnte!" inquit. "exspectātissimus es! cubiculum optimum tibi parāvimus."

Salvius Quīntum in tablīnum dūxit, ubi Rūfilla sedēbat. Rūfilla, 5 postquam familiārem suum salūtāvit, suāviter rīsit.

"cēnam modicam tibi parāvī," inquit. "tibi ostreās parāvī et garum Pompēiānum. post cēnam cubiculum tibi ostendere volō."

Salvius, postquam Quīntus cēnam cōnsūmpsit, dē urbe Pompēiīs quaerēbat. 10

"ubi in Campāniā mīlitābam, saepe urbem Pompēiōs vīsitābam. nōnne illa clādēs terribilis erat?"

Rūfilla interpellāvit,

"cūr Quīntum nostrum vexās? nōn decōrum est. difficile est Quīntō tantam clādem commemorāre." 15

Rūfilla ad Quīntum sē convertit.

"fortasse, mī Quīnte, fessus es. cubiculum tibi parāvī. cubiculum nōn est ōrnātum. in eō sunt armārium modicum et candēlābrum parvum."

Salvius īrātus nihil dīxit. 20

Quīntus, postquam cubiculum vīdit, exclāmāvit,

"quam ēlegāns est cubiculum! ego nihil ēlegantius vīdī."

"cōnsentiō," inquit Salvius. "cubiculum tuum ēlegantius est quam tablīnum meum."

exspectātissimus:		commemorāre	talk about
exspectātus	welcome	sē convertit:	
modicam	ordinary, little	sē convertere	turn
ostreās: ostrea	oyster	ōrnātum: ōrnātus	elaborately
garum	sauce		furnished,
clādēs	disaster		decorated
terribilis	terrible	ēlegantius	more tasteful
interpellāvit: interpellāre	interrupt		
tantam: tanta	so great, such a great		

Questions

1 Find four examples in this story where Salvius and Rufilla are not telling the truth. In each case explain why their words are untrue.
2 Why do you think Quintus says so little in this story? Think of two reasons.

About the Language III: Prepositional Phrases

Ablative

A Study the following examples:

1 Salvius ē **vīllā** contendit.
   Salvius hurried out of the house.
2 in **tablīnō** est armārium ēlegantissimum.
   In the study there is a very elegant cupboard.
3 haec vīlla ab **urbe** longē abest.
   This house is far from the city.
4 Bregāns prō **amphorīs** stat.
   Bregans is standing in front of the amphorae.
5 nōn decōrum est sine **amīcīs** habitāre.
   It is not right to live without friends.
6 dē **mercātōribus** audīre nōlō.
   I do not want to hear about the merchants.

The words in boldface are nouns in the ablative case.

B The ablative case is used with certain prepositions in Latin. These include:

ā/ab, cum, dē, ē/ex, in, prō, sine, sub.

C Here is a full list of the cases you have met. The new ablative forms are in boldface:

	FIRST DECLENSION	SECOND DECLENSION	THIRD DECLENSION
SINGULAR			
nominative	puella	servus	leō
dative	puellae	servō	leōnī
accusative	puellam	servum	leōnem
ablative	**puellā**	**servō**	**leōne**
PLURAL			
nominative	puellae	servī	leōnēs
dative	puellīs	servīs	leōnibus
accusative	puellās	servōs	leōnēs
ablative	**puellīs**	**servīs**	**leōnibus**

Accusative

D Study the following examples:

1 Quīntus ad **vīllam** advēnit.
  Quintus arrived at the house.
2 ego prope **urbem** habitāre volēbam.
  I wanted to live near the city.
3 vīlicus per **ōrdinēs** ambulābat.
  The manager was walking through the rows.
4 Salvius Quīntum in **tablīnum** dūxit.
  Salvius led Quintus into the study.

The words in boldface are in the **accusative case**. The accusative case is also used with certain prepositions in Latin. These include: **ad, apud, in, per, prope.** What deduction can you make about the preposition **in** when used in Latin?

tripodes argenteī

servī in cubiculō Quīntum vestiunt. ancilla eī togam fert. Anti-Loquāx celeriter intrat.

Anti-Loquāx: salvē! necesse est dominō meō ad aulam īre. rēx
               Cogidubnus omnēs nōbilēs ad sacrificium
               invītāvit.   5
Quīntus: rēgem hodiē vīsitāmus? ubi in urbe Londiniō
               habitābam, saepe dē hōc rēge audiēbam.

tripodes	*tripods*	**vestiunt: vestīre**	*dress*
argenteī:		**aulam: aula**	*palace*
argenteus	*made of silver*		

The Celtic chiefs loved Roman silver. This elegant wine cup was made about the time of our stories.

Anti-Loquāx:	ita vērō. quotannīs rēx sacrificium facit, quod imperātōrem Claudium honōrāre vult.	
Quīntus:	cūr Claudium honōrāre vult?	*10*
Anti-Loquāx:	decōrum est Cogidubnō Claudium honōrāre. nam Claudius erat imperātor quī Cogidubnum rēgem fēcit.	
Quīntus:	nunc rem intellegō. necesse est mihi dōnum rēgī ferre. in arcā meā sunt duo tripodes argenteī. illī tripodes sunt dōnum optimum.	*15*
	(*Anti-Loquāx ē cubiculō exit et Salviō dē tripodibus argenteīs nārrat. Salvius statim ad cellārium contendit.*)	
Salvius:	necesse est mihi rēgem Cogidubnum vīsitāre. dōnum eī ferre volō.	*20*
cellārius:	nōn difficile est nōbīs dōnum invenīre, domine. ecce! urna aēnea. antīquissima est. placetne tibi?	
Salvius:	mihi nōn placet. dōnum aēneum Cogidubnō ferre nōlō.	*25*
	(*cellārius Salviō amphoram dēmōnstrat.*)	
cellārius:	nōnne vīnum est dōnum optimum, domine?	
Salvius:	minimē! Cogidubnus multās amphorās habet, multumque vīnum. rēx vīnum ex Ītaliā cotīdiē importat.	*30*
	(*subitō Salvius statuam parvam cōnspicit.*) euge! hanc statuam rēgī ferre possum. aurāta est statua. Quīntus rēgī dōnum argenteum ferre vult; ego tamen aurātum dōnum ferre possum!	
cellārius:	domine! nōn dēbēs.	*35*
Salvius:	cūr nōn dēbeō?	
cellārius:	Cogidubnus ipse tibi illam statuam dedit!	
Salvius:	hercle! necesse est mihi istam urnam ad aulam ferre.	

quotannīs	*every year*	**urna**	*jar, jug*
imperātōrem:		**dēmōnstrat:**	
imperātor	*emperor*	**dēmōnstrāre**	*point out, show*
honōrāre	*honor*	**importat: importāre**	*import*
arcā: arca	*strong-box, chest*	**aurāta**	*gilded, gold-plated*
cellārium:		**nōn dēbēs**	*you should not,*
cellārius	*steward*		*you must not*

Practicing the Language

A Complete each sentence with the correct adjective. Then translate the sentence.

1 servī canem (ferōx, ferōcem) retrāxērunt.
2 ego (multī, multōs) iuvenēs in forō vīdī.
3 ōrnātrīx (laeta, laetam) coquō ōsculum dedit.
4 amīcī (fortēs, fortibus) lībertum servāvērunt.
5 māter (parvī, parvōs, parvīs) puerīs cibum parāvit.
6 Bregāns amphoram (gravis, gravem, gravī) portāre nōlēbat.
7 domina ancillae (fidēlis, fidēlem, fidēlī) stolam ēmit.

B Complete each sentence with the correct form of the imperfect tense from the list below and then translate.

eram	erāmus	poteram	poterāmus
erās	erātis	poterās	poterātis
erat	erant	poterat	poterant

1 "domina," inquit Domitilla, "nōs cubiculum tibi parāre ....., quod bene labōrāvimus."
2 servī ..... in āreā, ubi Salvium exspectābant.
3 Marcia urnam gravem vix portāre ....
4 vōsne canem retrahere .....? canis ..... ferōcissimus.
5 tū ..... anxius, quod celeriter prōcēdere nōn ....
6 ego servum īnsolentem pūnīre .....; nōnne ego ..... dominus?
7 vōs gladiōs habēbātis quod vōs ..... custōdēs.

C The following prepositions occur (in this order) in the story **Rūfilla** (page 30):

in, prope, ē, ad, in, sine, in, ad, prope, ab, in, in, cum, in

Make two lists of the prepositions in their respective phrases, according to whether they take the accusative or the ablative case.

For example: *Accusative*   *Ablative*
                prope eam   in cubiculō

Life in Roman Britain

Romans, like Salvius and Quintus, who found themselves living in Britain, would have experienced a lifestyle which differed greatly from life in Italy. They had to endure the weather, the distance from towns, the unfamiliar Celtic customs, the isolation from friends, and, especially, the lack of urban amenities. Most inhabitants of Roman Britain lived in the countryside. A typical small farm belonging to a native Briton would have provided for the basic needs of the farmer and his family and their slaves, with perhaps a little surplus left over for trade. His house consisted of a single round room where everyone in the family lived, worked, slept, and ate. Since there were no windows and only one low, narrow doorway, most of the light would have been provided by the open fire in the center of the room which also served as a place to cook and as a source of heat. Without a chimney the room must have been quite smoky inside.

About thirty years after the Roman invasion in A.D. 43, simple Romano-British "villas" began to appear in the countryside. Such a country estate was not a holiday retreat but the center of a working farm community. The majority of the estates discovered in Britain were the property not of Romans but of Romano-Britons. One of the signs of Roman influence is the replacement of round huts by rectangular buildings, erected using the new Roman tools, the new building methods, and the new materials such as brick and tile. The houses had

Wattle and daub: basketwork covered with clay.

A British farmhouse was circular, thereby minimizing heat loss through the walls, which were usually made of wattle and daub attached to a wooden frame. The steeply sloping thatched roof allowed rain and snow to run off quickly.

The inside of a large roundhouse. There is a coracle (a boat made of skins) hanging on the wall and a clay oven in the middle of the floor as well as an open hearth.

four or five rooms, sometimes linked by a corridor; they were built mainly of timber and wattle and daub, with roofs of thatch, stone slabs,

and later tiles. Some of these early villas are found on the sites of earlier British roundhouses. It is likely that the Britons were attempting to imitate the lifestyle of their Roman conquerors.

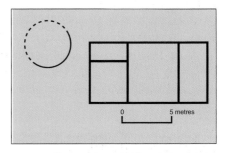

Plan of an early villa built beside a former roundhouse.

Gradually villas became more complicated in design and were built of cut stone and cement; the grandest ones might contain long colonnades, under-floor heating, an ornamental garden, mosaics, wall-paintings, flushing toilets, glass windows, and a set of baths complete with **tepidārium** and **caldārium**. They also had workshops, barns, living quarters for the farm laborers, and sheds for the animals. In choosing a place to build his villa, the owner would look not only for attractive surroundings but also for practical advantages, such as a nearby supply of running water and shelter from the cold north and east winds.

Reconstruction of a later villa.

Roman bronze model plowman, with a yoke of oxen.

Pre-Roman Britons probably had sheep like the Soay (top). During the Roman period a breed like the Shetland (above) was developed.

A pre-Roman British gold coin showing an ear of wheat. CAMV stands for Camulodunum (Colchester) where the coin was found.

Emmer, one of the kinds of wheat the Romans grew. It is bearded like barley.

A reconstruction of an early villa in Britain. How many different farming activities can you see?

Farming

The main crops grown in Britain at this time were cereal grains: barley, oats, rye, and especially wheat. Archaeologists have found seeds of all these crops, accidentally charred and thus preserved in the earth. Most farms seem to have kept animals such as cattle, sheep, goats, pigs, dogs, and horses, in addition to geese and hens. These animals could provide food (meat, milk, and eggs), transport, wool or leather clothing, fertilizer, and bone. Bees were kept to produce honey, which was used to sweeten food (there was no sugar at that time). Many fruits and vegetables were grown, including some (like cherries and peas) which had been brought to Britain by the Romans. As good iron tools and the new heavier plow became available, the yields of grain increased, encouraged by an expanding market. The expansion of farming into marshland was made possible by the Roman introduction of drainage tiles and dikes. The villas could not produce everything their owners needed, but home-grown products such as grain, leather, meat, timber, and honey could be traded for shellfish, salt, wine, pottery, and ironware.

A large villa like that belonging to Salvius would be supervised by a farm manager or overseer. He was often a slave like Varica. The manager was responsible for buying any food or other goods that could not be produced on the villa's own land and for looking after the buildings and slaves. Such country estates, rather than the towns, supported much of the industry of the province: market-gardening, fruit-growing, the wool and dye industry, potteries, tileries, even the raising of British hunting dogs.

The Slaves

Farm slaves were described by one Roman landowner as just "farming equipment with voices." The Celtic chieftains used and traded slaves taken in raids and inter-tribal warfare. Most of Salvius' farm slaves would also be British, whereas many of his skilled house slaves would be imported from abroad. Slaves working on the land lived a much harsher life than domestic slaves and slaves working in the mines had the harshest life of all. Many of these had been sent to work in the mines as a punishment, and conditions were so bad that this amounted to a death sentence. Some slaves were kept in chains. Slaves worked in state-operated iron works, state mines of tin, silver, and gold, and even state weaving mills, tileries, and potteries. But most of the population continued to work in agriculture.

In theory, the law gave slaves some protection: for example, any owner who killed a sick slave could be charged with murder. In practice, these laws were often ignored, as in the story of Salvius and the Cantiacan miners. However, in the first century A.D. slaves were becoming increasingly scarce and expensive; owners therefore had more motivation to look after the welfare of their slaves.

Some British slaves are known to us by name. For example, a gravestone from Chester was set up by a master in memory of three of his slaves who died young: a slave-boy aged twelve and two ten-year-olds called Atilianus and Anti-Atilianus, probably twins.

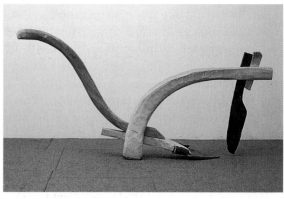

A weary young slave-boy waits with a lantern to light his master's way home.

Reconstruction of a Roman plow.

Word Study

A Give the Latin word in the Vocabulary Checklist from which each of these words is derived. Then give a definition of the English derivative.

1 lavatory
2 deleterious
3 quotidian
4 donation
5 indecorous
6 infidelity
7 deify
8 marital

B Give the Latin root found in the Vocabulary Checklist for the following English words; then match the definition to the English word.

1 astound   a friendly, intimate, close
2 regal   b to imply as a logical outcome
3 diligence   c characteristic of a king
4 deity   d to amaze, astonish greatly
5 ennoble   e to dignify
6 necessitate   f unable to be erased
7 familiar   g a god
8 indelible   h constant careful effort

C Match the definition to the derivative of **domina**.

1 belladonna   a a lady; an elderly woman
2 madam   b to rule by superior power, authority
3 damsel   c a girl, a maiden
4 dominate   d a woman, the lady of the house
5 dame   e a drug, originally used as a cosmetic

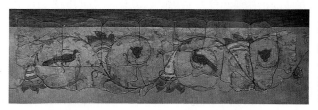

Detail from a wall-painting showing a leafy scroll with panther heads and birds.

Stage 14
Vocabulary Checklist

aliquid	*something*
apud (+ ACC)	*among, at the house of*
attonitus	*astonished*
aula	*palace*
cotīdiē	*every day*
decōrus	*right, proper*
dēleō, dēlēre, dēlēvī	*destroy*
deus [deī, dī (nom. pl.)]	*god*
difficilis	*difficult*
dīligenter	*carefully*
domina	*mistress*
dōnum	*present, gift*
familiāris: familiārem	*relative, relation*
fidēlis	*faithful, loyal*
ipse, ipsa	*himself, herself*
iste	*that*
lavō, lavāre, lāvī	*wash*
marītus	*husband*
necesse	*necessary*
nōbilis: nōbilem	*noble*
num?	*surely … not?*
quam	*how*
quamquam	*although*
-que	*and*
rēx: rēgem	*king*
ubi	*when*

Detail of a Roman cavalryman's gravestone. A conquered Briton cowers beneath the horse's hooves.

REX
COGIDUBNUS

1 multī Britannī ad aulam
   vēnērunt. senex, quī scēptrum
   tenēbat, erat rēx Cogidubnus.

2 fēmina prope Cogidubnum
   sedēbat. fēmina, quae corōnam
   gerēbat, erat rēgīna.

3 multī Rōmānī Cogidubnō rēs
   pretiōsās dabant. dōnum, quod
   rēgem maximē dēlectāvit, erat
   equus.

4 duae ancillae ad rēgem
  vēnērunt. vīnum, quod ancillae
  ferēbant, erat in paterā aureā.
  rēx vīnum lībāvit.

5 servus agnum ad āram dūxit.
  agnus, quem servus dūcēbat,
  erat victima.

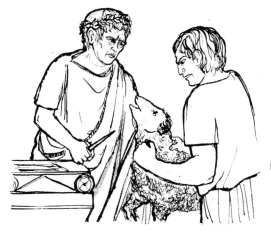

6 sacerdōs victimam īnspexit.
  victima, quam servus tenēbat,
  bālāvit. sacerdōs victimam
  interfēcit.

ad aulam

*agmen longissimum ad aulam prōcēdēbat. in prīmā parte ībant decem
servī. hī servī, quī virgās longās tenēbant, erant praecursōrēs. in mediō
agmine Salvius et Quīntus equitābant. post eōs ambulābant trēs ancillae,
quae urnam et tripodas portābant. aliae ancillae flōrēs et unguentum
ferēbant. postrēmō prōcēdēbant vīgintī servī. agmen, quod tōtam viam* 5
complēbat, erat splendidum.

*multī quoque Britannī cum uxōribus līberīsque ad aulam ībant.
magna turba erat in viā. tum Vārica, quī cum praecursōribus equitābat,
ad Salvium rediit.*

Vārica: domine, difficile est nōbīs prōcēdere, quod hī Britannī   *10*
                viam complent. ē viā exīre nōlunt. quid facere dēbeō?
Salvius: (*īrātus*) necesse est praecursōribus Britannōs ē viā
                ēmovēre. nōn decōrum est Britannīs cīvēs Rōmānōs
                impedīre. quam celerrimē īre volō. rēx nōs exspectat.

Vārica, quī dominum īrātum timēbat, ad praecursōrēs rediit.   *15*

Vārica: asinī estis! virgās habētis. ēmovēte Britannōs!

*tum praecursōrēs statim virgās vibrābant. multī Britannī in fossās
dēsiluērunt, quod virgās timēbant. duo iuvenēs tamen impavidī in viā
cōnsistēbant. prope iuvenēs erat plaustrum, quod tōtam viam claudēbat.*

Vārica: cūr viam clauditis? necesse est dominō meō   *20*
                         ad aulam īre.
iuvenis prīmus: nōs quoque rēgem vīsitāre volumus. sed
                         plaustrum movēre nōn possumus.
                         plaustrum rotam frāctam habet.
iuvenis secundus: amīcus noster, quem nōs exspectāmus, aliam   *25*
                         rotam quaerit. amīcum exspectāre dēbēmus.

Vārica anxius ad Salvium iterum rediit.

Vārica: plaustrum, quod vidēs, domine, rotam frāctam habet.
                difficile est nōbīs prōcēdere, quod hoc plaustrum tōtam
                viam claudit.   *30*
Salvius: (*īrātior quam anteā*) num surdus es? caudex! nōn
                commodum est mihi in hōc locō manēre. quam
                celerrimē prōcēdere volō.

Vārica ad praecursōrēs iterum rediit.

Vārica: caudicēs! ēmovēte hoc plaustrum! dēicite in fossam!   *35 praecursōrēs, postquam Vāricam audīvērunt, plaustrum in fossam dēiēcērunt. iuvenēs vehementer resistēbant. tum praecursōrēs iuvenēs quoque in fossam dēiēcērunt.*

Salvius: (*per viam prōcēdēns et cachinnāns*) Britannī sunt molestissimī. semper nōs Rōmānōs vexant.   *40*

agmen	*procession*
in prīmā parte	*in the forefront*
virgās: virga	*rod, stick*
praecursōrēs: praecursor	*forerunner (sent ahead of a procession to clear the way)*
equitābant: equitāre	*ride*
flōrēs: flōs	*flower*
unguentum: unguentum	*perfume*
līberīs: līberī	*children*
facere dēbeō	*ought to do*
ēmovēre	*move, clear away*
impedīre	*delay, hinder*
fossās: fossa	*ditch*
dēsiluērunt: dēsilīre	*jump down*
impavidī: impavidus	*fearless*
cōnsistēbant: cōnsistere	*stand one's ground, stand firm*
plaustrum	*wagon, cart*
claudēbat: claudere	*block*
movēre	*move*
rotam: rota	*wheel*
anteā	*before*
surdus	*deaf*
dēicite!	*throw!*
resistēbant: resistere	*resist*
cachinnāns	*laughing, cackling*
molestissimī: molestus	*troublesome*

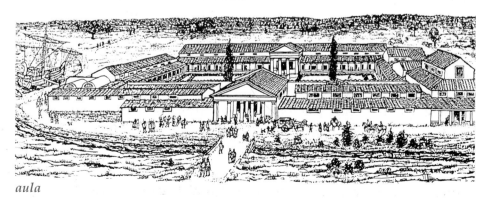

aula

caerimōnia

servus Salvium et Quīntum ad ātrium dūxit. illī, postquam ātrium
intrāvērunt, magnam turbam vīdērunt. multī prīncipēs Britannicī
in ātriō erant. multae fēminae cum prīncipibus sedēbant. sermōnēs
inter sē habēbant. aderant quoque multī Rōmānī, quī prope
prīncipēs sedēbant. haec multitūdō, quae ātrium complēbat,   5
magnum clāmōrem faciēbat.

in mediō ātriō Quīntus et Salvius lectum vīdērunt. in lectō erat
effigiēs cērāta. Quīntus effigiem agnōvit.

"bona est effigiēs!" inquit. "imperātor Claudius est!"

"ita vērō," respondit Salvius. "rēx Cogidubnus Claudium   10
quotannīs honōrat. fabrī perītissimī, quī ex Ītaliā veniunt, effigiem
quotannīs faciunt."

subitō turba, quae prope iānuam stābat, ad terram prōcubuit.
prīncipēs Britannicī, quī in mediō ātriō sedēbant, celeriter
surrēxērunt. etiam Rōmānī tacēbant.   15

"rēx adest," susurrāvit Salvius.

per iānuam intrāvit senex. parvus puer senem dūcēbat, quod
claudicābat. rēx et puer lentē per turbam prōcēdēbant. rēx,
postquam ad effigiem advēnit, vīnum lībāvit. tum sacerdōtēs, quī
prope effigiem stābant, victimās ad rēgem dūxērunt. Cogidubnus   20
victimās dīligenter īnspexit. victima, quam rēx ēlēgit, erat agnus
niveus. rēx eum sacrificāvit.

"decōrum est nōbīs Claudium honōrāre," inquit.

sacerdōtēs quoque victimās cēterās sacrificāvērunt. tum decem
prīncipēs Britannicī lectum in umerōs sustulērunt. effigiem ex   25
ātriō portāvērunt. post prīncipēs vēnērunt sacerdōtēs, quī
sollemniter cantābant.

in āreā erat rogus. prīncipēs, quī effigiem portābant, ad rogum
magnā cum dignitāte prōcessērunt. effigiem in rogum posuērunt.
servus rēgī facem trādidit. tum rēx facem in rogum posuit. mox   30
flammae rogum cōnsūmēbant. flammae, quae effigiem iam
tangēbant, cēram liquābant. omnēs effigiem intentē spectābant.
subitō aquila ex effigiē ēvolāvit. omnēs spectātōrēs plausērunt.

"ecce!" inquit rēx. "deī Claudium arcessunt. animus ad deōs
ascendit."   35

| caerimōnia | ceremony | prīncipēs: prīnceps | chief, chieftain |
| illī | they | Britannicī: Britannicus | British |

sermōnēs: sermō	conversation	facem: fax	torch
inter sē	among themselves, with each other	tangēbant: tangere	touch
		liquābant: liquāre	melt
multitūdō	crowd	aquila	eagle
effigiēs cērāta	wax image	ēvolāvit: ēvolāre	fly out
fabrī: faber	craftsman	arcessunt: arcessere	summon, send for
prōcubuit: prōcumbere	fall		
claudicābat: claudicāre	be lame	animus	soul, spirit
vīnum lībāvit	poured wine as an offering	ascendit: ascendere	climb, rise
sacerdōtēs: sacerdōs	priest		
victimās: victima	victim		
agnus	lamb		
niveus	snow-white		
sacrificāvit: sacrificāre	sacrifice		
umerōs: umerus	shoulder		
sustulērunt: tollere	raise, lift up		
sollemniter cantābant	were chanting solemnly		
rogus	pyre		
magnā cum dignitāte	with great dignity		

mox flammae rogum cōnsūmēbant.

Questions

1 Where was the crowd gathered for the ceremony? Which three groups of people did Salvius and Quintus see there (lines 2–4)?

2 Where was the wax image? Whom did it represent (lines 7–9)?

3 How did Salvius explain the good quality (**bona est effigiēs**) of the image (lines 11–12)?

4 In lines 13–15, how did the three different sections of the crowd behave?

5 Why was the king accompanied by a boy (lines 17–18)?

6 In lines 19–22 what two offerings did the king make? How did the priests assist the king in this ceremony (lines 19–24)?

7 What did the British chieftains do (lines 24–29)? What part did the priests play in this rite?

8 Where was the image placed (lines 28–29)?

9 After **servus rēgī facem trādidit**, what did the king do with the torch? What then happened to the image (lines 30–32)?

10 In lines 32–33, why did the spectators applaud?

11 What two things did the king say about Claudius (lines 34–35)? What did the **aquila** represent?

About the Language I: Relative Clauses

A Study the following pair of sentences:

> ancilla urnam portābat.
> *The slave-girl was carrying the jug.*

> ancilla, **quae post Salvium ambulābat**, urnam portābat.
> *The slave-girl, **who was walking behind Salvius**, was carrying the jug.*

The group of words in boldface is known as a relative clause, which is introduced by a relative pronoun.

B A relative clause is used to describe a noun. For example:

> vīlicus, **quī cum praecursōribus equitābat**, ad Salvium rediit.
> *The farm manager, **who was riding with the forerunners**, returned to Salvius.*

> prope iuvenēs erat plaustrum, **quod tōtam viam claudēbat**.
> *Near the young men was a wagon, **which was blocking the whole road**.*

In the first example, the relative clause describes the farm manager.

In the second example, the relative clause describes the wagon.

C Translate the following examples:

1 rēx, quī scēptrum tenēbat, in ātriō sedēbat.
2 vīnum, quod Salvius bibēbat, erat optimum.
3 ancillae, quae dominum timēbant, ē vīllā festīnāvērunt.
4 canis, quem Bregāns dūcēbat, ferōcissimus erat.
5 in viā erant multī Britannī, quī Rōmānōs impediēbant.
6 cēna, quam Volūbilis parābat, erat splendida.

For each example, write down the Latin relative clause and the Latin noun it describes.

A complete chart of the relative pronoun, **quī**, can be found on page 199.

About the Language II: Gender

A All Latin nouns belong to one of three genders: masculine, feminine, or neuter.

B Study the following examples:

1 aquila est animus, quī ad deōs ascendit.
The eagle is a soul which is ascending to the gods.
2 turba, quae prope iānuam stābat, ad terram prōcubuit.
The crowd which was standing near the doorway fell to the ground.
3 plaustrum, quod vidēs, rotam frāctam habet.
The cart which you see has a broken wheel.

In sentence 1, **animus** is masculine. Therefore the pronoun **quī** is used to introduce the relative clause.
In sentence 2, **turba** is feminine. Therefore the pronoun **quae** is used to introduce the relative clause.
In sentence 3, **plaustrum** is neuter. Therefore the pronoun **quod** is used to introduce the relative clause.

C Adjectives in Latin must agree in gender (as well as in case and number) with the nouns they describe. For example:

> **multōs prīncipēs vīdī.**   *I saw many chiefs.*
>
> **multās fēminās vīdī.**   *I saw many women.*

In the first sentence, **multōs** is accusative, plural, masculine to agree with **prīncipēs**.
In the second sentence, **multās** is accusative, plural, feminine to agree with **fēminās**.

D Further examples:

1 sacerdōtēs effigiem cērātam portābant.
2 rēx fabrōs callidōs laudāvit.
3 ancilla ignāva labōrāre nōlēbat.
4 Quīntus rēgī Britannicō dōnum ēlēgit.
5 Vārica contentiōnem cum praecursōribus īrātīs habēbat.
6 taurus horreum novum dēlēvit.

From each sentence, select the adjective–noun pair and indicate its case, number, and gender.

lūdī fūnebrēs

I

post caerimōniam rēx Cogidubnus pompam ad lītus dūxit. ibi Britannī lūdōs fūnebrēs celebrāvērunt. aderant Rēgnēnsēs, Cantiacī, et aliae gentēs Britannicae.

competītōrēs diū inter sē certābant. Cantiacī laetissimī erant, quod semper vincēbant. āthlēta Cantiacus celerius quam cēterī   5
cucurrit. pugil Cantiacus, quī rōbustissimus erat, cēterōs pugilēs facile superāvit. alius āthlēta Cantiacus discum longius quam cēterī ēmīsit.

post haec certāmina, Cogidubnus certāmen nāvāle inter Cantiacōs et Rēgnēnsēs nūntiāvit. nautae Cantiacī nāvem   10
caeruleam parābant, nautae Rēgnēnsēs nāvem croceam. Dumnorix, prīnceps Rēgnēnsis, quī nāvī croceae praeerat, gubernātor perītissimus erat. Belimicus, prīnceps Cantiacus, nāvī caeruleae praeerat. homō superbus et īnsolēns erat. nautae, postquam nāvēs parāvērunt, signum intentē exspectābant.   15

subitō tuba sonuit. nāvēs statim prōsiluērunt; per undās ruēbant. rēmī undās vehementer pulsābant. spectātōrēs, quī in lītore stābant, magnōs clāmōrēs sustulērunt.

Cantiacī clāmābant, "nōs Belimicō favēmus! Belimicus vincere potest! nautae nostrī sunt optimī!"   20

Rēgnēnsēs tamen Dumnorigī favēbant:

"nōs optimam nāvem habēmus! nōs optimum gubernātōrem habēmus! gubernātor Cantiacus est stultior quam asinus!"

certāmen nāvāle.

lūdī fūnebrēs	*funeral games*	certāmen nāvāle	*boat-race*
pompam: pompa	*procession*	caeruleam:	
ad lītus	*to the seashore*	caeruleus	*blue*
Rēgnēnsēs	*Regnenses*	croceam:	
	(a British tribe)	croceus	*yellow*
gentēs: gēns	*tribe*	gubernātor	*helmsman*
competītōrēs:		superbus	*arrogant, proud*
competītor	*competitor*	prōsiluērunt:	
certābant: certāre	*compete*	prōsilīre	*leap forward*
vincēbant: vincere	*be victorious, win*	undās: unda	*wave*
celerius	*faster*	rēmī: rēmus	*oar*
longius	*further*	in lītore	*on the shore*
certāmina:			
certāmen	*contest*		

II

procul in marī erat saxum ingēns. hoc saxum erat mēta. nāvēs ad mētam ruēbant. nāvis Rēgnēnsis, quam Dumnorix dīrigēbat, iam prior erat. ā tergō Belimicus, gubernātor Cantiacus, nautās suōs vituperābat.

Dumnorix, ubi saxō appropinquāvit, nāvem subitō ad dextram 5 vertit.

"ecce!" inquit Dumnorix. "perīculōsum est nōbīs prope saxum nāvigāre, quod multa saxa minōra sub undīs latent. necesse est nōbīs saxa vītāre."

Belimicus tamen, quī haec saxa ignōrābat, cursum rēctum 10 tenēbat.

procul	*far off*
in marī	*in the sea*
saxum	*rock*
mēta	*turning point*
dīrigēbat: dīrigere	*steer*
prior	*in front, first*
ā tergō	*from behind, in the rear*
ad dextram	*to the right*
nāvigāre	*sail*
minōra: minor	*smaller*
sub	*under*
vītāre	*avoid*
ignōrābat	*did not know of*
cursum rēctum: cursus rēctus	*a straight course*

"comitēs," clāmāvit, "ecce! nōs vincere possumus, quod Dumnorix ad dextram abiit. hī Rēgnēnsēs sunt timidī; facile est nōbīs vincere, quod nōs sumus fortiōrēs."

nautae Cantiacī Belimicō crēdēbant. mox nāvem Rēgnēnsem superāvērunt et priōrēs ad mētam advēnērunt. Belimicus, quī saxa perīculōsa nōn vīdit, Dumnorigem dērīdēbat. subitō nāvis Cantiaca in saxa incurrit. nautae perterritī clāmāvērunt; aqua nāvem complēbat. Belimicus et Cantiacī nihil facere poterant; nāvis mox summersa erat.

intereā Dumnorix, quī summā cum cūrā nāvigābat, circum mētam nāvem dīrēxit. nāvis ad lītus incolumis pervēnit. multī spectātōrēs Dumnorigem victōrem laudāvērunt. Rēgnēnsēs laetī, Cantiacī miserī erant. tum omnēs ad mare oculōs vertēbant. difficile erat eīs nautās vidēre, quod in undīs natābant. omnēs tamen Belimicum vidēre poterant, quod summō in saxō sedēbat. madidus ad saxum haerēbat et auxilium postulābat.

comitēs: comes	*comrade, companion*
timidī: timidus	*fearful, frightened*
superāvērunt: superāre	*overtake*
dērīdēbat: dērīdēre	*mock, make fun of*
incurrit: incurrere	*run onto, collide*
summersa	*sunk*
intereā	*meanwhile*
summā cum cūrā	*with the greatest care*
circum	*around*
incolumis	*safe*
oculōs: oculus	*eye*
eīs	*for them*
natābant: natāre	*swim*
summō in saxō	*on the top of the rock*
madidus	*soaked through*
haerēbat: haerēre	*cling*

Practicing the Language

A Complete each sentence with the correct form of the noun and then translate.

1 ubi sacerdōtēs erant parātī, servī vīnum (rēgem, rēgī) dedērunt.
2 Cogidubnus, quī prope effigiem stābat, (victimam, victimae) ēlēgit.
3 Dumnorix (amīcōs, amīcīs) nāvem ostendit.
4 facile erat (spectātōrēs, spectātōribus) Belimicum vidēre, quod ad saxum haerēbat.
5 post certāmen nāvāle, rēx (nautās, nautīs) ad aulam invītāvit.

B Translate the following sentences:

1 difficile est Cogidubnō festīnāre, quod senex est.
2 spectāculum vidēre nōlumus.
3 necesse est nōbīs fugere.
4 pecūniam reddere dēbēs.
5 Salvius est dominus; decōrum est Salviō servōs pūnīre.
6 commodum est tibi in aulā manēre.
7 victimam sacrificāre vīs?

C Complete each sentence with the correct form of the relative pronoun and then translate the sentence.

1 sacerdōs, (quī, quae) victimam sacrificābat, Claudium honōrābat.
2 canis, (quam, quem) Bregāns tenēbat, erat dōnum.
3 Dumnorix nāvī, (quī, quae) prīma ad lītus pervēnit, praeerat.
4 in fossam praecursōrēs plaustrum, (quī, quod) viam claudēbat, dēiēcērunt.
5 nautae, (quōs, quās) spectātōrēs vix vidēre poterant, in undīs natābant.
6 lectus, in (quō, quā) Quīntus recumbit, est in triclīniō.

D Refer to **ad aulam** on page 54. List different examples of prepositional phrases, two with the ablative, four with the accusative, and one each with **in** and the accusative and ablative. Translate each phrase.

The Celts: Friend or Foe?

The Romans, as with most conquerors in the ancient world, exhibited a certain arrogance and insensitivity when dealing with conquered subjects. The Celts must have found Roman imperial arrogance exasperating. In their belief that only their culture was significant, the Romans thoughtlessly drove one of their major roads, the Fosse Way, straight through lands sacred to Sulis, one of the most revered of the Celtic gods. Once an area had been pacified and the army moved on, it left behind a **colōnia**, or town with farm allotments for its veterans. This also annoyed the Celts. In general, however, the Romans treated the Celtic tribes tolerantly provided that they fit into the Roman system of law, order, and profitable trade. In fact, the Romans actively encouraged the Britons to take over civil administration in their own regions. Some British rulers, such as Caratacus and Queen Boudica, resisted the Romans bitterly but unsuccessfully. Others, like King Cogidubnus and Queen Cartimandua, chose to co-operate with the invaders and become allies or dependants of Rome.

Boudica and Cartimandua

The Iceni, a tribe to the east, were at first friendly to Rome. When their king, Prasutagus, died, he made the emperor co-heir, hoping thereby to save his kingdom from harm. The local Roman administrators ignored the will and confiscated all the king's lands and property. When Boudica protested, she was flogged and her daughters raped. Boudica and the Iceni would not let these unprovoked insults go unavenged and, joining with other discontented tribes, they raised a rebellion (A.D. 60).

At first the rebels were very successful. They met with no effective opposition, since Suetonius Paulinus, the Roman governor, was far away fighting the Druids and their supporters. Boudica's forces looted and destroyed the Roman town of Camulodunum (Colchester), burning the temple dedicated to Claudius and killing all the inhabitants. Londinium (London) and Verulamium (St. Albans) suffered the same fate.

Boudica leading her warriors, according to this sculpture in London, England.

Eventually Suetonius Paulinus confronted Boudica and her forces with his legions. Although the Roman troops were heavily outnumbered, their superior training and tactics won them a decisive victory. Rather than face the humiliation of being forced to walk in a triumphal procession as a Roman prisoner of war, Boudica committed suicide by taking poison.

In Roman eyes, Boudica was a remarkable and fearsome figure, not only because she brought them to the brink of disaster, but also because she was a woman who wielded real power. In this she was not alone among British women. From the little we know of their lives, some of the more wealthy had equal rights with men. They could own property in their own right within marriage, divorce their husbands, and be buried with precious possessions and the same funeral rites as their menfolk. Although some Roman women enjoyed these same rights, no Roman woman ever ruled her people and led them into battle. It is not surprising therefore that Boudica was regarded by the Romans as an unnatural, dangerous, but fascinating woman.

On the other hand, Cartimandua, queen of the Brigantes, openly welcomed the Romans. The Romans were glad to have a buffer between them and the wilder tribes of the far north. Caratacus, a Welsh leader who had been fighting the Romans for seven years, fled to her for refuge. Cartimandua showed her loyalty to Rome by handing Caratacus over to them. In spite of the trouble Caratacus had caused, Claudius, after parading Caratacus and his family in his triumph at Rome, allowed him to live in honorable retirement. For supporting Rome, Cartimandua twice received Roman help in quelling rebellions in her own tribe.

Aerial view of Chichester (ancient Noviomagus), showing the traditional Roman grid pattern for the main streets.

Cogidubnus, King of the Regnenses

To Neptune and Minerva, for the welfare of the Divine House, by the authority of Tiberius Claudius Cogidubnus, great king of the Britons, the Association of Craftsmen and those in it gave this temple at their own expense. ...ens, son of Pudentinus, presented the forecourt.

A slab of stone inscribed with these Latin words was discovered in Chichester near the south-east coast in 1723. When found, the slab was broken, but as soon as the pieces had been fitted together it was clear that this was the dedication stone of a temple built at the request of Cogidubnus in honor of Neptune, god of the sea, and Minerva, goddess of wisdom and craftsmanship. Roman dedication stones are rather like the foundation stones which are laid nowadays when an important public building, such as a church, school, or city hall, is being erected. They state the name of the person or group of people who gave the site and paid for the building. This particular temple was paid for by the local **collēgium** or association of craftsmen.

The inscription helps us to reconstruct part of Cogidubnus' life story. He was probably a member of the family that ruled the Atrebates. After the Roman invasion in A.D. 43 the Romans appointed him king of this tribe and the tribe was renamed the Regnenses. Cogidubnus was a faithful supporter of the Romans, and the kingship may have been a reward from the Emperor Claudius for helping them at the time of the invasion. He was granted the privilege of Roman citizenship and allowed to add two of the emperor's names (Tiberius Claudius) to his own. He became a "client king," which meant that he ruled on behalf of the emperor and that he was responsible for collecting the taxes and keeping the peace in his part of Britain. In this way he played an important part in keeping the southern region loyal to Rome, while the legions advanced to conquer the tribes in the north.

As well as his native Celtic gods, Cogidubnus worshiped Roman ones: Neptune and Minerva.

By dedicating the new temple to Neptune and Minerva rather than British gods, Cogidubnus publicly declared his loyalty to Rome. The temple was a reminder of Roman power. Its priests may well have been selected from the local British chieftains, many of whom were quick to see the advantages of supporting the new government. And when the inscription goes on to say that the temple was intended "for the welfare of the Divine House," Cogidubnus is suggesting that the emperor himself is related to the gods and should be worshiped. The Romans encouraged the people of their empire to respect and worship the emperor in this way, because it helped to ensure obedience and to build up a sense of unity in a large empire that contained many tribes, many languages, and many religions.

The Regnenses received not only a new king, but also a new capital town, Noviomagus. It was founded on the south-east coast, where Chichester now stands. Three miles (five kilometers) to the west is the modern village of Fishbourne, where the remains of a remarkably large Roman building were found in 1960 by a workman digging a trench. This was a palace as large and splendid as the fashionable houses in Rome itself, with one set of rooms after another, arranged round a huge courtyard. No inscription has been found to reveal the owner's name, but the palace was so large, so magnificent, and so near to Noviomagus that Cogidubnus seems the likeliest owner. The palace itself was evidence of the benefits of accepting or tolerating the Roman presence in Britain.

Vespasian and the Durotriges

Vespasian (inset) found the Durotriges defended by hill forts surrounded by huge banks and ditches, like Maiden Castle (above). Roundhouses filled the space inside the ditches. After the Roman victory, the defenders were buried by the fort entrance (left).

The Second Legion built a camp in the corner of a British hill fort (right).

Word Study

A Give a derivative from the Vocabulary Checklist to match each definition. Use the underlined word as a clue.

1. fear of being <u>shut</u> in
2. a pipe for bringing <u>water</u> from a distant source
3. <u>conveniently</u> roomy
4. something <u>owed</u> to another
5. to overflow or overwhelm like a <u>wave</u>
6. one who rides a <u>horse</u>
7. the <u>chief</u> person in a school

B Match the definition to the derivative. Give the Latin root and its meaning.

1. principle   **a** to enclose
2. fracture   **b** to obstruct
3. debenture   **c** a rule of conduct
4. tenacious   **d** priestly
5. alias   **e** a break
6. include   **f** another, often false, name
7. sacerdotal   **g** like a horse
8. equine   **h** persistent, stubborn
9. impede   **i** to billow
10. undulate   **j** a certificate indicating something owed

C Explain why the name saxifrage is so appropriate for this plant.

Stage 15
Vocabulary Checklist

The gender of each noun will now be indicated. Adjectives will be listed by their nominative singular masculine, feminine, and neuter forms.

alius, alia, aliud	*other, another*
aqua, f.	*water*
claudō, claudere, clausī	*shut, block*
commodus, commoda, commodum	*convenient*
dēbeō, dēbēre, dēbuī	*owe, ought*
effigiēs: effigiem, f.	*image, statue*
equus, m.	*horse*
etiam	*even*
frāctus, frācta, frāctum	*broken*
impediō, impedīre, impedīvī	*delay, hinder*
lectus, m.	*couch*
lentē	*slowly*
mare, n.	*sea*
miser, misera, miserum	*miserable, wretched*
nauta, m.	*sailor*
plaustrum, n.	*wagon, cart*
praesum, praeesse, praefuī (+DAT)	*be in charge of*
prīnceps: prīncipem, m.	*chief, chieftain*
quī, quae, quod	*who, which*
redeō, redīre, rediī	*return, go back*
sacerdōs: sacerdōtem, m.	*priest*
saxum, n.	*rock*
teneō, tenēre, tenuī	*hold*
unda, f.	*wave*
vincō, vincere, vīcī	*win*

A Roman arrowhead was found in the spine of a Celtic warrior.

IN AULA

Stage 16

1 Cogidubnus Quīntum per
aulam dūcēbat. in aulā erant
multae pictūrae, quās pictor
Graecus pīnxerat.

2 rēx iuvenem in hortum dūxit.
in hortō erant multī flōrēs,
quōs Cogidubnus ex Ītaliā
importāverat.

3 tum ad ātrium vēnērunt.
mediō in ātriō erat fōns
marmoreus, quem fabrī
Rōmānī fēcerant.

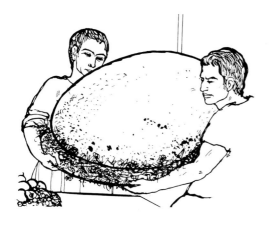

4 rēx et hospitēs in aulā
cēnābant. cēna, quam coquī
Graecī parāverant, optima
erat. servī magnum ōvum in
mēnsam posuērunt.

5 ex ōvō, quod servī in
mēnsam posuerant, appāruit
saltātrīx.

6 tum pūmiliōnēs, quōs rēx in
Ītaliā ēmerat, intrāvērunt.
pūmiliōnēs pilās iactābant.

Belimicus ultor

Belimicus, prīnceps Cantiacus, postquam Dumnorix in certāmine nāvālī vīcit, rem graviter ferēbat. īrātissimus erat. omnēs hospitēs, quōs rēx ad aulam invītāverat, eum dērīdēbant. Cantiacī quoque eum dērīdēbant et vituperābant. etiam servī, quī dē naufragiō cognōverant, clam rīdēbant. 5

"iste Dumnorix mē dēcēpit," Belimicus sibi dīxit. "mē in saxa impulit et praemium iniūstē cēpit. decōrum est mihi eum pūnīre."

Belimicus sēcum cōgitāvit et cōnsilium callidum cēpit. erant in aulā multae bēstiae, quās rēx ē multīs terrīs importāverat. inter haec animālia erat ursa ingēns, quam servus Germānicus 10 custōdiēbat. Belimicus ad hunc servum adiit.

"hoc animal est magnificum," inquit. "mē valdē dēlectat. ursam tractāre volō; eam nōn timeō."

itaque prīnceps ad ursam cotīdiē veniēbat; ursae cibum et aquam dabat. paulātim ursam mānsuētam fēcit. tandem sōlus 15 ursam tractāre potuit.

mox Cogidubnus cēnam et spectāculum nūntiāvit. amīcōs ad aulam invītāvit. Belimicus statim ad servum Germānicum contendit.

"rēx hodiē spectāculum dat," inquit. "hodiē hanc ursam in 20 aulam dūcere volō. nunc eam tractāre possum. hospitibus eam ostendere volō."

servus invītus cōnsēnsit. Belimicus cachinnāns sibi dīxit, "parātus sum. nunc Dumnorigem pūnīre possum."

ultor	avenger
graviter ferēbat	took badly
dē naufragiō	about the shipwreck
cognōverant: cognōscere	find out, get to know
clam	secretly, in private
impulit: impellere	push, force
praemium	prize
iniūstē	unfairly
sēcum	to himself
ursa	bear
Germānicus	German
adiit: adīre	approach, go up to
tractāre	handle
paulātim	gradually
mānsuētam: mānsuētus	tame

ursa

saltātrīx

rēx spectāculum dat

I

rēx cum multīs hospitibus in aulā cēnābat. Salvius et Quīntus
prope rēgem recumbēbant. Britannī cibum laudābant, Rōmānī
vīnum. omnēs hospitēs rēgī grātiās agēbant.

subitō Belimicus tardus intrāvit.

"ecce! naufragus noster intrat," clāmāvit Dumnorix. "num tū   5
aliam nāvem āmīsistī?"

cēterī Belimicum dērīsērunt et Dumnorigī plausērunt.
Belimicus tamen Dumnorigī nihil respondit, sed tacitus cōnsēdit.

rēx hospitibus suīs spectāculum nūntiāvit. statim pūmiliōnēs
cum saltātrīcibus intrāvērunt et hospitēs dēlectāvērunt. deinde,   10
ubi rēx eīs signum dedit, omnēs exiērunt. Salvius, quem
pūmiliōnēs nōn dēlectāverant, clāmāvit,

"haec cēna est bona. numquam cēnam meliōrem cōnsūmpsī.
sed ursam, quae saltat, vidēre volō. illa ursa mē multō magis
dēlectat quam pūmiliōnēs et saltātrīcēs."   15

tardus	*late*
naufragus	*shipwrecked*
	sailor
tacitus	*silent, in silence*
cōnsēdit:	
cōnsīdere	*sit down*
pūmiliōnēs:	
pūmiliō	*dwarf*
cum saltātrīcibus	*with dancing-*
	girls
saltat: saltāre	*dance*
multō magis	*much more*

*Salvius et Quīntus prope
rēgem recumbēbant.*

II

When you have read this part of the story, answer the questions at the end.

rēx servīs signum dedit. servus, quī hoc signum exspectābat, statim cum ursā intrāvit et hospitibus eam ostendit.

Belimicus, simulatque hoc vīdit, surrēxit, et ad medium triclīnium prōcessit.

"mī Dumnorix!" clāmāvit. "facile est tibi iocōs facere. sed ursam   5
tractāre nōn audēs! ego nōn timeō. ego, quem tū dērīdēs, ursam tractāre audeō."

omnēs Belimicum spectābant attonitī. Belimicus, quī servum Germānicum iam dīmīserat, ursam ad Dumnorigem dūxit.

"nōnne tū quoque ursam tractāre vīs?" rogāvit īnsolēns. "nōnne   10
tū hospitibus spectāculum dare vīs?"

Dumnorix impavidus statim surrēxit et Belimicum dērīsit.

"facile est mihi hanc ursam superāre. tē quoque, homuncule, superāre possum."

tum cēterī, quī anteā timuerant, valdē cachinnāvērunt.   15
Belimicus, ubi cachinnōs audīvit, furēns ursam pulsāvit, et eam ad Dumnorigem impulit. subitō ursa saeva sē vertit, et Belimicum ferōciter percussit. tum prīncipēs perterritī clāmōrem magnum sustulērunt et ad iānuās quam celerrimē cucurrērunt. etiam inter sē pugnābant, quod exīre nōn poterant. ursa, quam hic clāmor   20
terruerat, ad lectum currēbat, ubi rēx sedēbat.

rēx tamen, quod claudicābat, effugere nōn poterat. Dumnorix in ursam frūstrā sē coniēcit. Salvius immōtus stābat. sed Quīntus hastam, quam servus tenēbat, rapuit. hastam celeriter ēmīsit et bēstiam saevam trānsfīxit. illa dēcidit mortua.   25

Mosaic tendril border from Fishbourne showing a bird, which probably served as the mosaicist's signature or trademark.

iocōs: iocus	*joke*	saeva: saevus	*savage*
audēs: audēre	*dare*	sē vertit: sē vertere	*turn around*
homuncule: homunculus	*little man*	coniēcit: conicere	*hurl, throw*
cachinnāvērunt: cachinnāre	*roar with laughter*	immōtus	*still, motionless*
cachinnōs: cachinnus	*laughter*	hastam: hasta	*spear*
furēns	*furious, in a rage*		

Questions

1 What two things did the German slave do at the king's signal?
2 What boast did Belimicus make (lines 6–7)? How did he show in lines 8–9 that he meant what he said?
3 What two challenges did Belimicus make to Dumnorix (lines 10–11)?
4 Look at lines 13–14. What two things did Dumnorix say that showed he was **impavidus**?
5 What two things did Belimicus do when he heard the guests laughing at him (lines 16–17)?
6 What unexpected effect did this have on the bear? Give two details.
7 What actions of the chiefs show that they were **perterritī** (lines 18–20)?
8 Why did the guests fight among themselves?
9 Why did the bear run towards the king's couch?
10 Why could the king not escape?
11 In lines 22–25 how did each of the following people react?
   a) Dumnorix   b) Salvius   c) Quintus
12 What do their reactions show about each of their characters?

Exotic animals and birds were collected from Africa and Asia and other parts of the ancient world. Some were destined for collections like that of King Cogidubnus; others ended up being hunted and killed in the amphitheater. This mosaic shows two ostriches being carried up the gangplank of a ship.

About the Language I: Pluperfect Tense

A In this Stage, you have met examples of the **pluperfect** tense. They looked like this:

> in aulā erat ursa ingēns, quam rēx ex Ītaliā **importāverat**.
> *In the palace was a huge bear, which the king **had imported** from Italy.*

> sacerdōtēs, quī ad āram **prōcesserant**, victimās sacrificāvērunt.
> *The priests, who **had advanced** to the altar, sacrificed the victims.*

B The complete pluperfect tense is as follows:

portāveram	*I had carried*
portāverās	*you (s.) had carried*
portāverat	*s/he had carried*
portāverāmus	*we had carried*
portāverātis	*you (pl.) had carried*
portāverant	*they had carried*

C Further examples:

1 Rūfilla ancillās, quae cubiculum parāverant, laudāvit.
2 in ātriō sedēbant hospitēs, quōs rēx ad aulam invītāverat.
3 agricola nōs laudāvit, quod per tōtum diem labōrāverāmus.
4 Belimicus, quī nāvem āmīserat, īrātissimus erat.
5 Salvius mē pūnīvit, quod ē vīllā fūgeram.

D Study the differences among the present, perfect, and pluperfect tenses:

	PRESENT	PERFECT	PLUPERFECT
first conjugation	portat *s/he carries*	portāvit *s/he carried*	portāverat *s/he had carried*
second conjugation	docet *s/he teaches*	docuit *s/he taught*	docuerat *s/he had taught*
third conjugation	trahit *s/he drags*	trāxit *s/he dragged*	trāxerat *s/he had dragged*
fourth conjugation	audit *s/he hears*	audīvit *s/he heard*	audīverat *s/he had heard*

Quīntus dē sē

postrīdiē Quīntus per hortum cum rēge ambulābat, flōrēsque variōs spectābat. deinde rēx

"quō modō," inquit, "ex urbe Pompēiīs effūgistī? paterne et māter superfuērunt?"

Quīntus trīstis   5

"periit pater," inquit. "māter quoque in urbe periit. ego et ūnus servus superfuimus. ex urbe vix effūgimus. simulac tūtī erāmus, servum, quī tam fortis et tam fidēlis fuerat, līberāvī."

"quid deinde fēcistī?" inquit rēx. "pecūniam habēbās?"

"omnēs vīllās, quās pater in Campāniā possēderat, vēndidī. ita   10
multam pecūniam comparāvī. tum ex Ītaliā discēdere voluī, quod trīstissimus eram. ego igitur et lībertus meus urbem Brundisium petīvimus et nāvem cōnscendimus.

"prīmō ad Graeciam vēnimus et in urbe Athēnīs habitābāmus. haec urbs erat pulcherrima, sed cīvēs turbulentī. multī philosophī,   15
quī forum cotīdiē frequentābant, contrōversiās inter sē habēbant. post paucōs mēnsēs, aliās urbēs vidēre voluimus. ad Aegyptum igitur nāvigāvimus, et mox ad urbem Alexandrīam advēnimus."

variōs: varius	*different*
quō modō	*how*
superfuērunt: superesse	*survive*
vix	*with difficulty*
tam	*so*
fuerat	*had been*
possēderat: possidēre	*possess*
comparāvī: comparāre	*obtain*
Brundisium	*Brindisi (a port on the Adriatic Sea)*
cōnscendimus: cōnscendere	*embark on, go on board*
prīmō	*first*
Athēnīs: Athēnae	*Athens*
frequentābant: frequentāre	*crowd*
mēnsēs: mēnsis	*month*
Aegyptum: Aegyptus	*Egypt*

The Acropolis (or citadel) of Athens. The prominent building is the Parthenon, the temple of Athena (whom the Romans called Minerva).

About the Language II: Questions

A In Unit 1, you met the question-word **num** which is used to suggest that the anticipated answer to the question will be *no*. Notice again the different ways of translating it:

> **num** tū servus es?
> *Surely you're not a slave?*
> *You're not a slave, are you?*

> **num** tū sellam extrāxistī?
> *Surely you didn't take away the chair?*
> *You didn't take away the chair, did you?*

B In Unit 1 you also met **-ne** which is used to elicit the answer *yes* or *no* to a question.

> pater**ne** et māter superfuērunt?
> *Did your father and mother survive?*

C From Stage 13 onwards, you have met the question-word **nōnne** which is used to suggest that the anticipated answer will be *yes*. Notice the different ways of translating it:

> **nōnne** tū hospitibus spectāculum dare vīs?
> *Surely you want to give a show to the guests?*
> *You want to give a show to the guests, don't you?*

> **nōnne** haec vīlla est ēlegāns?
> *Surely this house is elegant?*
> *This house is elegant, isn't it?*

D Further examples:

1 nōnne haec pictūra est pulchra?
2 num perterritus es?
3 tūne effugere poterās?
4 num Bregāns labōrat?
5 nōnne rēx tibi illum canem dedit?

Practicing the Language

A Complete each sentence by selecting the correct pluperfect verb form in the relative clause. Then translate into English:

For example: fabrī, quōs imperātor (mīserat, mīserant), aulam
aedificāvērunt.
fabrī, quōs imperātor mīserat, aulam
aedificāvērunt.
The craftsmen whom the emperor had sent built the palace.

1 rēx, quī multōs hospitēs (invītāverat, invītāverant), eīs cēnam optimam dedit.
2 prīncipēs, quī ex ātriō (discesserat, discesserant), in āream prōcessērunt.
3 dōnum, quod ego rēgī (dederam, dederat), pretiōsum erat.
4 ancillae, quae ad aulam (vēnerāmus, vēnerant), nōs dēlectāvērunt.
5 nōs, quī Belimicum (cōnspexerāmus, cōnspexerant), valdē rīsimus.
6 tū, quī ursam (tractāverās, tractāverat), nōn timēbās.

B Complete each sentence with the correct word from those given below, and then translate. You will have to use some words more than once.

NOMINATIVE   Rōmānī   Britannī
DATIVE   Rōmānīs   Britannīs

1 Rōmānī et Britannī ad aulam vēnerant. Cogidubnus Rōmānīs et . . . . . cēnam splendidam dabat.
2 rēx Rōmānīs favēbat. multī . . . . . prope rēgem sedēbant. rēx . . . . . vīnum optimum obtulit.
3 rēx . . . . . nōn favēbat. Cogidubnus Britannīs vīnum pessimum obtulit.
4 multī . . . . . erant īrātī. mox Britannī et . . . . . inter sē pugnābant.

obtulit: offerre *offer*

C Translate into English:

Cogidubnus et Vespasiānus

Cogidubnus Quīntō dē vītā suā nārrābat:

"ubi Rōmānī in Britanniam invāsērunt, Claudius legiōnem secundam contrā Durotrigēs mīsit. Vespasiānus, quī hanc legiōnem dūcēbat, ad mē vēnit et auxilium rogāvit. ego Vespasiānō auxilium dedī. Rōmānīs frūmentum comparāvī. 5
Rōmānīs explōrātōrēs dedī. hī explōrātōrēs Rōmānōs celeriter dūxērunt ad regiōnem, ubi Durotrigēs habitābant. Durotrigēs diū resistēbant sed Rōmānī tandem victōrēs erant. Vespasiānus ad mē epistulam scrīpsit.

"'Durotrigēs fortiter pugnāvērunt, sed nōs eōs tandem 10
superāvimus. multōs Durotrigēs necāvimus; multās fēminās līberōsque cēpimus; multōs vīcōs incendimus. nōs Rōmānī fortiōrēs erāmus quam barbarī. facile erat nōbīs eōs superāre.'

"post multōs annōs Rōmānī Vespasiānum imperātōrem fēcērunt. Vespasiānus, quī mihi amīcus fidēlissimus erat, mē 15
honōrāvit. aliam epistulam ad mē mīsit.

"'tē honōrāre volō, quod mihi auxilium ōlim dedistī. decōrum est tibi in aulā habitāre. architectum igitur ex Graeciā arcessīvī, et fabrōs Ītalicōs comparāvī. eōs ad tē mīsī.'

"architectus et fabrī, quōs Vespasiānus mīsit, callidissimī 20
erant. dīligenter labōrāvērunt et hanc aulam aedificāvērunt. ita Vespasiānus mihi benignitātem summam ostendit."

Vespasiānus	Vespasian (Roman general in British campaigns, A.D. 43; emperor A.D. 69–79)
invāsērunt: invādere	invade
legiōnem: legiō	legion
contrā	against
Durotrigēs	Durotriges (name of a British tribe)
explōrātōrēs: explōrātor	scout, spy
regiōnem: regiō	region
cēpimus: capere	take, capture
vīcōs: vīcus	village
incendimus: incendere	burn, set fire to
annōs: annus	year
Ītalicōs: Ītalicus	Italian
benignitātem: benignitās	kindness

The Palace at Fishbourne

On the Fishbourne site, underneath the palace, excavators have found the remains of earlier wooden buildings, dating back to the time of the Roman invasion or very shortly afterwards. One of them was a granary. Pieces of metal and a helmet were also found nearby. These discoveries indicate the presence of soldiers; they may have been the soldiers of the Second Legion, commanded by Vespasian, a brilliant young general who led the attack against the Durotriges in the southwest. There was a harbor nearby, where Roman supply ships docked. It is therefore likely that the Romans first used Fishbourne as a military port and supply base.

When the Roman soldiers moved on from Fishbourne, they left behind them a few buildings and some roads. During the next thirty years many improvements were made. The roads were resurfaced and the drainage of this low-lying, rather marshy site was improved. The harbor was developed and merchant ships called regularly. A fine new villa with a set of baths was built in the late sixties. This could have been a residence built by Cogidubnus for himself just three miles (five kilometers) from his new capital town, Noviomagus.

In A.D. 69, Vespasian himself became emperor, and renewed work began on the Fishbourne site about A.D. 75. Perhaps Vespasian was remembering the loyalty of Cogidubnus and was now presenting him with this palace in return for his continued support of the Romans. A vast area of about ten acres was cleared, leveled, and landscaped. The original villa and its baths became part of the southeast corner of a huge new palace.

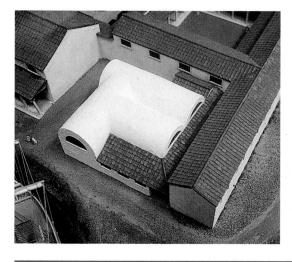

The bath house (with the white roof) of the original villa was incorporated into the later palace. Notice how close to the sea the palace was.

A Roman Palace for a British King

The palace at Fishbourne was laid out in four long wings around a central garden.

The north wing contained three suites of rooms arranged around two internal courtyards where important guests could stay.

The aisled hall, which had access only from outside the palace, was probably a public assembly hall.

Visitors entered the palace through the imposing entrance hall in the middle of the east wing. Some other rooms in this wing may have provided guest accommodations for less important visitors.

The west wing was built on a platform five feet (1.5 meters) higher than the rest of the palace. In the center stood the impressive audience chamber where the king received his subjects and interviewed officials; the other rooms may have been used as offices.

Today the south wing lies under a modern road and houses, but excavations suggest that it may have been the residential suite for King Cogidubnus and his family, with a colonnaded veranda overlooking an informal terraced garden extending to the sea.

The bath house in the south-east corner was part of the original villa.

Elegant Walls

The Romans' decorative schemes have been reconstructed from fragments.

One fragment of painted wall plaster from Fishbourne (left) is similar in size to a painting from Stabiae (right).

A frieze made of fine plaster and some of the marble pieces that decorated the walls (right).

Fashionable Floors

Above and right: Cogidubnus' floors were covered with elegant black-and-white mosaics in geometric patterns. Try drawing the different shapes and work out how they fit together.

This floor, laid by a later owner, had a more complicated pattern. In the center, Cupid rides a dolphin, and legendary sea creatures swim in the semi-circular spaces around.

Specialist craftsmen were brought in from Italy: makers of mosaics, marble-workers, plasterers to make friezes, painters, carpenters, iron-smiths, hydraulic engineers to construct the fountains, and many others. All the construction and detailed manufacturing was carried out on the site itself, where the builders lived and worked for many years. Many traces of the activity of these craftsmen have been found. The floor of the area used by the stonemasons was littered with fragments of marble and colored stone which had been imported from quarries in Italy, the Greek island of Scyros, Asia Minor, and elsewhere. In another area were signs of iron-working where the smiths had manufactured door-hinges, handles, and bolts.

The Palace Gardens

Like the palace, the garden was planned, laid out, and decorated in the most fashionable Italian style. Whoever the owner was, he wanted his palace in Britain to be as Roman as possible.

The open area, which measured approximately 100 by 80 yards (90 by 70 meters), was laid out as a formal garden. The two lawns were not rolled and cut like a modern lawn, but the grass was kept short and tidy. Along the edges of the lawns archaeologists have found deep bedding trenches filled with a mixture of loam and crushed chalk where shrubs

Box hedges have been planted exactly where the Roman bedding trenches were found.

The reconstruction of the garden at Fishbourne features plants which Cogidubnus might have had in his garden. They have been planted there now. Clockwise from top left: acanthus, lily, rose, hyssop, grapevine.

and flowers such as roses, flowering trees, box, rosemary, lilies, and acanthus would probably have been planted.

A line of deep-set post holes across the eastern side of the garden shows where wooden poles and trellises supported fruit trees and climbing plants. Some of these may have been rambler roses: the Romans were fond of roses and good at growing them.

A broad path, approximately 13 yards (12 meters) wide and surfaced with stone chippings, ran through the middle of the garden leading from the entrance hall to the audience chamber. Paths ran around the outside of the lawns. The garden had drains and was irrigated by spring water through ceramic pipes. A system of underground pipes brought water to the fountains which stood at intervals along the paths. Small marble and bronze statues provided further decoration.

A slave working in the potting shed: a reconstruction at Fishbourne today.

Word Study

A What do the following derivatives of **pōnō, pōnere, posuī** mean?

1	composition	6	exponent
2	indisposed	7	impose
3	opponent	8	proposition
4	juxtaposition	9	appositive
5	deposit	10	repository

B Use derivatives from the Latin words below (listed in order of appearance) to fill in the blanks in the following sentences:

cōnsilium   flōs   dēlectāre   parātus   aedificāre   vertere tollere   vertere   dērīdēre   pūnīre

Cogidubnus' social _____ put forth his suggestions for a banquet. He would create a wonderful _____ display for the triclinium from the garden. The chef would concoct a thoroughly _____ repast of meat, fruit, and wine. After intense _____ and for the _____ of the guests, Etruscan dancers would present their _____ of the Romulus and Remus story to _____ the heroes of old Rome. Should anyone _____ to barbaric behavior during the entertainment and react to the presentation with _____, severe _____ measures would be taken.

C Copy the following words and put parentheses around the Latin root. Then write the Latin root word and its meaning for each derivative.

e.g. conservation   con(serva)tion   servāre – save

1 consensual
2 incontrovertible
3 consummate (adjective)
4 intolerable
5 ameliorate
6 navigable
7 intervention
8 auxiliary
9 fabricate
10 impunity

Stage 16
Vocabulary Checklist

aedificō, aedificāre, aedificāvī	build
auxilium, n.	help
cōnsentiō, cōnsentīre, cōnsēnsī	agree
cōnsilium, n.	plan, idea
deinde	then
dēlectō, dēlectāre, dēlectāvī	delight
dērīdeō, dērīdēre, dērīsī	mock, make fun of
dīmittō, dīmittere, dīmīsī	send away, dismiss
effugiō, effugere, effūgī	escape
faber, fabrum, m.	craftsman
flōs, flōrem, m.	flower
imperātor, imperātōrem, m.	emperor
inter (+ ACC)	among
ita	in this way
melior, melior, melius	better
nāvigō, nāvigāre, nāvigāvī	sail
nōnne?	surely?
parātus, parāta, parātum	ready, prepared
pereō, perīre, periī	die, perish
pōnō, pōnere, posuī	place, put
postrīdiē	on the next day
pūniō, pūnīre, pūnīvī	punish
simulac, simulatque	as soon as
summus, summa, summum	highest, greatest, top
supersum, superesse, superfuī	survive
tollō, tollere, sustulī	raise, lift up
vertō, vertere, vertī	turn

Detail from the Cupid and Dolphin mosaic at Fishbourne (pictured on page 86), showing a fabulous sea-panther.

ALEXANDRIA

Quīntus dē Alexandrīā

1 Alexandrīa magnum portum habet. prope portum est īnsula. facile est nāvibus ad portum pervenīre, quod in hāc īnsulā est pharus ingēns. multae nāvēs in portū Alexandrīae sunt.

2 Alexandrīa est urbs turbulenta. ingēns turba semper urbem complet. multī mercātōrēs per viās ambulant. multī servī per urbem currunt. multī mīlitēs per viās urbis incēdunt. mīlitēs Rōmānī urbem custōdiunt.

3 ego et Clēmēns, postquam ad urbem pervēnimus, templum vīdimus. ad hoc templum, quod Augustus Caesar prope lītus aedificāverat, festīnāvimus. prō templō Caesaris erat āra. ego vīnum in āram fūdī.

4 prope hanc urbem habitābat Barbillus, vir dīves. Barbillus negōtium cum patre meō saepe agēbat. vīllam splendidam habēbat. ad vīllam Barbillī mox pervēnī. facile erat mihi vīllam invenīre, quod Barbillus erat vir nōtissimus.

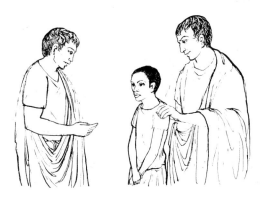

5 Barbillus multōs servōs habēbat, ego nūllōs. "decōrum est tibi servum Aegyptium habēre," inquit Barbillus. inter servōs Barbillī erat puer Aegyptius. Barbillus, vir benignus, mihi hunc puerum dedit.

tumultus

I

in vīllā Barbillī diū habitābam. ad urbem cum servō quondam contendī, quod Clēmentem vīsitāre volēbam. ille tabernam prope portum Alexandrīae possidēbat. servus, quī mē dūcēbat, erat puer Aegyptius.

in urbe erat ingēns multitūdō, quae viās complēbat. mercātōrēs 5 per viās ambulābant et negōtium inter sē agēbant. fēminae et ancillae tabernās frequentābant; tabernāriī fēminīs et ancillīs stolās ostendēbant. multī servī per viās urbis currēbant. difficile erat nōbīs per viās ambulāre, quod maxima erat multitūdō. tandem ad portum Alexandrīae pervēnimus. plūrimī Aegyptiī aderant, sed 10 nūllōs Graecōs vidēre poterāmus. puer, postquam hoc sēnsit, anxius

"melius est nōbīs," inquit, "ad vīllam Barbillī revenīre. ad tabernam Clēmentis īre nōn possumus. viae sunt perīculōsae, quod Aegyptiī īrātī sunt. omnēs Graecī ex hāc parte urbis 15 fūgērunt."

"minimē!" puerō respondī. "quamquam Aegyptiī sunt īrātī, ad vīllam redīre nōlō. longum iter iam fēcimus. paene ad tabernam Clēmentis pervēnimus. necesse est nōbīs cautē prōcēdere."

tumultus	*riot*	plūrimī	*very many*
quondam	*one day, once*	sēnsit: sentīre	*notice*
ille	*he*	melius est	*it would be better*
tabernāriī:		parte: pars	*part*
tabernārius	*shopkeeper*		

II

When you have read this part of the story, answer the questions at the end.

itaque ad tabernam Clēmentis contendimus, sed in triviīs plūrimī Aegyptiī nōbīs obstābant. in multitūdine Aegyptiōrum erat senex, quī Graecōs Rōmānōsque vituperābat. omnēs eum intentē audiēbant.

ubi hoc vīdī, sollicitus eram. puer Aegyptius, quī sollicitūdinem 5 meam sēnserat, mē ad casam proximam dūxit.

"domine, in hāc casā habitat faber, quī Barbillum bene nōvit. necesse est nōbīs casam intrāre et perīculum vītāre."

faber per fenestram casae forte spectābat. ubi puerum agnōvit, nōs in casam suam libenter accēpit. 10

postquam casam intrāvimus, susurrāvī,

"quis est hic faber?"

"est Diogenēs, faber Graecus,"respondit puer.

ubi hoc audīvī, magis timēbam. nam in casā virī Graecī eram; extrā iānuam casae Aegyptiī Graecōs vituperābant. subitō servus 15 clāmāvit,

"ēheu! Aegyptiī īnfestī casam oppugnant."

Diogenēs statim ad armārium contendit. in armāriō erant quīnque fūstēs, quōs Diogenēs extrāxit et nōbīs trādidit.

Aegyptiī iānuam effrēgērunt et in casam irrūpērunt. nōs 20 Aegyptiīs fortiter resistēbāmus, sed illī erant multī, nōs paucī. septem Aegyptiī mē circumveniēbant. duōs graviter vulnerāvī, sed cēterī mē superāvērunt. prōcubuī exanimātus. ubi animum recēpī, casam circumspectāvī. fenestrae erant frāctae, casa dīrepta. Diogenēs mediā in casā stābat lacrimāns. prope mē iacēbat puer 25 meus.

"puer mortuus est," inquit Diogenēs. "Aegyptiī eum necāvērunt, quod ille tē dēfendēbat."

in triviīs	*at the crossroads*
nōbīs obstābant	*blocked our way, obstructed us*
sollicitūdinem: sollicitūdō	*anxiety*
casam: casa	*small house*
nōvit	*knows*
perīculum	*danger*
fenestram: fenestra	*window*
forte	*by chance*
accēpit: accipere	*take in, receive*
magis	*more*
extrā iānuam	*outside the door*
īnfestī: īnfestus	*hostile*
oppugnant: oppugnāre	*attack*
effrēgērunt: effringere	*break down*
irrūpērunt: irrumpere	*burst in*
septem	*seven*
circumveniēbant: circumvenīre	*surround*
animum recēpī: animum recipere	*recover consciousness*
dīrepta: dīreptus	*pulled apart, ransacked*
dēfendēbat: dēfendere	*defend*

Questions

1 What was happening at the crossroads (lines 1–2)?
2 What was the old man doing? What was the crowd's reaction to him (lines 3–4)?
3 **ubi hoc vīdī, sollicitus eram** (line 5). Why do you think Quintus was worried?
4 **puer … mē ad casam proximam dūxit** (lines 5–6). Explain why the boy did this (lines 7–8).
5 Why were Quintus and the boy taken into the house (lines 9–10)?
6 **magis timēbam** (line 14). Why was Quintus more frightened now?
7 How had Diogenes prepared for an Egyptian attack on the house? What does this imply about recent events in this part of the city?
8 How did the Egyptians get into the house (line 20)?
9 Why was it difficult to resist the Egyptians (line 21)?
10 Describe the part Quintus played in the fight (lines 22–23).
11 In what condition was the house when Quintus looked around it (line 24)?
12 Who was killed? Why do you think he was killed and not anyone else?

Egypt, especially Alexandria, had a very mixed population. Many were Greeks like Artemidorus in the portrait on the left. The sculpture of the African man on the right was found in Alexandria itself.

About the Language: Genitive Case

A Study the following sentences:

ad portum **Alexandrīae** mox pervēnimus.
We soon arrived at the harbor of Alexandria.

in vīllā **Barbillī** erant multī servī.
In the house of Barbillus were many slaves.

mīlitēs Rōmānī per viās **urbis** incēdēbant.
Roman soldiers were marching through the streets of the city.

in multitūdine **Aegyptiōrum** erat senex.
In the crowd of Egyptians was an old man.

agmen **mīlitum** per urbem incēdit.
A column of soldiers is marching through the city.

The words in boldface are in the genitive case.

B Here is a full list of the cases you have met. The new genitive forms are in boldface.

	SINGULAR			PLURAL		
	first declension	*second declension*	*third declension*	*first declension*	*second declension*	*third declension*
nominative	puella	servus	leō	puellae	servī	leōnēs
genitive	**puellae**	**servī**	**leōnis**	**puellārum**	**servōrum**	**leōnum**
dative	puellae	servō	leōnī	puellīs	servīs	leōnibus
accusative	puellam	servum	leōnem	puellās	servōs	leōnēs
ablative	puellā	servō	leōne	puellīs	servīs	leōnibus

C In future Vocabulary Checklists and in the Complete Vocabulary, the genitive singular of a noun is listed along with the nominative. The genitive indicates the declension (family) to which a noun belongs, and it also shows the stem of nouns like **leō, leōnis**.

D Further examples:

1 Quīntus per multitūdinem servōrum contendit.
2 Aegyptiī in casam fabrī ruērunt.
3 nūllī Graecī in illā parte urbis habitābant.
4 multī Aegyptiī in fundō fēminae labōrābant.
5 puer Quīntum per turbam mīlitum dūxit.
6 iuvenēs et puerī ad tabernam mercātōris contendērunt.

ad templum

per viās urbis quondam cum Barbillō ībam. in multitūdine, quae viās complēbat, Aegyptiōs, Graecōs, Iūdaeōs, Syrōs vīdī. subitō vir quīdam nōbīs appropinquāvit. Barbillus, simulatque eum cōnspexit, magnum gemitum dedit.

Barbillus:	ēheu! quam miserī sumus! ecce Plancus, vir doctissimus, quī numquam tacet! semper dē portū Alexandrīae et dē templīs deōrum et dē aliīs monumentīs garrīre vult.	5
Plancus:	salvē, mī dulcissime! quid hodiē agis? quō contendis?	
Barbillus:	(*invītus*) ad templum.	10
Plancus:	ad templum Augustī?	
Barbillus:	minimē, ad templum Serāpidis īmus. nunc festīnāre dēbēmus, quod iter longum est. nōnne tū negōtium cum aliīs mercātōribus agere dēbēs? valē!	
Plancus:	hodiē ōtiōsus sum. commodum est mihi ad templum Serāpidis īre. dē Serāpide vōbīs nārrāre possum. (*Plancus nōbīscum ībat garriēns. nōbīs dē omnibus monumentīs urbis nārrāre coepit. Barbillus rem graviter ferēbat.*)	15
Barbillus:	(*susurrāns*) amīcus noster loquācior est quam psittacus et obstinātior quam asinus.	20
Plancus:	nunc ad templum Serāpidis advēnimus. spectāte templum! quam magnificum! spectāte cellam! statuamne vīdistis, quae in cellā est? deus ibi magnā cum dignitāte sedet. in capite deī est canistrum. Serāpis enim est deus quī segetēs cūrat. opportūnē hūc vēnimus. hōra quārta est. nunc sacerdōtēs in ārā sacrificium facere solent. (*subitō tuba sonuit. sacerdōtēs ē cellā templī ad āram prōcessērunt.*)	25

30 |
| sacerdōs: | tacēte vōs omnēs, quī adestis! tacēte vōs, quī hoc sacrificium vidēre vultis! (*omnēs virī fēminaeque statim tacuērunt.*) | |
| Barbillus: | (*rīdēns et susurrāns*) ehem! vidēsne Plancum? ubi sacerdōs silentium poposcit, etiam ille dēnique tacuit. mīrāculum est. deus nōs servāvit. | 35 |

Iūdaeōs: Iūdaeī	*Jews*	
Syrōs: Syrī	*Syrians*	
vir quīdam	*one man, a certain man, someone*	

gemitum: gemitus	*groan*
doctissimus: doctus	*learned, clever*
monumentīs: monumentum	*monument*
garrīre	*chatter, gossip*
mī dulcissime	*my very dear friend*
quid ... agis?	*how are you?*
Serāpidis: Serāpis	*Serapis (an Egyptian god)*
garriēns	*chattering*
coepit	*began*
susurrāns	*whispering*
loquācior: loquāx	*talkative*
psittacus	*parrot*
obstinātior: obstinātus	*obstinate, stubborn*
cellam: cella	*sanctuary*
in capite	*on the head*
canistrum	*basket*
enim	*for*
opportūnē	*just at the right time*
hōra	*hour*
quārta	*fourth*
ārā: āra	*altar*
facere solent	*are accustomed to make, usually make*
rīdēns	*smiling*
ehem!	*well, well!*
silentium	*silence*
dēnique	*at last, finally*
mīrāculum	*miracle*

Portrait of a priest of Serapis.

This sphinx marks the site of a Temple of Serapis.

Left: *The god Serapis, crowned with a basket for measuring grain, was associated with agricultural prosperity.*

mercātor Arabs

ego cum Barbillō cēnāre solēbam. Barbillus mihi gemmās suās quondam ostendit. gemmās attonitus spectāvī, quod maximae et splendidae erant. Barbillus hās gemmās ā mercātōre Arabī ēmerat. dē hōc mercātōre fābulam mīrābilem nārrāvit.

mercātor ōlim cum merce pretiōsā Arabiam trānsībat. in merce   5
erant stolae sēricae, dentēsque eburneī. multōs servōs quoque habēbat, quī mercem custōdiēbant. subitō latrōnēs, quī īnsidiās parāverant, impetum fēcērunt. mercātor servīque latrōnibus ācriter resistēbant, sed latrōnēs tandem servōs superāvērunt. tum latrōnēs cum servīs et cum merce mercātōris effūgērunt.   10
mercātōrem exanimātum relīquērunt.

ille tamen nōn erat mortuus. mox animum recēpit. sōlus erat in dēsertīs, sine aquā, sine servīs. dē vītā suā paene dēspērābat. subitō mōnstrum terribile in caelō appāruit; ālae longiōrēs erant quam rēmī, unguēs maiōrēs quam hastae. in capite mōnstrī erant oculī,   15
quī flammās ēmittēbant. mōnstrum mercātōrem rēctā petīvit. mercātor, postquam hoc mōnstrum dēscendēns vīdit, ad terram exanimātus prōcubuit.

ubi animum recēpit, anxius circumspectāvit. iterum dē vītā dēspērābat, quod iam in nīdō ingentī iacēbat. nīdus in monte   20
praeruptō haerēbat. in nīdō mōnstrī mercātor cumulum lapidum fulgentium cōnspexit.

"nunc rem intellegere possum," mercātor sibi dīxit. "hoc mōnstrum, sīcut pīca, rēs fulgentēs colligere solet. mōnstrum mē petīvit, quod zōna mea fulgēbat."   25

postquam lapidēs īnspexit, laetus sibi, "hercle!" inquit. "fortūna fortibus favet!" nōnnūllās gemmās in saccō celeriter posuit. tum post cumulum gemmārum sē cēlāvit. mōnstrum mox cum aliā gemmā revēnit, et in nīdō cōnsēdit.

postquam nox vēnit, mercātor audāx in mōnstrum dormiēns   30
ascendit, et in tergō iacēbat. in tergō mōnstrī per tōtam noctem haerēbat. māne hoc mōnstrum cum mercātōre, quī in tergō etiam nunc iacēbat, ēvolāvit. quam fortūnātus erat mercātor! mōnstrum ad mare tandem advēnit, ubi nāvis erat. mercātor, postquam nāvem vīdit, dē tergō mōnstrī dēsiluit. in undās maris prope   35
nāvem cecidit. ita mercātōrem fortūna servāvit.

Arabs	*Arabian*	**praeruptō:**	
gemmās: gemma	*jewel, gem*	**praeruptus**	*steep*
merce: merx	*goods, merchandise*	**cumulum: cumulus**	*pile*
trānsībat: trānsīre	*cross*	**lapidum: lapis**	*stone*
sēricae: sēricus	*silk*	**fulgentium:**	*shining,*
dentēs ... eburneī	*ivory tusks*	**fulgēns**	*glittering*
latrōnēs: latrō	*robber*	**sīcut pīca**	*like a magpie*
īnsidiās: īnsidiae	*trap, ambush*	**colligere**	*gather, collect*
ācriter	*keenly, fiercely*	**zōna**	*belt*
relīquērunt:		**fulgēbat:**	
relinquere	*leave*	**fulgēre**	*shine*
in dēsertīs	*in the desert*	**fortūna**	*fortune, luck*
mōnstrum	*monster*	**saccō: saccus**	*bag, purse*
ālae: āla	*wing*	**audāx**	*bold*
unguēs: unguis	*claw*	**dormiēns**	*sleeping*
rēctā	*directly, straight*	**in tergō**	*on its back*
dēscendēns	*coming down*	**cecidit: cadere**	*fall*
nīdō: nīdus	*nest*		

The Great Harbor in Alexandria today.

Practicing the Language

A Complete each sentence with the correct noun and then translate.

1 in multitūdine (Aegyptiōrum, Aegyptiī) stābat senex.
2 faber per fenestram (casārum, casae) spectābat.
3 Alexandrīa erat urbs turbulenta. in viīs (urbis, urbium) erant multī mercātōrēs īrātī.
4 domina per turbam (ancillae, ancillārum) festīnāvit.
5 nōs ad templum Serāpidis pervēnimus. prō templō (deī, deōrum) stābant multī cīvēs.
6 prīncipēs vīllās splendidās habēbant. in vīllīs (prīncipis, prīncipum) erant statuae pretiōsae.

B Complete each sentence with the correct form of the verb and then translate.

1 ubi Diogenēs hoc dīxit, nōs casam (intrāvī, intrāvimus).
2 Aegyptiī tabernam vestram oppugnāvērunt, ubi vōs in Arabiā (aberās, aberātis).
3 ego, ubi in urbe eram, tēcum negōtium (agēbam, agēbāmus).
4 tū senem, quī Rōmānōs vituperābat, (audīvistī, audīvistis).
5 nōs (tacēbāmus, tacēbam) quod sacerdōtēs ad āram prōcēdēbant.
6 vōs auxilium mihi semper (dabātis, dabās).
7 pestis es! togās sordidās mihi (vēndidistis, vēndidistī).
8 ad portum ambulābam. multōs mīlitēs Rōmānōs (vīdī, vīdimus).

C Match the following examples of the imperfect and pluperfect verb tenses, and then translate each verb.

tollēbat   perveniēbat   poterat   restiterat   effūgerat
pōnēbat   erat   pervēnerat   fuerat   effugiēbat
potuerat   resistēbat   posuerat   sustulerat

D Complete each sentence with the correct verb from the box below and then translate.

volō	volumus	possum	possumus
vīs	vultis	potes	potestis
vult	volunt	potest	possunt

1 māne ad portum ambulāre soleō, quod nāvēs spectāre . . . . . .

2 mihi valdē placet puellam audīre, quae suāviter cantāre . . . . . .

3 Barbille! nōnne dē monumentīs audīre . . . . . ?

4 iter longum iam fēcistis; ad vīllam hodiē pervenīre nōn . . . . . .

5 multī virī fēminaeque ad templum contendunt, quod sacrificium vidēre . . . . . .

6 paucī sumus. Aegyptiōs superāre nōn . . . . . .

7 māter, quae fīliō dōnum dare . . . . . , togās in tabernā īnspicit.

8 Aegyptiī fūstēs habent; Graecī eīs resistere nōn . . . . . .

This mosaic floor comes from the dining-room of a rich Alexandrian. It shows the head of Medusa, which could turn those who looked at it to stone.

Alexandria

Alexandria had three harbors. The Great Harbor and the Western Harbor lay on either side of a breakwater three-quarters of a mile (1.2 kilometers) long which joined Pharos island to the mainland. The third harbor was on the large lake which lay behind the city and was connected by canals to the river Nile. From here goods could be brought by a further canal, or overland, to the Red Sea; this was the route that led to India.

Alexandria

The site of this famous city was chosen by the Greek king, Alexander the Great, when he conquered Egypt in 331 B.C. Alexander noted both the excellent agricultural land and the fine harbor of a small fishing village west of the mouth of the Nile. Here there was good anchorage, a healthy climate, fresh water, and limestone quarries nearby to provide stone for building. He commanded his architect to plan and build a city which was to be a new center of trade and civilization.

Alexander the Great.

Alexander died while the city was still developing, but the city was named after him and his body was later buried there in a magnificent tomb. He was succeeded as ruler by Ptolemy, one of his generals, whose descendants governed Alexandria and Egypt for the next three hundred years. The last Ptolemaic ruler was Queen Cleopatra. With her defeat in 30 B.C., Egypt became a Roman province.

By the first century A.D., Alexandria was probably as large and splendid as Rome itself; it was certainly the greatest city in the eastern part of the empire, with perhaps a million inhabitants. Much of its wealth and importance was due to its position. It stood at a meeting-place of great trade routes and was therefore excellently placed for trading on a large scale. Merchants and businessmen were attracted to the city because it offered them safe harbors for their ships, a large number of dock-workers to handle their cargoes, huge warehouses for storage, and a busy market for buying and selling.

Into Alexandria came luxury goods such as bronze statues from Greece or fine Italian wines, and raw materials such as wood and marble to be used by craftsmen in the local workshops. Out to other countries went wheat in enormous quantities, papyrus, glassware, and much else. A list in the Red Sea Guide Book, written by an Alexandrian merchant in the first century A.D., gives some idea of the vast range of goods bought and sold in the city: "clothes, cotton, skins, muslins, silks, brass, copper, iron, gold, silver, silver plate, tin, axes, adzes, glass, ivory, tortoise shell, rhinoceros horn, wine, olive oil, sesame oil, rice, honey, wheat, myrrh, frankincense, cinnamon, fragrant gums, papyrus."

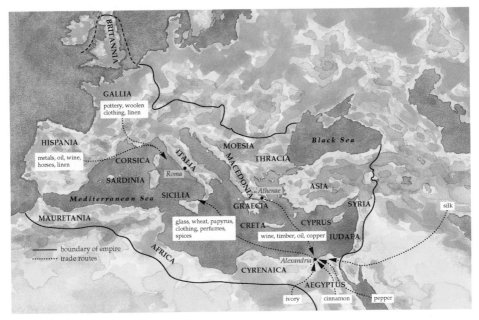

Alexandria and trade in the first century A.D.

Travelers from Greece or Italy would approach Alexandria by sea. From 70 miles (88 kilometers) away, they would be welcomed by a beacon from the Pharos, a huge lighthouse named for the little island on which it stood. Like the Statue of Liberty on Liberty Island in New York Harbor, Pharos marked the entrance to a safe ocean port at the mouth of a great river, each beacon lighting the way to a vast cosmopolitan center. The three-tiered marble-faced Pharos was one of the seven wonders of the ancient world. Day and night the fire in the lantern level sent out a blaze of light which, enhanced by highly polished bronze mirrors, guided the thousands of ships that used the port each year.

Alexander's architect planned the city carefully, with its streets set out in a grid system, crossing each other at right angles as in many modern North American cities. The main street, Canopus Street, was more than 100 feet (30 meters) wide, wider than any street in Rome and four times the size of any street that Quintus would have known in Pompeii. Some of the houses were several stories high, and many of the public buildings were built of marble. By the Great Harbor was the Royal Quarter, an area of more than one square mile (260 hectares) containing palaces, temples, administrative offices, and gardens. West of the Royal Quarter was the Caesareum, where Quintus, in the paragraph on page 93, made his offering of wine. The Caesareum was a shrine begun by Queen Cleopatra in honor of the Roman general Marc Antony and completed by the

The Pharos

Right: *A model of the Pharos based on evidence like the coin on page 91, with a cut-away drawing. The Pharos was over 440 feet (135 meters) high, with a fire constantly alight at the top. A spiral ramp inside the lowest stage allowed fuel to be carried up by animals. Statues of Ptolemy II and his queen can be seen at the base of the lighthouse.*

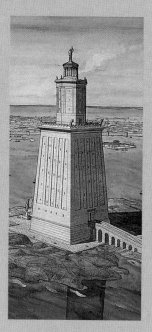

Below: *A 15th-century fort was built on the ruins of the Pharos.*

Emperor Augustus as a temple dedicated to himself. In the words of the Jewish writer Philo, it was "wonderfully high and large, full of precious paintings and statues, and beautiful all over with gold and silver; it contains colonnades, libraries, courtyards, and sacred groves, all made as skillfully as possible with no expense spared."

In front of the Caesareum stood two obelisks, each a tall narrow pillar cut from a single slab of granite and pointed at the top. They were brought from an ancient Egyptian temple and put in position by a Roman engineer in 13 B.C. In the nineteenth century one was removed to London, England, and the other was taken to Central Park, New York City. They are known as Cleopatra's Needles.

But Alexandria was more than a city of fine streets, glittering marble, and busy trading; it was a center of education and study. The university, known as the Museum and situated in the Royal Quarter, had the largest library in the ancient world with more than half a million volumes. As well as the Great Library, the Museum had lecture halls, laboratories, observatories, a park, and a zoo. Professional scholars were employed to do research in a wide range of subjects – mathematics, astronomy, anatomy, geography, literature, and languages. Here mapping techniques were improved, based on travelers' reports; here Euclid wrote his famous geometry textbook, and Aristarchus put forward his theory that the Earth goes round the Sun.

Alexandria was a city of many different races, including Egyptians, Jews, Romans, Africans, and Indians. But, on the whole, the

Left: *The Caesareum obelisks as they appeared at the end of the 18th century; one is lying on the ground.*

Cleopatra's Needle in Central Park, New York City.

people with most power and influence were the Greeks. They had planned the city and built it; they had ruled it before the Romans came and continued to play a part in running it under the Romans; theirs was the official language; they owned great wealth in Alexandria and enjoyed many privileges. These factors caused jealousy among the other nationalities and races, and were among the reasons why quarrels and riots frequently broke out. The Roman governor, or even the emperor himself, often had to step in and try to settle such disputes as fairly and peacefully as possible. After one violent riot, the Emperor Claudius included the following stern warning in a letter to the Alexandrians:

> **Although I am very angry with those who stirred up the trouble, I am not going to enquire fully into who was responsible for the riot – I might have said, the war – with the Jews. But I tell you this, once and for all: if you do not stop quarrelling with each other, I shall be forced to show you what even a kind emperor can do when he has good reason to be angry.**

A reconstruction of the Great Hall of the ancient Library of Alexandria.

Underwater Discoveries

Underwater excavations in the Great Harbor are now bringing much of the waterfront of ancient Alexandria back to life.

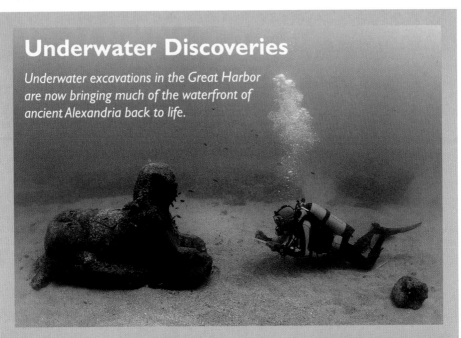

Top: A diver examining a sphinx underwater.

Above: Raising from the water part of a statue of one of the Greek rulers of Egypt, perhaps Ptolemy II. The Pharos was completed in his reign.

Right: Several parts of the statue have been found, enabling it to be rebuilt. The over life-sized figure, dressed in the traditional royal dress of the Pharaohs, probably stood at the foot of the great lighthouse.

Word Study

A Match each word to its definition.

1. a manner to which one is not accustomed
2. scarcity
3. a land formation which is almost an island
4. spiritless or inert
5. grouped in clusters
6. a shore or coastal region
7. a position which requires little effort but draws good pay

a. agminate
b. exanimate
c. insolence
d. littoral
e. paucity
f. sinecure
g. peninsula

B For each of the following words, find the Latin root from the Vocabulary Checklist. Then give the definition for each English word.

1. beneficent
2. benevolent
3. inherent
4. coherent
5. adherent
6. recipient
7. unanimity
8. equanimity
9. magnanimity

C Give an English derivative from the following Latin words for the following definitions:

benignus faber facilis graviter impetus

1. kind
2. rash, impulsive
3. a woven cloth
4. seriousness
5. to make easy, assist or help

Warships in a harbor. Wall-painting from the Temple of Isis at Pompeii.

Stage 17 Vocabulary Checklist

Nouns in the checklists for Stages 17–20 are usually listed in the form of their nominative and genitive singular.

ā, ab (+ ABL)	*from, away from*
agmen, agminis, n.	*column (of people), procession*
animus, animī, m.	*spirit, soul, mind*
appropinquō, appropinquāre, appropinquāvī (+ DAT)	*approach, come near to*
āra, ārae, f.	*altar*
bene	*well*
benignus, benigna, benignum	*kind*
diū	*for a long time*
exanimātus, exanimāta, exanimātum	*unconscious*
facilis, facilis, facile	*easy*
graviter	*seriously*
haereō, haerēre, haesī	*stick, cling*
hūc	*here, to this place*
impetus, impetūs, m.	*attack*
īnsula, īnsulae, f.	*island*
invītus, invīta, invītum	*unwilling*
itaque	*and so*
lītus, lītoris, n.	*shore*
maximus, maxima, maximum	*very big, very large, very great*
multitūdō, multitūdinis, f.	*crowd*
numquam	*never*
paucī, paucae, pauca	*few, a few*
perveniō, pervenīre, pervēnī	*reach, arrive at*
quondam	*one day, once*
recipiō, recipere, recēpī	*recover, take back*
resistō, resistere, restitī (+ DAT)	*resist*
sine (+ ABL)	*without*
soleō, solēre	*be accustomed, usually*

Lantern in the shape of the Pharos.

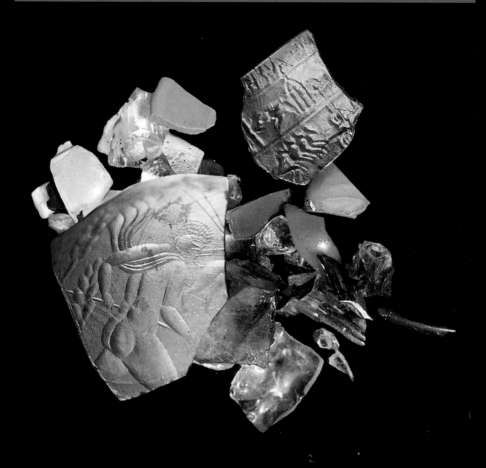

EUTYCHUS ET CLEMENS

Stage 18

taberna

postquam ad urbem advēnimus, ego Clēmentī diū tabernam quaerēbam. tandem Barbillus, quī multa aedificia possidēbat, mihi tabernam optimam obtulit. haec taberna prope templum Īsidis erat. in hāc parte urbis via est, in quā omnēs tabernāriī vitrum vēndunt. facile est illīs tabernāriīs mercem vēndere, quod vitrum 5 Alexandrīnum nōtissimum est. taberna, quam Barbillus mihi offerēbat, optimum situm habēbat, optimum lucrum. Barbillus tamen dubitābat.

"sunt multae operae," inquit, "in illā parte urbis. tabernāriī operās timent, quod pecūniam extorquent et vim īnferunt. operae 10 lībertum meum interfēcērunt, quī nūper illam tabernam tenēbat. eum in viā invēnimus mortuum. lībertus, quī senex obstinātus erat, operīs pecūniam dare nōluit. operae eum necāvērunt tabernamque dīripuērunt."

"Clēmēns vir fortis, nōn senex īnfirmus est," ego Barbillō 15 respondī. "fortūna semper eī favet. hanc tabernam Clēmentī emere volō. tibi centum aureōs offerō. placetne?"

"mihi placet," respondit Barbillus. "centum aureī sufficiunt."

Barbillō igitur centum aureōs trādidī.

vitrum	*glass*
Alexandrīnum: Alexandrīnus	*Alexandrian*
situm: situs	*position, site*
lucrum	*profit*
dubitābat: dubitāre	*be doubtful*
operae	*hired thugs*
extorquent: extorquēre	*extort*
vim īnferunt: vim īnferre	*use force, violence*
tenēbat: tenēre	*own*
dīripuērunt: dīripere	*ransack*
īnfirmus	*weak*
centum aureōs	*a hundred gold pieces*
sufficiunt: sufficere	*be enough*

Alexandria, Home of Luxury Glass

Alexandrian glass was traded widely, even outside the Roman Empire. The glass beaker on the right was made in Alexandria, but was found in Afghanistan. It has a painted design showing the princess Europa being carried off on the back of a bull, which is Jupiter in disguise.

The disc below is cameo glass, carved in two layers, white on blue. It shows Paris pondering the judgment of Juno, Minerva, and Venus.

in officīnā Eutychī

I

postquam tabernam Clēmentī dedī, ille mihi grātiās maximās ēgit.
statim ad viam, in quā taberna erat, festīnāvit: adeō cupiēbat
tabernam tenēre.

in viā vitreāriōrum erat ingēns turba. ibi Clēmēns tabernam
suam prope templum Īsidis cōnspexit. valvās ēvulsās vīdit,   5
tabernam dīreptam. īrātus igitur Clēmēns tabernārium vīcīnum
rogāvit,

"quis hoc fēcit?"

tabernārius perterritus nōmina dare nōluit. tandem "rogā
Eutychum!" inquit.   10

Clēmēns statim Eutychum quaesīvit. facile erat Clēmentī eum
invenīre, quod officīnam maximam possidēbat. prō officīnā
Eutychī stābant quattuor servī Aegyptiī. Clēmēns numquam
hominēs ingentiōrēs quam illōs Aegyptiōs vīderat. eōs autem nōn
timēbat. ūnum servum ex ōrdine trāxit.   15

"heus! Atlās!" inquit Clēmēns. "num dormīs? Eutychum,
dominum tuum, interrogāre volō. cūr mihi obstās? nōn decōrum
est tibi lībertō obstāre."

tum Clēmēns servōs attonitōs praeteriit, et officīnam Eutychī
intrāvit.   20

officīnā: officīna	*workshop*
adeō	*so much, so greatly*
in viā vitreāriōrum	*in the street of the glassmakers*
valvās: valvae	*doors*
ēvulsās: ēvulsus	*wrenched off*
vīcīnum: vīcīnus	*neighboring, nearby*
nōmina: nōmen	*name*
prō officīnā	*in front of the workshop*
quattuor	*four*
autem	*however, but*
interrogāre	*question*
praeteriit: praeterīre	*go past*

II

Eutychus in lectō recumbēbat; cibum ē canistrō gustābat. valdē
sūdābat, et manūs in capillīs servī tergēbat. postquam Clēmentem
vīdit,

"quis es, homuncule?" inquit. "quis tē hūc admīsit? quid vīs?"

"Quīntus Caecilius Clēmēns sum," respondit Clēmēns. "dē   5
tabernā, quam latrōnēs dīripuērunt, cognōscere volō. nam illa
taberna nunc mea est."

Eutychus, postquam hoc audīvit, Clēmentem amīcissimē
salūtāvit, et eum per officīnam dūxit. ipse Clēmentī fabrōs suōs
dēmōnstrāvit. in officīnā erant trīgintā vitreāriī Aegyptiī, quī ōllās   10
ōrnātās faciēbant. dīligenter labōrābant, quod aderat vīlicus, quī
virgam vibrābat.

Eutychus, postquam Clēmentī officīnam ostendit, negōtium
agere coepit.

"perīculōsum est, mī amīce, in viā vitreāriōrum," inquit. "multī   15
fūrēs ad hanc viam veniunt, multī latrōnēs. multa aedificia dēlent.
omnēs igitur tabernāriī auxilium ā mē petunt. tabernāriī mihi
pecūniam dant, ego eīs praesidium. tabernam tuam servāre
possum. omnēs tabernāriī mihi decem aureōs quotannīs dare
solent. paulum est. num tū praesidium meum recūsāre vīs?"   20

Clēmēns tamen Eutychō nōn crēdēbat.

"ego ipse tabernam, in quā habitō, servāre possum," inquit
Clēmēns. "praesidium tuum operāsque tuās floccī nōn faciō."

tum lībertus sēcūrus exiit.

sūdābat: sūdāre	*sweat*
manūs ... tergēbat	*was wiping his hands*
capillīs: capillī	*hair*
admīsit: admittere	*let in*
amīcissimē: amīcē	*in a friendly way*
ōllās: ōlla	*vase*
ōrnātās: ōrnātus	*decorated*
praesidium	*protection*
paulum	*little*
floccī nōn faciō	*I don't give a hoot about*
sēcūrus	*without a care*

About the Language I: Neuter Nouns

A Study the following examples:

1 plaustrum viam claudēbat.	*A cart was blocking the road.*
2 plaustra viam claudēbant.	*Carts were blocking the road.*
3 Vārica plaustrum ēmōvit.	*Varica removed the cart.*
4 Vārica plaustra ēmōvit.	*Varica removed the carts.*

B **plaustrum** is a typical example of a **neuter noun**. The accusative singular of neuter nouns is always the same as the nominative singular (sentences 1 and 3). The nominative and accusative plural of neuter nouns are also identical to each other, and they always end in -a (sentences 2 and 4).

C Compare the following forms:

	SECOND DECLENSION		THIRD DECLENSION	
	masculine	*neuter*	*masculine*	*neuter*
singular nom.	servus	templum	leō	nōmen
singular acc.	servum	templum	leōnem	nōmen
plural nom.	servī	templa	leōnēs	nōmina
plural acc.	servōs	templa	leōnēs	nōmina

D Further examples:

1 Salvius horrea nova īnspexit.
2 Cogidubnus pompam ad lītus dūxit.
3 prīncipēs dōna ad aulam tulērunt.
4 nōmenne senis mortuī scīs?
5 Plancus monumenta urbis dēmōnstrāvit.
6 animālia hospitēs terruērunt.

Detail of a mosaic panel, using colored glass pieces.

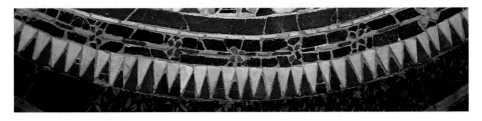

Egyptian Cats

The Egyptians kept cats both as pets and to control rats and mice in their granaries and food stores. They also venerated cats as sacred mammals as they thought they were earthly forms of the goddess Isis and another goddess called Bastet. When cats died they were mummified; vast numbers of them have been excavated.

This expensive bronze cat was made as an offering to the goddess Bastet around 600 BC.

In Egyptian legend, each night a cat kills an evil snake that tries to prevent the sun from rising.

Clēmēns tabernārius

Clēmēns mox tabernam suam renovāvit. fabrōs condūxit, quī valvās mūrōsque refēcērunt. multās ōllās ōrnāmentaque vitrea ēmit. cēterī tabernāriī, quamquam Eutychum valdē timēbant, Clēmentem libenter adiuvābant. nam Clēmēns cōmis erat et eīs invicem auxilium dabat. facile erat eī lucrum facere, quod pretia   5
aequa semper postulābat.

haec taberna, ut dīxī, prope templum deae Īsidis erat. ad hoc templum Clēmēns, quī pius erat, cotīdiē adībat. ibi deam Īsidem adōrābat et eī ōrnāmentum vitreum saepe cōnsecrābat.

sacerdōtēs, quī templum administrābant, mox Clēmentem   10
cognōvērunt. deinde Clēmēns Īsiacīs sē coniūnxit. sacerdōtēs eī librum sacrum dedērunt, in quō dē mystēriīs deae legere poterat. Clēmēns in templō cum sacerdōtibus cēnāre solēbat. in cellā templī habitābat fēlēs sacra. Clēmēns eam semper mulcēbat, et eī semper aliquid ex paterā suā dabat.   15

mox plūrimōs amīcōs Clēmēns habēbat. nam tabernāriī, quī Eutychō pecūniam invītī dabant, paulātim Clēmentī cōnfīdēbant. tabernāriī Eutychum inimīcum putābant, Clēmentem vindicem. tandem omnēs Eutychō pecūniam trādere nōluērunt.

Eutychus, ubi dē hīs rēbus cognōvit, operās Aegyptiās collēgit   20
et eīs fūstēs dedit.

"iste Clēmēns," inquit Eutychus, "molestissimus est. necesse est eī poenās dare. ille impetūs nostrōs diūtius vītāvit."

operae, postquam fūstēs cēpērunt, ad tabernam Clēmentis contendērunt.   25

renovāvit: renovāre	restore	adōrābat: adōrāre	worship
condūxit: condūcere	hire	cōnsecrābat:	
refēcērunt: reficere	repair	cōnsecrāre	dedicate
ōrnāmenta:		Īsiacīs: Īsiacī	followers of Isis
ōrnāmentum	ornament	sē coniūnxit:	
vitrea: vitreus	glass, made	sē coniungere	join
	of glass	sacrum: sacer	sacred
invicem	in turn	mystēriīs:	mysteries,
aequa: aequus	fair	mystēria	secret worship
ut	as	mulcēbat: mulcēre	pet, pat
pius	respectful to	paterā: patera	bowl
	the gods		

cōnfīdēbant:		poenās dare	*pay the penalty,*
cōnfīdere	*trust*		*be punished*
putābant: putāre	*think, consider*	diūtius	*for too long*
vindicem: vindex	*champion, defender*		

Questions

1 How did Clemens get his shop repaired and restocked?
2 Why did the other shopkeepers help Clemens (lines 4–5)?
3 What policy allowed him to make a good profit?
4 Where was Clemens' shop? Why was this convenient for him (lines 7–8)?
5 How did he show his respect for the goddess (lines 8–9)?
6 How did the priests help Clemens to learn more about the goddess (lines 11–12)?
7 Where did the sacred cat live? In what ways did Clemens show kindness to it?
8 **mox plūrimōs amīcōs Clēmēns habēbat** (line 16). Who were these friends?
9 From line 18, pick out the Latin word that shows how Clemens' friends regarded Eutychus. How did they finally oppose Eutychus?
10 What conclusion did Eutychus come to about Clemens (lines 22–23)? Give two details.
11 Read the last sentence. Suggest two things the thugs might do.

About the Language II: Fourth and Fifth Declensions

A While most nouns in Latin belong to the first, second, or third declension, there are two other less commonly seen declensions. Study the following charts:

	FOURTH DECLENSION		FIFTH DECLENSION	
	singular	*plural*	*singular*	*plural*
nominative	portus	portūs	rēs	rēs
genitive	portūs	portuum	reī	rērum
dative	portuī	portibus	reī	rēbus
accusative	portum	portūs	rem	rēs
ablative	portū	portibus	rē	rēbus

B The genitive case of a noun indicates the declension to which it belongs:

First declension: puell**ae**
Second declension: serv**ī**
Third declension: leō**nis**
Fourth declension: port**ūs**
Fifth declension: r**eī**

C Translate the following sentences:

1 in portū Alexandrīae erant multae nāvēs.
2 sacerdōtēs effigiem in rogum posuērunt.
3 tumultūsne in hāc urbe cotīdiē vidēs?
4 servī fūstēs in manibus tenēbant.
5 puerī nōmina diērum recitant.
6 tabernāriī Clēmentī dē impetibus nārrābant.

Practice in determining the declension of a noun by means of the genitive is given on pages 215–216 of the Complete Vocabulary.

prō tabernā Clēmentis

Clēmēns in templō deae Īsidis cum cēterīs Īsiacīs saepe cēnābat. quondam, ubi ā templō, in quō cēnāverat, domum redībat, amīcum cōnspexit accurrentem. amīcus clāmābat.

"taberna ardet! taberna tua ardet! tabernam tuam dīripiunt Eutychus et operae. eōs vīdī valvās ēvellentēs, vitrum frangentēs, 5 tabernam incendentēs. fuge! fuge ex urbe! Eutychus tē interficere vult. nēmō eī operīsque resistere potest."

Clēmēns tamen nōn fūgit, sed ad tabernam quam celerrimē contendit. postquam illūc advēnit, prō tabernā stābat immōtus. valvās ēvulsās, tabernam dīreptam vīdit. Eutychus extrā tabernam 10 cum operīs Aegyptiīs stābat, rīdēbatque.

Eutychus cachinnāns "mī dulcissime!" inquit. "nōnne tē dē hāc viā monuī? nōnne amīcōs habēs quōs vocāre potes? cūr absunt? fortasse sapientiōrēs sunt quam tū."

Clēmēns summā cum tranquillitāte eī respondit, 15

"absunt amīcī, sed deī mē servāre possunt. deī hominēs scelestōs pūnīre solent."

Eutychus īrātissimus "quid dīcis?" inquit. "tūne mihi ita dīcere audēs?"

domum: domus	*home*	**illūc**	*there, to that place*
accurrentem: accurrēns	*running up*	**monuī: monēre**	*warn*
ēvellentēs: ēvellēns	*wrenching off*	**sapientiōrēs: sapiēns**	*wise*
frangentēs: frangēns	*breaking*	**tranquillitāte:**	
incendentēs: incendēns	*burning, setting on fire*	**tranquillitās**	*calmness*
		scelestōs: scelestus	*wicked*

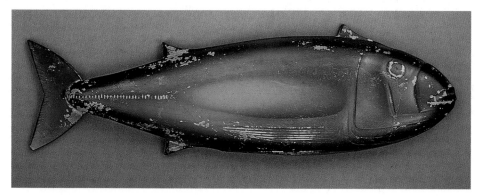

When this fish-shaped cover was removed, an actual cooked fish would be found underneath.

tum Eutychus operīs signum dedit. statim quattuor Aegyptiī, qui fūstēs vibrābant, Clēmentī appropinquābant. Clēmēns *20* cōnstitit. via, in quā stābat, erat dēserta. tabernāriī perterritī per valvās tabernārum spectābant. omnēs invītī Clēmentem dēseruerant, simulatque Eutychus et operae advēnērunt.

subitō fēlēs sacra, quam Clēmēns mulcēre solēbat, ē templō exiit. Clēmentem rēctā petīvit. in manūs Clēmentis īnsiluit. omnēs *25* Aegyptiī statim fūstēs abiēcērunt et ad pedēs Clēmentis prōcubuērunt. Clēmentem, quem fēlēs sacra servābat, laedere nōn audēbant.

saeviēbat Eutychus, sīcut taurus īrātus. tum fēlēs in Eutychum īnsiluit, et caput vehementer rāsit. *30*

"melius est tibi fugere," inquit Clēmēns.

Eutychus cum operīs suīs perterritus fūgit. posteā neque Clēmentem neque tabernāriōs laedere temptābat. mox etiam ex urbe discessit. nunc Clēmēns est prīnceps tabernāriōrum.

dēseruerant: dēserere	*desert*
īnsiluit: īnsilīre	*jump onto, jump into*
abiēcērunt: abicere	*throw away*
laedere	*harm*
sīcut taurus	*like a bull*
rāsit: rādere	*scratch*
neque ... neque	*neither ... nor*
temptābat: temptāre	*try*

Practicing the Language

A Complete each sentence with the correct form of the adjective in parentheses and then translate. Remember that adjectives agree with nouns in case, number, and gender. You may need to check the Complete Vocabulary for gender.

1 (multī, multae) tabernāriī Eutychō pecūniam dedērunt.
2 Quīntus templa (magnificōs, magnifica) prope portum vīsitāvit.
3 quō operae senem (obstinātum, obstinātam) trāxērunt?
4 Clēmēns sacerdōtēs (doctōs, doctī) cognōvērunt.
5 mercātor lībertō (fidēlī, fidēlibus) praemium obtulit.
6 Eutychus manūs (sordidās, sordidōs) in capillīs tergēbat.
7 prīncipēs effigiēī (cērātae, cērātō) appropinquāvērunt.
8 Clēmēns cōnsilium (audāx, audācem) cēpit.
9 servus ē vīllā dominī (crūdēlem, crūdēlis) fūgit.
10 mīlitēs hastās (gravis, gravēs) tenēbant.

B Complete each sentence with the correct form of the verb and then translate.

1 Clēmēns ad tabernam, quam Quīntus (ēmerat, ēmerant), festīnāvit.
2 ingēns turba, quae viam (complēverat, complēverant), tabernam spectābat.
3 Clēmēns ad Eutychum, quī operās (mīserat, mīserant), contendit.
4 Eutychus Clēmentem, quem servī nōn (terruerat, terruerant), amīcissimē salūtāvit.
5 Eutychus dē tabernāriīs, quī praesidium (petīverat, petīverant), Clēmentī nārrāvit.
6 Clēmēns tamen praesidium, quod Eutychus eī (obtulerat, obtulerant), recūsāvit.

Pick out the Latin word for "who" or "which" (**quī, quae**, etc.) at the beginning of each relative clause and the noun it refers to. Write down the gender of each pair.

C Complete the sentences of the story with the correct word from the following list, and then translate.

mīsī	frēgī	vituperāvī
mīsistī	frēgistī	vituperāvistī

Eutychus in officīnā stābat. vīlicum ad sē vocāvit.

"ego amīcō meō ducentās ōllās herī prōmīsī," inquit Eutychus. "quot ōllās ad tabernam amīcī meī mīsistī?"

"ego centum ōllās ad eum . . . . . ," respondit vīlicus.

"centum ōllās!" exclāmāvit Eutychus. "cūr tū centum   5
sōlum ōllās ad amīcum meum . . . . . ?"

"servus canistrum, in quō ōllae erant, stultissimē omīsit. multae ōllae sunt frāctae," respondit vīlicus.

"ubi est iste servus, quī ōllās frēgit?" rogāvit Eutychus.

vīlicus statim servum ad Eutychum trāxit.   10

"cūr tū tot ōllās . . . . . ?" rogāvit Eutychus.

"ego ōllās . . . . . , quod vīlicus mē terruit," inquit servus. "vīlicus virgam vibrāvit et mē vituperāvit."

"cūr tū virgam vibrāvistī et hunc servum . . . . . ?" rogāvit Eutychus.   15

"ego servum . . . . . , quod ignāvus erat," respondit vīlicus.

"servus ignāvus erat, tū neglegēns," inquit Eutychus. "necesse est vōbīs per tōtam noctem labōrāre."

ducentās: ducentī	*two hundred*	**stultissimē: stultē**	*foolishly*
quot?	*how many?*	**omīsit: omittere**	*drop*
sōlum	*only*	**frēgit: frangere**	*break*

D Pick the odd one out from the following groups of words. Explain your choice.

1 tumultus   situs   portus   lītus   manus   impetus
2 agmen   fabrum   mīlitum   effigiem   negōtium   caput
3 favet   placet   obstat   petit   cōnfīdit   resistit
4 petīverat   pervēnerat   recūsāverat   cognōverat   poterat discesserat
5 nōbīs   tibi   eī   vōbīs   mē   eīs
6 aedificia   tempora   nōmina   amphora   itinera   lītora

Glassmaking

In the stories in this Stage, Quintus established Clemens in what is thought to have been one of Alexandria's oldest and most successful industries – glassmaking. The earliest Egyptian glass vessels, discovered in tombs, date from about 1500 B.C., and glass continued to be made in Egypt through the period of the Pharaohs, the Ptolemaic kings, and the Roman conquest and occupation.

Glass is made from sand, plant ash or natron, and lime. The earliest use of glass was as a colored, opaque, or transparent glaze applied to ceramics before they were fired (as is still done today). Small pieces of colored glass were considered valuable and often rivaled precious gems as jewelry items.

As time passed, it was discovered – perhaps by a potter – that if glass is heated until it becomes semi-liquid, it can be shaped and left to cool in a new, solid, independently standing shape. At first this shaping was carried out by wrapping a coil of molten glass around a clay or sand core.

A scent-bottle made around a sand core.

This core had been molded around a rod into the shape of a vase or any other object which was required. When the glass had cooled, the rod was

This ribbon-glass bowl was made by lining a mold with differently colored sticks of glass, then heating them until they melted and fused together.

This bowl is decorated in a typical Alexandrian style known as "millefiori" (Italian for "a thousand flowers"). Small pieces of colored glass were arranged in a mold and then heated until they fused together.

pulled out from the core and the remaining parts of the core were scraped or washed out. This method was suitable only for making small luxury items, such as perfume containers.

As the art of glassmaking progressed, glassmakers developed a second technique known as casting and cutting. In this process, glass was cast into a mold the approximate shape of the object desired. When the blank cooled, excess glass was cut away by a workman using a hand lathe or other tools. Magnificent specimens such as cameo glass and cage cups were created by ancient craftsmen using this technique. Variations on the casting technique were used in the creation of millefiori glass in which short sections of multi-colored canes were placed into a mold and heated and fused, or ribbon glass, in which heated canes were sagged over a mold until they fused. As was the case with core-forming, these techniques were labor-intensive and time-consuming, had a high breakage rate, and therefore resulted in expensive products.

In the first century B.C., somewhere at the eastern end of the Mediterranean, a new invention caused a true revolution in the glass industry. This was the discovery of glassblowing, both free-blowing and mold-blowing. The line drawing on page 129 demonstrates the process of free-blowing. The craftsman at the back has picked up a gob of molten glass on the end of a hollow iron rod. The craftsman at the front has produced a hollow bubble of glass by blowing steadily through his rod. With repeated heating and blowing, the bubble can be made quite large and even shaped by swinging or by using various tools. Then the glassworker can add handles, bases, and decorations, such as trails of colored glass applied like piped icing on a cake. The very same processes are still in use today in modern facilities such as the Corning Glass Center, New York (below right).

In the mold-blowing technique, hot glass is blown into a mold, then shaped and finished as in free-blowing. With the invention of free-blowing and mold-blowing, the earlier methods died out almost completely. Since glassblowing was faster and less labor-intensive, with low production costs, it was the basis of the mass production which characterized the Roman industry and made glass vessels more readily available and affordable.

The color of "natural" glass is green to bluish-green. This color is caused by the varying amounts of naturally occurring iron impurities in the sand. Glassmakers learned to make colored glass by adding metallic compounds and mineral oxides to produce brilliant hues of red, green, and blue – the colors of gemstones. Glassmakers also learned to decolor glass to neutralize the effects of the impurities in the sand. When gemcutters learned to cut glass, they found that clear glass was an excellent refractor of light. The popularity of cut clear glass soared, that of colored glass diminished.

A modern glass-blower at work in the Corning Glass Center, Corning, New York.

Above: *This small scent-bottle in the shape of a bunch of grapes is made of purple glass which has been blown into a mold.*

Left: *A blown jug in white glass with trailed decoration in blue.*

Soon after Alexandria's foundation it became a dominant center for the production of glass. With the introduction of glassblowing from the Near East, the industry spread within a hundred and fifty years to Rome, northern Italy, Gaul, and the Rhineland with a widespread effect on most social classes. Glass tableware became common. The strength of glass, combined with its light weight, its resistance to retaining the odors and residue of its contents, and its transparency made glass containers reusable. Furthermore, about the time of our stories, the Romans discovered that panes could be made for windows out of glass instead of the more expensive quartz, thereby allowing architects to make windows larger and rooms brighter, especially in the **thermae** where illumination was dependent on oil lamps.

The art and skill of the ancient glassmakers were not equaled or surpassed in Europe until the rise of the Venetian glass industry during the Renaissance. In fact, the ancient methods of making cameo glass, gold band glass, and the cage cups were not duplicated until the late nineteenth and the twentieth centuries.

A bubble of clear bluish glass has been shaped into a bird.

Egypt

South of Alexandria stretched the fertile valley of the river Nile. Every year the Nile flooded, watering the land and depositing rich new soil on the fields. This produced not only enough grain to supply the whole of Egypt but also a large surplus to be exported. However, the profits from the grain trade benefited only a small number of people.

The Nile. Notice the fertile agricultural land between the desert and the river.

Peasants harvesting wheat under supervision.

Everything the peasants did was checked by the officials.

Before the Romans came to Egypt, the country had been ruled by Egyptian "pharaohs" (kings), then by Persians, then by Greeks. These rulers had worked out a system for making the fullest possible use of the land for their own advantage. They regarded the whole country as their own property and treated the peasant farmers as their private force of

Above: *The god of the Nile bearing the river's rich harvest.*

Left: *Part of an Egyptian official document. This papyrus was written in Greek during the Roman period of rule, and concerns work done on a canal.*

workers. The peasants were not allowed to leave their villages without permission; they had to plant whatever crop they were told; and they did not receive their share of the harvest until the ruler had received his. They were also responsible for the upkeep and repair of the country's canals and dikes. In addition, the Egyptians were taxed to provide money needed to maintain the Pharos, the police, and the huge numbers of government officials who continually checked all activities of the people.

When the Romans came, they did nothing to improve the life of the peasants. Like the previous rulers, the Romans were more concerned with using the land for their own benefit than with improving the working conditions of peasant farmers. Above all, they wanted to ensure a steady supply of grain to Rome. Without the grain from Egypt and North Africa, the huge population of Rome would have starved and rioted. To avoid this danger the emperors made sure that Egypt was under their personal control.

Given these conditions and the fact that the Greek and Roman communities had special legal and tax privileges, it is not surprising that many letters of complaint have been found addressed by peasants to government officials; that bribery and corruption were common; and that, as in the story in Stage 17, there was social and racial unrest in Alexandria.

Emperor as Horus. This hawk-headed emperor wears Roman sandals and a toga.

The Romans not only imported grain, papyrus, gold, marble, and granite from Egypt. They were also influenced by Egyptian culture. The worship of Serapis, Isis, and Osiris was enthusiastically adopted all over the Roman world. In imitation of the ancient pharaohs, Roman emperors had their names inscribed in hieroglyphs in the temples they built in Egypt where they might be portrayed in the Egyptian fashion, for instance, as the hawk-headed god, Horus. The Emperor Trajan built a Kiosk, complete with Egyptian architectural features, beside the sanctuary of Isis on the Island of Philae near Egypt's southern border. Egypt was also a pleasure ground for upper class Romans and we can imagine Quintus sailing up the Nile some 100 miles (160 km) from Alexandria to the Giza plateau, lured by the ancient wonders of the Sphinx and the pyramids built thousands of years before his time.

There was even a melding of the Roman taste for highly individualized portraiture with the Egyptian funerary practice of mummification or embalming of the dead. The method of mummification, however, differed considerably from that practiced in ancient Egypt. Rather than lavishly preparing the body itself, attention was given to the exterior appearance of the mummy and its wrappings. Wealthy families commissioned artists to paint portraits on thin wooden panels or linen using encaustic (paint mixed with hot beeswax). These hung in the home until, at death, the portrait was cut down and fitted into the linen mummy wrappings. The faces of Greeks, Egyptians, Romans, Syrians, Libyans, Nubians, Jews, and others testify to communities of peoples from remarkably diverse origins.

Word Study

A For each definition below, give an English word derived from one of the following Latin words:

audēre caput cōnsistere frangere nox pars petere

1 period of equal day and night on all parts of the earth
2 a solemn, formal request
3 affecting only a part
4 a piece which is broken away
5 punishable by death
6 daring
7 standing firm in all types of circumstances

B Match the following definitions to the derivatives of **manus**.

1 manumission   a handcuffs
2 manicure   b evident, clear, plain
3 manipulate   c freeing of a slave
4 manacles   d to make by hand
5 manufacture   e to keep up, carry on
6 amanuensis   f care of one's hands and nails
7 manifest   g to control, often by unfair means
8 maintain   h secretary, one who copies what is
                     already written

C Write a definition for each of the following words, including in your definition some reference to the meaning of the Latin root (which appears in the Vocabulary Checklist for this Stage).

For example: president: a person who acts as a <u>protector</u> for a group of people

cognizance   demonstrable   militant   obstacle   sacrilege

Stage 18
Vocabulary Checklist

audeō, audēre	dare
caput, capitis, n.	head
coepī	I began
cognōscō, cognōscere, cognōvī	get to know, find out
cōnsistō, cōnsistere, cōnstitī	stand one's ground, stand firm
dea, deae, f.	goddess
dēmōnstrō, dēmōnstrāre, dēmōnstrāvī	point out, show
discēdō, discēdere, discessī	depart, leave
fortasse	perhaps
frangō, frangere, frēgī	break
ibi	there
libenter	gladly
manus, manūs, f.	hand
mīles, mīlitis, m.	soldier
nam	for
nēmō	no one
nox, noctis, f.	night
obstō, obstāre, obstitī (+ DAT)	obstruct, block the way
pars, partis, f.	part
petō, petere, petīvī	beg for, ask for
posteā	afterwards
postrēmō	finally, lastly
praesidium, praesidiī, n.	protection
prō (+ ABL)	in front of
quō?	where? where to?
recūsō, recūsāre, recūsāvī	refuse
sacer, sacra, sacrum	sacred
saeviō, saevīre, saeviī	be in a rage

A Roman mosaic uses millefiori glass pieces for the clothes of these Egyptian characters.

ISIS

Stage 19

1 hic vir est Aristō. Aristō est amīcus Barbillī. in vīllā splendidā habitat, sed miserrimus est.

2 haec fēmina est Galatēa. Galatēa est uxor Aristōnis. Galatēa marītum saepe castīgat, numquam laudat.

3 haec puella est Helena. Helena est fīlia Aristōnis et Galatēae. multī iuvenēs hanc puellam amant, quod pulcherrima est.

4 pompa splendida per viās
Alexandrīae prōcēdit. omnēs
Alexandrīnī hanc pompam
spectāre volunt.

5 hī virī sunt sacerdōtēs deae
Īsidis. Aristō hōs virōs intentē
spectat. sacerdōtēs statuam
deae per viās portant.

6 hae puellae prō pompā currunt.
Helena hās puellās intentē
spectat. puellae corōnās
rosārum gerunt.

7 pompa ad templum Augustī
advenit. prope hoc templum
stant duo iuvenēs. hī iuvenēs
tamen pompam nōn spectant.

Aristō

Aristō vir miserrimus est, quod vītam dūram vīvit. pater Aristōnis scrīptor nōtissimus erat, quī in Graeciā habitābat. tragoediās optimās scrībēbat. Aristō, quod ipse tragoediās scrībere vult, vītam quiētam quaerit; sed uxor et fīlia eī obstant.

Galatēa, uxor Aristōnis, amīcōs ad vīllam semper invītat. amīcī   5
Galatēae sunt tībīcinēs et citharoedī. hī amīcī in vīllā Aristōnis semper cantant et iocōs faciunt. Aristō amīcōs uxōris semper fugit.

Helena quoque, fīlia Aristōnis et Galatēae, patrem vexat. multōs iuvenēs ad vīllam patris invītat. amīcī Helenae sunt poētae. in vīllā Aristōnis poētae versūs suōs recitant. Aristō hōs versūs nōn amat,   10
quod scurrīlēs sunt. saepe hī poētae inter sē pugnant. saepe Aristō amīcōs fīliae ē vīllā expellit. difficile est Aristōnī vītam quiētam vīvere.

vīvit: vīvere	*live*
scrīptor	*writer*
tragoediās: tragoedia	*tragedy*
tībīcinēs: tībīcen	*pipe player*
citharoedī: citharoedus	*cithara player*
amat: amāre	*love, like*
expellit: expellere	*throw out*

The Roman theater at Alexandria.

A writer of plays.

diēs fēstus

I

cīvēs laetī erant. nam hiems erat cōnfecta. iam prīmus diēs vēris aderat. iam sacerdōtēs deam Īsidem per viās urbis portāre solēbant. sacerdōtēs effigiem deae ad portum quotannīs ferēbant. pompa, quam plūrimī Alexandrīnī spectāre volēbant, splendida erat.

hanc pompam autem Barbillus spectāre nōlēbat.

"nōn commodum est mihi hodiē ad urbem īre," inquit. "ego hanc pompam saepe vīdī, tū tamen numquam. amīcus meus igitur, Aristō, tē ad pompam dūcere vult."

Barbillō grātiās ēgī, et cum Aristōne ad portum ībam. Galatēa et fīlia, Helena, nōbīscum ībant. viās urbis iam complēbant cīvēs Alexandrīnī. ubi portuī appropinquābāmus, Galatēa fīliam et marītum assiduē castīgābat:

"Helena! nōlī festīnāre! tolle caput! Aristō! ēmovē hanc turbam! turba Alexandrīnōrum tōtam viam complet. in magnō perīculō sumus."

diēs fēstus	*festival, holiday*
cōnfecta: cōnfectus	*finished*
vēris: vēr	*spring*
assiduē	*continually*
castīgābat: castīgāre	*scold, nag*
tolle!	*hold up!*

This portrait of a young woman called Eirene ("Peace") might help us to picture Helena in our stories. Portraits like this (and those on page 134) enable us to visualize the varied faces in the Alexandrian crowd at the festival of Isis.

II

postquam ad templum Augustī vēnimus, Galatēa

"locum optimum nōvimus," inquit, "unde tōtum spectāculum vidēre solēmus. illinc pompam et nāvem sacram vidēre possumus. servus nōbīs illum locum servat. Aristō! nōnne servum māne ēmīsistī?"   5

"ēheu!" Aristō sibi dīxit.

ubi ad illum locum, quem Galatēa ēlēgerat, tandem pervēnimus, Galatēa duōs iuvenēs cōnspexit. hī iuvenēs locum tenēbant, ubi Galatēa stāre volēbat.

"marīte!" inquit. "ēmovē illōs iuvenēs! ubi est servus noster?   10 nōnne servum ēmīsistī?"

Aristō, quī anxius circumspectābat, respondit. "cārissima, melius est nōbīs locum novum quaerere. iste servus sānē neglegēns erat."

Galatēa tamen, quae iam īrātissima erat, Aristōnem incitāvit.   15 ille igitur iuvenibus appropinquāvit et cōmiter locum poscēbat. uxor tamen vehementer clāmāvit,

"iuvenēs! cēdite! nōlīte nōbīs obstāre!"

iuvenēs, quamquam rem graviter ferēbant, cessērunt. iuvenēs Galatēam spectābant timidī, Helenam avidī.   20

subitō spectātōrēs pompam cōnspexērunt. statim multitūdō spectātōrum clāmōrem sustulit.

"ecce pompa! ecce! dea Īsis!"

unde	*from where*
illinc	*from there*
sānē	*obviously*
cōmiter	*politely, courteously*
avidī: avidus	*eager*

Questions

1 **ad templum Augustī vēnimus** (line 1). Write down one thing you already know about this temple.
2 **locum optimum nōvimus** (line 2). Why did Galatea think the place was **optimum**?
3 What was the slave's job (line 4)?
4 Why do you think Aristo said "**ēheu!**" to himself (line 6)?
5 In lines 7–9, what unpleasant surprise did Galatea have?
6 What did Galatea tell her husband to do? What suspicion did she have (lines 10–11)?
7 What alternative suggestion did Aristo make? How did he try to avoid blame?
8 After going up to the young men, how did Aristo carry out his wife's instruction (line 16)?
9 What did Galatea do that showed her attitude was different from her husband's? What did she tell the young men to do (line 18)?
10 Why do you think they finally gave up the place (lines 19–20)?
11 Why do you think Galatea at last stopped nagging everyone?
12 Having read this part of the story, how would you describe Aristo's character? Make three points and give evidence for each one.

About the Language I: hic and ille

A You have now met the Latin word for *this* (plural *these*):

	SINGULAR			PLURAL		
	masculine	*feminine*	*neuter*	*masculine*	*feminine*	*neuter*
nominative	hic	haec	hoc	hī	hae	haec
accusative	hunc	hanc	hoc	hōs	hās	haec

> **hic** vir est Barbillus.   *This man is Barbillus.*
> **hanc** pompam vīdī.   *I saw this procession.*
> **hae** stolae sunt sordidae!   *These dresses are dirty!*
> tibi **hōs** flōrēs trādō.   *I hand these flowers to you.*

B You have also met the Latin word for *that* (plural *those*):

	SINGULAR			PLURAL		
	masculine	*feminine*	*neuter*	*masculine*	*feminine*	*neuter*
nominative	ille	illa	illud	illī	illae	illa
accusative	illum	illam	illud	illōs	illās	illa

> **illa** fēmina est Galatēa.   *That woman is Galatea.*
>
> Clēmēns **illōs** sacerdōtēs saepe adiuvābat.   *Clemens often used to help those priests.*
>
> **illae** viae sunt perīculōsae.   *Those roads are dangerous.*
>
> multī Aegyptiī **illud** templum vīsitābant.   *Many Egyptians used to visit that temple.*

C For a complete chart of the forms for **hic** and **ille**, see page 200. Note that **hic** and **ille** agree in case, number, and gender with the nouns they describe.

D Further examples:

1 haec cēna est optima.
2 latrōnēs illum mercātōrem vituperant.
3 haec templa laudābāmus; illa aedificia vidēre nōn poterāmus.
4 hī servī sunt Aegyptiī.
5 Plancus illud monumentum dēmōnstrāvit.
6 Galatēa hunc iuvenem ēmovēre voluit.
7 ille poēta Aristōnem vexat.

pompa

pompa adveniēbat. prō pompā currēbant multae puellae, quae flōrēs in canistrīs ferēbant. puellae flōrēs spectātōribus dabant et in viam spargēbant. post multitūdinem puellārum tubicinēs et puerī prōcēdēbant. puerī carmina dulcia cantābant. tubicinēs tubās īnflābant. nōs, quī pompam plānē vidēre poterāmus, assiduē plaudēbāmus. duo iuvenēs tamen, quōs Galatēa ē locō ēmōverat, pompam vidēre vix poterant. 5

Helena:	spectā illās rosās, quās fēminae in viam spargunt! rosās pulchriōrēs quam illās numquam vīdī.
iuvenis prīmus:	pompam vidēre nōn possum. sed spectā 10 illam puellam! puellam pulchriōrem quam illam rārō vīdī.
Galatēa:	Helena! hūc venī! stā prope mē! Aristō! cūr fīliam tuam in tantā multitūdine nōn cūrās? *(subitō omnēs tubicinēs tubās vehementer* 15 *īnflābant.)*
Galatēa:	ō mē miseram! ō caput meum! audīte illōs tubicinēs! audīte illum sonitum! quam raucus est sonitus tubārum!
iuvenis secundus:	tubicinēs vix audīre possum. quam raucae 20 sunt vōcēs fēminārum Graecārum! *(post turbam puerōrum tubicinumque vēnit dea ipsa. quattuor sacerdōtēs effigiem deae in umerīs ferēbant.)*

pompa	*procession*
canistrīs: canistrum	*basket*
spargēbant: spargere	*scatter*
tubicinēs: tubicen	*trumpeter*
carmina: carmen	*song*
dulcia: dulcis	*sweet*
īnflābant: īnflāre	*blow*
plānē	*clearly*
rosās: rosa	*rose*
rārō	*rarely*
sonitum: sonitus	*sound*
raucus	*harsh*
vōcēs: vōx	*voice*

Galatēa:	spectā illam stolam croceam! pulcherrima	25
	est illa stola, pretiōsissima quoque. ēheu!	
	vīlēs sunt omnēs stolae meae, quod marītus	
	avārus est.	
	(*subitō iuvenēs, quī effigiem vidēre nōn*	
	poterant, Galatēam trūsērunt. iuvenis forte	30
	pedem Galatēae calcāvit.)	
Galatēa:	ō iuvenem īnsolentissimum! nōlī mē vexāre!	
	nōn decōrum est mātrōnam trūdere. num	
	bēstia es?	
Helena:	māter! hic iuvenis forte tibi nocuit.	35
	spectātōrēs nōs premunt, quod pompam	
	vidēre cupiunt.	
Galatēa:	Helena! nōlī istum iuvenem dēfendere!	
	īnsolentissimus est. Aristō! cūr mē nōn	
	servās? uxōrem fīliamque flōccī nōn facis.	40
	miserrima sum!	
Aristō:	ēheu! uxor mē vexat, fīlia mātrem. clāmōrēs	
	eārum numquam effugere possum. facile est	
	mihi tragoediās scrībere. tōta vīta mea est	
	tragoedia!	45

vīlēs: vīlis	*cheap*
trūsērunt: trūdere	*push, shove*
calcāvit: calcāre	*tread on*
nocuit: nocēre	*hurt*
premunt: premere	*push*
eārum	*their*

tōta vīta mea est tragoedia!

About the Language II: Imperatives

A In the following sentences, people are told to do something:

māter! **spectā** hoc!	amīcī! **spectāte** hoc!
*Mother! **Look at** this*	*Friends! **Look at** this!*
Helena! **venī** ad mē!	servī! **venīte** ad mē!
*Helena! **Come** to me!*	*Slaves! **Come** to me!*

The form of the verb in boldface is known as the imperative. It can be singular or plural, depending on who is being ordered.

B Compare the imperative forms with the infinitive:

	IMPERATIVE		INFINITIVE
	SINGULAR	PLURAL	
first conjugation	portā!	portāte!	portāre
	carry!	*carry!*	*to carry*
second conjugation	docē!	docēte!	docēre
	teach!	*teach!*	*to teach*
third conjugation	trahe!	trahite!	trahere
	drag!	*drag!*	*to drag*
fourth conjugation	audī!	audīte!	audīre
	listen!	*listen!*	*to listen*

C Study the way in which people are ordered *not* to do things:

SINGULAR	nōlī currere!	*Don't run!*
	nōlī cantāre!	*Don't sing!*
PLURAL	nōlīte festīnāre!	*Don't hurry!*
	nōlīte trūdere!	*Don't push!*

nōlī and **nōlīte**, the imperative forms of **nōlō**, are used with the infinitive. **nōlī currere** means literally "be unwilling to run."

D Further examples:

1 iuvenēs! tacēte!
2 dīligenter labōrā!
3 date mihi pecūniam!
4 mē adiuvā!
5 nōlī dormīre!
6 nōlīte discēdere!
7 nōlīte Rōmānōs interficere!
8 nōlī mē pūnīre!

nāvis sacra

sacerdōtēs, ubi ad portum pervēnērunt, effigiem deae Īsidis
dēposuērunt. in portū stābat nāvis, quae ōrnātissima erat. tōta
puppis erat aurāta. corōna rosārum dē mālō nāvis pendēbat. nūllī
tamen nautae in nāve erant.

sacerdōtēs cum effigiē deae ad hanc nāvem prōcessērunt.   5
deinde pontifex ipse deae Īsidī precēs adhibēbat. cīvēs
sacerdōtēsque rosās in nāvem et in mare iēcērunt. tum nautae
rudentēs solvere coepērunt. ventus secundus nāvem in altum lentē
impellēbat. spectātōrēs iterum iterumque plaudēbant. clāmor
spectātōrum precēsque sacerdōtum aurēs nostrās implēbant.   10

"nunc nāvis solūta est; nunc mare placidum. dea Īsis nōbīs
favet. dea cīvibus Alexandrīnīs favet."

sacerdōtēs, postquam nāvem sacram ita ēmīsērunt, effigiem
deae ad templum reportāvērunt. cīvēs per viās urbis laetī
currēbant.   15

ad vīllam Aristōnis lentē reveniēbāmus. Helena cum illīs
iuvenibus ambulābat, quōs Galatēa ē locō ēmōverat. hoc tamen
Galatēa nōn sēnsit, quod assiduē marītum castīgābat:

"in hāc urbe diūtius manēre nōlō. tū nihil facis, nihil cūrās.
servum nōn ēmīsistī, quamquam tē saepe monēbam. ēheu! cīvēs   20
Alexandrīnī sunt bēstiae. fīliam nostram vexābant illī iuvenēs.
Helena ērubēscēbat; paene lacrimābat. cūr eam numquam servās?
mihi semper necesse est fīliam nostram cūrāre."

"ubi est Helena?" rogāvit Aristō.

"nōnne tēcum ambulābat?" respondit Galatēa. "ēheu! illī   25
iuvenēs columbam meam iterum agitant."

"stultissima es, uxor!" respondit ille. "columba iuvenēs agitat,
nōn iuvenēs columbam."

puppis	stern	impellēbat:	drive forward,
corōna	garland, wreath	impellere	carry
dē mālō	from the mast	aurēs: auris	ear
pendēbat: pendēre	hang	implēbant: implēre	fill
pontifex	high priest	solūta: solūtus	untied, cast off
precēs adhibēbat	offered prayers	placidum: placidus	calm, peaceful
iēcērunt: iacere	throw	reportāvērunt:	
rudentēs: rudēns	cable, rope	reportāre	carry back
solvere	untie, cast off	ērubēscēbat:	
ventus	wind	ērubēscere	blush
secundus	favorable, following		
in altum	onto the deep, towards the open sea		

vēnātiō

I

Barbillus mē ad vēnātiōnem invītāvit. māne vīlicum Phormiōnem cum multīs servīs ēmīsit. Phormiō sēcum duōs haedōs dūxit. sed, ubi ē vīllā discēdēbāmus, astrologus Barbillī commōtus ad nōs cucurrit.

"domine, quō festīnās?" clāmāvit. "cūr ē vīllā hodiē exīre vīs?"   *5*
"ad praedium meum iter facimus," Barbillus respondit.

"sed, domine," inquit astrologus, "immemor es. perīculōsum est tibi hodiē ē vīllā exīre, quod hodiē sōl Arietī appropinquat."

ubi hoc audīvī, astrologum dērīsī. Barbillus, quamquam eī crēdēbat, mē offendere nōluit. postquam rem diū cōgitāvit,   *10*
"mihi placet exīre," inquit.

astrologus igitur, ubi dominō persuādēre nōn potuit, amulētum, quod Chaldaeī fēcerant, eī dedit. tum sēcūrī ad praedium Barbillī contendimus. per partem praediī flūmen Nīlus lēniter fluēbat.   *15*

ubi illūc advēnimus, multōs servōs vīdimus collēctōs. in hāc multitūdine servōrum erant nōnnūllī Aethiopes, quī hastās in manibus tenēbant. prope Aethiopas stābat Phormiō.

Phormiō "salvē, domine!" inquit. "omnia tibi parāvimus. scaphās, quās postulāvistī, comparāvimus."   *20*

"haedōs cecīdistis?" rogavit Barbillus.

"duōs haedōs cecīdimus, domine," inquit vīlicus. "eōs in scaphās iam posuimus."

haedōs: haedus	*kid, young goat*	**flūmen Nīlus**	*river Nile*
astrologus	*astrologer*	**lēniter**	*gently*
commōtus	*alarmed, excited*	**collēctōs: collēctus**	*assembled*
praedium	*estate*	**Aethiopes**	*Ethiopians*
immemor	*forgetful*	**omnia**	*everything,*
Arietī: Ariēs	*the Ram (sign of the*		*all things*
	zodiac)	**scaphās: scapha**	*punt,*
offendere	*displease*		*small boat*
persuādēre	*persuade*	**cecīdistis: caedere**	*kill*
amulētum	*amulet, lucky charm*		
Chaldaeī	*Chaldeans (an ancient*		
	people of Babylon)		

II

tum Phormiō nōs ad rīpam flūminis dūxit, ubi scaphae, quās comparāverat, dēligātae erant. postquam scaphās cōnscendimus, ad palūdem, in quā crocodīlī latēbant, cautē nāvigāvimus. ubi palūdī appropinquāvimus, aqua līmōsior fiēbat, harundinēsque dēnsiōrēs. postquam ad mediam palūdem nāvigāvimus, Barbillus 5 Phormiōnī signum dedit. haedōs Phormiō in aquam iniēcit. sanguis haedōrum crocodīlōs trahēbat, quī praecipitēs haedōs petēbant. tum Aethiopes crocodīlōs agitāre coepērunt. hastās ēmittēbant et crocodīlōs interficiēbant. magna erat fortitūdō crocodīlōrum, maior tamen perītia Aethiopum. mox multī 10 crocodīlī mortuī erant.

subitō ingentem clāmōrem audīvimus. Phormiō dominum vocābat, quod hippopotamus, quem Aethiopes ē palūde excitāverant, scapham Barbillī ēverterat. Barbillum et trēs servōs in aquam dēiēcerat. 15

quamquam ad Barbillum et ad servōs, quī in aquā natābant, celeriter nāvigāvimus, crocodīlī iam eōs circumvēnerant. hastās in crocodīlōs statim ēmīsimus. ubi crocodīlōs dēpulimus, Barbillum et ūnum servum servāre potuimus. sed postquam Barbillum ex aquā trāximus, eum invēnimus vulnerātum. hasta, quam servus 20 ēmīserat, umerum Barbillī percusserat. Barbillus ā servō suō graviter vulnerātus erat.

rīpam: rīpa	*bank*
dēligātae: dēligātus	*tied up, moored*
palūdem: palūs	*marsh, swamp*
crocodīlī: crocodīlus	*crocodile*
līmōsior: līmōsus	*muddy*
fiēbat	*became*
harundinēs: harundō	*reed*
iniēcit: inicere	*throw in*
praecipitēs: praeceps	*headlong, straight for*
fortitūdō	*courage*
perītia	*skill*
hippopotamus	*hippopotamus*
ēverterat: ēvertere	*overturn*
dēpulimus: dēpellere	*drive off*
ā servō suō	*by his own slave*

An amulet, in the form of the hippopotamus god Thueris.

About the Language III: Vocative Case

A In each of the following sentences, somebody is being spoken to:

Aristō! quam stultus es!   *Aristo! How stupid you are!*
quid accidit, **Barbille**?   *What happened, Barbillus?*
contendite, **amīcī**!   *Hurry, friends!*
cūr rīdētis, **cīvēs**?   *Why are you laughing, citizens?*

The words in boldface are in the vocative case. If only one person is spoken to, the vocative singular is used; if more than one person, the vocative plural is used.

B The vocative case has the same form as the nominative with the exception of the vocative singular of words in the second declension.

C Compare the nominative singular and vocative singular of second declension nouns like **servus** and **Salvius**:

nominative	*vocative*
servus labōrat.	cūr labōrās, **serve**?
amīcus gladium habet.	dā mihi gladium, **amīce**!
Eutychus est in viā.	ubi sunt latrōnēs, **Eutyche**?
Salvius est īrātus.	quid accidit, **Salvī**?
fīlius currit.	cūr curris, **fīlī**?
Holcōnius in lectō recumbit.	**Holcōnī**! surge!

D The vocative plural always has the same form as the nominative plural:

nominative	*vocative*
custōdēs dormiunt.	vōs semper dormītis, **custōdēs**.
puerī in forō stant.	ubi est theātrum, **puerī**?
puellae ad pompam festīnant.	nōlīte currere, **puellae**!

A Nile crocodile in a painting in the Temple of Isis at Pompeii.

Practicing the Language

A Complete each sentence with the correct form of **hic** or **ille** and then translate. If you are not sure of the gender of a noun, you will find it in the vocabulary at the end of the book.

1 (hic, hoc) astrologus Barbillō dē perīculō persuādēre nōn potuit.
2 Phormiō (illōs, illās) servōs ad flūmen Nīlum mīsit.
3 (hic, hoc) flūmen est perīculōsum.
4 (hī, hae) servī prope flūmen stābant.
5 Phormiō (illōs, illās) scaphās in rīpā īnstrūxit.
6 (illī, illae) crocodīlī haedōs petīvērunt.
7 Aethiopes (illum, illam, illud) hippopotamum ē palūde excitāvērunt.
8 (hic, haec, hoc) hasta umerum Barbillī percussit.

B This exercise is based on the story **diēs fēstus** on pages 141–142. Read the story again. Complete each of the sentences below with one of the following groups of words and then translate. Use each group of words once only.

postquam ad illum locum pervēnērunt
quod pompam vidēre volēbat
simulac prīmus diēs vēris advēnit
postquam marītum vituperāvit
quamquam Galatēa eum saepe monēbat
quod valdē īrāta erat

1 sacerdōtēs . . . . . deam Īsidem ad portum ferre solēbant.
2 Galatēa Aristōnem iussit servum māne ēmittere et locum servāre . . . . . .
3 sed Aristō . . . . . servum nōn ēmīsit.
4 Aristō et Galatēa . . . . . duōs iuvenēs ibi cōnspexērunt.
5 Galatēa marītum vituperāre coepit . . . . . .
6 Galatēa . . . . . iuvenēs ēmōvit.

C Complete each sentence with the correct form of the verb. Then translate the sentence.

1 Barbillus: Quīnte! mēcum ad vēnātiōnem (venī, venīte)!
2 Phormiō: servī! ad flūmen Nīlum (prōcēde, prōcēdite)!
3 astrologus: domine! (nōlī, nōlīte) ē vīllā discēdere!
4 Quīntus: amīce! nōlī astrologō (crēde, crēdere).
5 Phormiō: servī! ad mediam palūdem cautē (nāvigā, nāvigāte)!
6 Barbillus: Aethiopes! hastās (ēmitte, ēmittite)!
7 Quīntus: servī! (nōlī, nōlīte) hippopotamum vexāre!
8 Barbillus: Quīnte! vulnerātus sum. mē (servā, servāte)!

Procession of priests and priestesses carrying sacred objects: the sistrum, ladle, jug, sacred scroll, sacred cobra, water pot.

The Worship of Isis

Isis was one of Egypt's oldest and most important goddesses. The Egyptians worshiped her as the devoted wife and loving mother and for her power to give new life; they believed that just as she had given new life to Osiris (whom the Romans called Serapis), she was also responsible for the new life which followed the annual flooding of the Nile waters. They believed also that she offered a hope of life after death for those who became her followers. Within the cult of Isis, women enjoyed an equal position with men, even becoming priestesses.

One of the most important festivals of Isis was held at the beginning of spring. It took place annually on March 5th, when the sailing season opened and the large grain ships, so crucial to Rome's food supply, could once again set off safely across the Mediterranean. A statue of Isis was carried in procession down to the Great Harbor.

The procession was headed by dancers and musicians playing pipes, trumpets, and castanets. Female attendants scattered roses in the road and over the tightly packed crowd. The statue of Isis was carried high on the shoulders of her priests, so that everyone could get a glimpse of the goddess and her splendid robe. Next came more priests and priestesses and more trumpeters and finally the high priest, wearing garlands of roses and shaking a sacred rattle known as a **sistrum**.

At the harbor, a special newly built ship was moored. Its stern was shaped like a goose's neck and covered with gold plate. First the high priest dedicated the ship to Isis and offered prayers; then the priests and people loaded it with gifts of spices and flowers; finally the mooring-ropes were unfastened and the wind carried the ship out to sea.

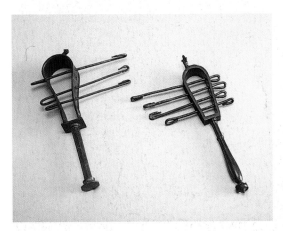
Two bronze sistra.

Woman holding a sistrum.

Isis

According to the Egyptians, Isis loved her brother, the god Osiris, who appeared on earth in the form of a man. However, Osiris was murdered; his body was cut up and the pieces were scattered throughout the world. Overcome with grief, Isis set out on a search for the pieces of Osiris' corpse. When at last she had found them all, a miracle took place: the dead Osiris was given new life and became the father of the child Horus.

Osiris and Isis.

Isis, as protector of shipping, holds a billowing sail in this Alexandrian coin. The Pharos can be seen on the right.

Isis was often portrayed as a loving mother, nursing her child, Horus.

Mosaic showing the Nile in flood. Isis was believed to send these floods, which brought Egypt its fertile soil.

After the ceremony at the harbor, the statue of Isis was taken back to the temple. The spectators crowded into the open area in front of the temple, and the priests replaced the statue in the **cella** or sanctuary of the temple. Then a priest read to the people from a sacred book and recited prayers for the safety of the Roman people and their emperor, and for sailors and ships.

The festival was noisy and colorful. Everybody had the day off, and although the religious ceremony was serious, it was also good entertainment. When the ceremony was over, the Alexandrians continued to enjoy themselves in a lively and spirited way. Their behavior was sometimes criticized, for example by the writer Philo:

> **They give themselves up to heavy drinking, noisy music, amusements, feasting, luxury, and rowdy behavior, eager for what is shameful and neglecting what is decent. They wake by night and sleep by day, turning the laws of nature upside down.**

But in spite of these words of Philo, a festival of Isis was not just an excuse for a holiday. The worship of the goddess was taken seriously by many Egyptians, who went regularly to her temple, prayed to her statue, and made offerings. Some of them, like Clemens in Stage 18, went further and became **Īsiacī**, members of the special fellowship of Isis; this involved a long period of preparation leading up to an initiation ceremony in the temple.

Those who wished to become initiates had to begin with an act of repentance for the sins they had committed in the past; for example, they might offer a sacrifice, or fast from food, or go on a pilgrimage. In a Latin

A ceremony outside a temple of Isis.

As the worship of Isis spread from Egypt into the Greek and Roman world, new ways were found of picturing the goddess. This Egyptian drawing shows her with her hieroglyph, a throne, above her head; she carries a scepter in one hand and an ankh, the symbol for life, in the other. On the right is a Roman painting of Isis holding the sacred cobra of Egypt. It was found in her temple at Pompeii.

novel known as *The Golden Ass*, the main character becomes a follower of Isis. He explains to his readers how he prepared to be admitted to the brotherhood. First his body was washed by the priests in a ceremony of baptism; next he was taught the sacred mysteries of the goddess, and forbidden to reveal them to anyone outside the brotherhood; then he fasted for ten days; and finally he underwent the initiation ceremony in the temple.

This was a ceremony of mystery and magic, full of strange and emotional experiences for the worshipers: those who were initiated believed that they had personally met Isis and that by dedicating themselves as her followers they could hope for life after death. But the exact details of the ceremony were kept strictly secret, as the narrator of *The Golden Ass* explains:

> If you are interested in my story, you may want to know what was said and done in the temple. I would tell you if I were allowed to tell, you would learn if you were allowed to hear; but your ears and my tongue would suffer for your foolish curiosity.

Roman statue of the goddess Isis with sistrum and jug for sacred water.

In Egyptian mythology, the male hippopotamus was identified with Seth, god of storms, and enemy of Isis and Osiris. Small figures like this are often found in tombs to placate Seth and keep him from injuring the owner.

By the time of our stories, the worship of Isis had spread from Alexandria and was flourishing across the ancient world. Temples to Isis have been found in places as far apart as London and the Black Sea area. A group of priests serving in a temple of Isis at Pompeii suffered a miserable death when the city was destroyed in the eruption of Vesuvius. They collected the sacred objects and treasures and fled from the temple, but by then it was too late. Their bodies were found along the route of their flight across the city, each corpse surrounded by the valuables he had tried to save.

Mosaic from Pompeii of the River Nile with Egyptian animals, including a hippopotamus and a crocodile.

Word Study

A Based on your knowledge of the Stage 19 Vocabulary Checklist, give an English word to match each of the following definitions. Use the underlined words as a help.

1 one who does something for the <u>love</u> of it
2 extreme <u>danger</u>
3 one who <u>looks after</u> a museum or house, for example
4 using the <u>voice</u>
5 a plan or outline of a <u>journey</u>
6 occurring by <u>chance</u>
7 <u>flowing</u> like honey

B Based on your knowledge of previous Checklists and the verb **caedō, caedere** suggest meanings for the following words:

1 infanticide	4 deicide	7 regicide	10 uxoricide
2 homicide	5 pesticide	8 suicide	
3 matricide	6 fratricide	9 parricide	

C Match the definitions to the following **-ate** words:

1 affiliate   **a** to bring into another's favor
2 castigate   **b** to think seriously, to ponder
3 cogitate   **c** to avoid committing oneself
4 curate   **d** to rebuke or punish
5 equivocate   **e** an assistant clergyman
6 hastate   **f** spear-shaped
7 ingratiate   **g** to find
8 locate   **h** an associate

Stage 19
Vocabulary Checklist

amō, amāre, amāvī	love, like
caedō, caedere, cecīdī	kill
cārus, cāra, cārum	dear
castīgō, castīgāre, castīgāvī	scold, nag
cōgitō, cōgitāre, cōgitāvī	think, consider
comparō, comparāre, comparāvī	obtain
cōnficiō, cōnficere, cōnfēcī	finish
cūrō, cūrāre, cūrāvī	look after
dulcis, dulcis, dulce	sweet
fīlia, fīliae, f.	daughter
fluō, fluere, flūxī	flow
forte	by chance
grātiās agō	I thank, give thanks
hasta, hastae, f.	spear
illūc	there, to that place
iter, itineris, n.	journey
locus, locī, m.	place
māne	in the morning
neglegēns, neglegēns, neglegēns, *gen.* neglegentis	careless
nōvī	I know
perīculum, perīculī, n.	danger
plūrimus, plūrima, plūrimum	very much
plūrimī, plūrimae, plūrima	very many
poscō, poscere, poposcī	demand, ask for
sonitus, sonitūs, m.	sound
tot	so many
umerus, umerī, m.	shoulder
vexō, vexāre, vexāvī	annoy
vīvō, vīvere, vīxī	live
vix	hardly, scarcely
vōx, vōcis, f.	voice

MEDICUS

1 servī ad vīllam revēnērunt,
Barbillum portantēs.

2 ancillae prope lectum
stābant, lacrimantēs.

3 astrologus in cubiculum
irrūpit, clāmāns.

4 Barbillus, in lectō recumbēns,
astrologum audīvit.

5 Phormiō ad urbem
contendit, medicum
quaerēns.

remedium astrologī

ego et servī cum Barbillō ad vīllam quam celerrimē rediimus.
multus sanguis ex vulnere Barbillī effluēbat. Phormiō, quī servōs
vulnerātōs sānāre solēbat, tunicam suam sciderat; partem tunicae
circum umerum Barbillī dēligāverat. fluēbat tamen sanguis.

servī, quī Barbillum portābant, ubi cubiculum intrāvērunt, in   5
lectum eum lēniter posuērunt. duae ancillae prope lectum stābant
lacrimantēs. Phormiō ancillās ē cubiculō ēmīsit et servōs ad sē
vocāvit.

"necesse est vōbīs," inquit, "magnum numerum arāneārum
quaerere. ubi sanguis effluit, nihil melius est quam arāneae."   10

servī per tōtam vīllam contendēbant, arāneās quaerentēs;
magnum clāmōrem tollēbant. Phormiō, postquam servī multās
arāneās ad cubiculum tulērunt, in umerum dominī eās collocāvit.

astrologus ancillās lacrimantēs vīdit, servōsque clāmantēs
audīvit. statim in cubiculum Barbillī irrūpit, exclāmāns: 15

"nōnne hoc prōvīdī? ō nefāstum diem! ō dominum īnfēlīcem!"

"habēsne remedium?" rogāvī anxius.

"remedium certum habeō," respondit astrologus. "facile est
mihi Barbillum sānāre, quod nōs astrologī sumus vērī medicī.

remedium	*cure*
vulnere: vulnus	*wound*
effluēbat: effluere	*pour out, flow out*
sānāre	*heal, cure*
sciderat: scindere	*tear up*
dēligāverat: dēligāre	*bind, tie*
lectum: lectus	*bed*
numerum: numerus	*number*
arāneārum: arānea	*spider's web*
tollēbant: tollere	*raise*
collocāvit: collocāre	*place*
prōvīdī: prōvidēre	*foresee*
nefāstum: nefāstus	*dreadful*
certum: certus	*certain, infallible*
vērī: vērus	*true, real*
medicī: medicus	*doctor*

remedium igitur Barbillō comparāre possum. est remedium, quod 20
Chaldaeī nōbīs trādidērunt. prīmō necesse est mihi mūrem nigrum
capere. deinde mūrem captum dissecāre volō. postrēmō eum in
umerum Barbillī pōnere volō. hoc sōlum remedium est."

subitō, Barbillus, quī astrologum audīverat, oculōs aperuit.
postquam mihi signum languidum dedit, in aurem meam 25
susurrāvit,

"quaere Petrōnem, medicum bonum!"

Phormiōnem, quī Petrōnem bene nōverat, ē vīllā statim ēmīsī.
itaque vīlicus medicum quaerēbat, astrologus mūrem.

mūrem: mūs	*mouse*
nigrum: niger	*black*
captum: captus	*captured, caught*
dissecāre	*cut up*
languidum: languidus	*weak, feeble*

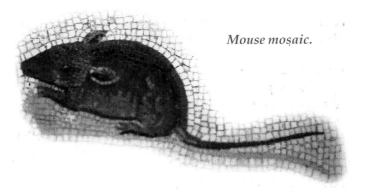

Mouse mosaic.

Petrō

Petrō, postquam dē vulnere Barbillī audīvit, statim ad vīllam eius
festīnāvit. ubi cubiculum intrāvit, astrologum vīdit, quī Barbillum
sānāre temptābat. astrologus mūrem dissectum in vulnus dominī
collocābat, versum magicum recitāns. Petrō, simulac mūrem
cōnspexit, īrātissimus erat; astrologum verberāvit et ē cubiculō 5
expulit.

tum Petrō, postquam umerum Barbillī īnspexit, spongiam cēpit
et in acētō summersit. eam in vulnus collocāvit. Barbillus
exanimātus reccidit.

Petrō ad mē sē vertit. 10

"necesse est tibi mē adiuvāre," inquit. "difficile est mihi
Barbillum sānāre. dē vītā eius dēspērō, quod tam multus sanguis
etiam nunc effluit."

itaque medicō auxilium dedī. Petrō, postquam aquam ferventem postulāvit, manūs forcipemque dīligenter lāvit. deinde, forcipem firmē tenēns, vulnus summā cum cūrā īnspexit. postquam hoc cōnfēcit, umerum Barbillī lāvit; cutem, quam hasta servī secuerat, perītē cōnseruit. dēnique fasciam lātam cēpit, umerumque firmē dēligāvit. *15*

mē ita monuit Petrō: *20*

"nunc necesse est Barbillō in hōc lectō manēre; necesse est eī quiēscere et dormīre. nātūra sōla eum sānāre potest, nōn astrologus."

Petrōnī grātiās maximās ēgī. apud Barbillum diū manēbam, negōtium eius administrāns. Barbillus enim mihi sōlī cōnfīdēbat. *25* cotīdiē ad cubiculum, ubi iacēbat aeger, veniēbam. multōs sermōnēs cum Barbillō habēbam, prope lectum sedēns. postquam Barbillum familiārissimē cognōvī, ille mihi dē vītā suā multum nārrāvit. sine dubiō fortūna eum graviter afflīxerat.

eius	*his*	cōnseruit: cōnserere	*stitch*
dissectum: dissectus	*cut up, dismembered*	fasciam: fascia	*bandage*
		lātam: lātus	*wide*
versum magicum:		monuit: monēre	*advise*
versus magicus	*magic spell*	quiēscere	*rest*
spongiam: spongia	*sponge*	nātūra	*nature*
acētō: acētum	*vinegar*	familiārissimē:	*closely,*
summersit:		familiāriter	*intimately*
summergere	*dip*	afflīxerat: afflīgere	*afflict, hurt*
reccidit: recidere	*fall back*		
ferventem: fervēns	*boiling*		
forcipem: forceps	*doctor's tongs, forceps*		
firmē	*firmly*		
cutem: cutis	*skin*		
perītē	*skillfully*		

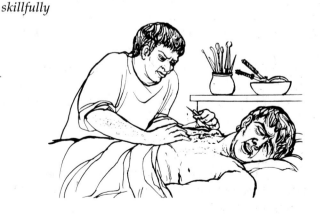

About the Language I: Present Participles

A Study the following sentences:

medicus, per forum **ambulāns**, Phormiōnem cōnspexit.
*The doctor, **walking** through the forum, caught sight of Phormio.*

Clēmēns Eutychum in mediā viā **stantem** invēnit.
*Clemens found Eutychus **standing** in the middle of the road.*

servī, Barbillum **portantēs**, vīllam intrāvērunt.
*The slaves, **carrying** Barbillus, entered the house.*

Phormiō ancillās in cubiculō **lacrimantēs** audīvit.
*Phormio heard the slave-girls **crying** in the bedroom.*

The words in boldface are present active participles. A participle is part verb and part adjective. For example, **ambulāns** is part of the verb **ambulāre**; as an adjective, **ambulāns** describes the noun **medicus**.

B Further examples:

1 astrologus in cubiculum irrūpit, clāmāns.
2 puerī, per urbem currentēs, Petrōnem cōnspexērunt.
3 spectātōrēs sacerdōtem ē templō discēdentem vīdērunt.
4 Galatēa iuvenēs in locō optimō stantēs vituperāvit.
5 Quīntus Phormiōnem umerum Barbillī dēligantem spectābat.

Pick out the present participle in each sentence and find the noun which it describes.

C Study these forms of the present participle:

	SINGULAR			
	masculine and feminine			
nominative	portāns	docēns	trahēns	audiēns
accusative	portantem	docentem	trahentem	audientem
	PLURAL			
	masculine and feminine			
nominative	portantēs	docentēs	trahentēs	audientēs
accusative	portantēs	docentēs	trahentēs	audientēs

D Further examples:

1 fūr ē vīllā effūgit, cachinnāns.
2 rēx mīlitēs, prō templō sedentēs, spectābat.
3 Helena in hortō ambulābat, cantāns.
4 puellae, in pompā ambulantēs, rosās spargēbant.
5 Clēmēns fēlem sacram in tabernā iacentem invēnit.

Pick out the present participle in each sentence and find the noun which the participle is describing. State whether each noun and participle pair is singular or plural.

fortūna crūdēlis

When you have read this story, answer the questions on page 169.

Barbillus uxōrem fidēlem fīliumque optimum habēbat. Plōtīna, uxor Barbillī, erat fēmina placida, quae domī manēbat contenta. Rūfus, fīlius eōrum, erat iuvenis impiger. ad palaestram cum amīcīs saepe adībat; in dēsertīs equitāre solēbat, bēstiās ferōcissimās agitāns. aliquandō, sīcut aliī iuvenēs, contentiōnēs 5 cum parentibus habēbat. sed parentēs Rūfī eum maximē amābant, et ille eōs.

  inter amīcōs Rūfī erat iuvenis Athēniēnsis, nōmine Eupor. hic Eupor ad urbem Alexandrīam vēnerat et medicīnae studēbat. saepissimē domum Barbillī vīsitābat. tandem ad urbem Athēnās 10 rediit, ubi artem medicīnae exercēbat. Eupor mox epistulam scrīpsit, in quā Rūfum parentēsque ad nūptiās suās invītāvit. Rūfus ad Graeciam īre valdē cupiēbat, sed Barbillus nāvigāre timēbat, quod hiems iam appropinquābat. astrologum suum igitur arcessīvit, et sententiam eius rogāvit. astrologus, postquam diū 15 cōgitāvit, Rūfō parentibusque respōnsum dedit.

domī	*at home*	medicīnae: medicīna	*medicine*
eōrum	*their*	studēbat: studēre	*study*
impiger	*lively, energetic*	artem: ars	*art*
aliquandō	*sometimes*	exercēbat: exercēre	*practice,*
maximē	*very much*		*exercise*
Athēniēnsis	*Athenian*	nūptiās: nūptiae	*wedding*
nōmine	*named, by name*	respōnsum	*answer*

"rem perīculōsam suscipitis. lūna Scorpiōnem iam intrat. tūtius est vōbīs domī manēre."

Barbillus et uxor astrologō, quī erat vir doctissimus, libenter crēdidērunt, sed Rūfus rem graviter ferēbat. ubi Barbillus aberat, 20 Rūfus saepe ad mātrem ībat, patrem dēplōrāns:

"pater stultissimus est, quod astrologō crēdit. astrologī nōn sunt nautae. nihil dē arte nāvigandī sciunt."

itaque Rūfus Plōtīnae persuāsit, sed patrī persuādēre nōn poterat. Barbillus obstinātus nāvigāre nōluit. Rūfus igitur et 25 Plōtīna Barbillum domī relīquērunt, et ad Graeciam nāvigābant. ubi tamen nāvis, quae eōs vehēbat, Graeciae appropinquābat, ingēns tempestās eam obruit. Rūfus ad lītus natāre poterat, sed Plōtīna, quam Barbillus valdē amābat, in magnīs undīs periit.

ubi Barbillus dē naufragiō, in quō uxor perierat, audīvit, 30 maximē commōtus erat. fīlium iterum vidēre nōlēbat. Rūfus, quamquam domum redīre volēbat, patrī pārēbat. in Graeciā diū manēbat; sed tandem iter in Britanniam fēcit, ubi in exercitū Rōmānō mīlitāvit.

Scorpiōnem: Scorpiō	*the Scorpion (sign of the zodiac)*
tūtius est	*it would be safer*
nāvigandī	*of sailing*
vehēbat: vehere	*carry*
tempestās	*storm*
obruit: obruere	*overwhelm*
commōtus	*upset, distressed*
pārēbat: pārēre	*obey*
exercitū: exercitus	*army*

Questions

1 Give three details we are told about Plotina's character.
2 Give two reasons why Rufus could be called **iuvenis impiger**.
3 What kind of a relationship did Rufus have with his parents?
4 What was Eupor doing in Alexandria?
5 When did Eupor write his letter? What did the letter contain?
6 Why did Barbillus ask for the opinion of his astrologer?
7 What was the astrologer's reply?
8 **Rūfus rem graviter ferēbat.** Why do you think Rufus was upset? What did he do? What success did he have?
9 What happened when the ship was approaching Greece? What happened to Rufus and Plotina?
10 Why did Rufus not return home? What did he do after leaving Greece?
11 Rufus said, **"pater stultissimus est, quod astrologō crēdit."** From what has happened to Barbillus and his family since that comment was made, do you think Rufus was right? Give a reason for your answer.

Plotina and Rufus would have sailed in a cargo ship like this one. There were no ships that carried only passengers in the Roman world.

About the Language II: Personal Pronouns

A You have now met various forms of the Latin word for "him," "her," "it," "them," etc.

Clēmēns officīnam intrāvit. Eutychus **eum** salūtāvit.
*Clemens entered the workshop. Eutychus greeted **him**.*

servī ingentēs erant. Clēmēns tamen **eōs** neglēxit.
*The slaves were huge. However, Clemens ignored **them**.*

Barbillus mē ad cēnam invītāvit. ego ad vīllam **eius** contendī.
*Barbillus invited me to dinner. I hurried to **his** house.*

operae celeriter convēnērunt. Eutychus **eīs** fūstēs trādidit.
*The thugs assembled quickly. Eutychus handed out clubs **to them**.*

B Here is a complete chart of the forms:

	SINGULAR			PLURAL		
	masculine	*feminine*	*neuter*	*masculine*	*feminine*	*neuter*
nominative	is	ea	id	eī	eae	ea
genitive	eius	eius	eius	eōrum	eārum	eōrum
dative	eī	eī	eī	eīs	eīs	eīs
accusative	eum	eam	id	eōs	eās	ea
ablative	eō	eā	eō	eīs	eīs	eīs

C Further examples:
1. Barbillus in cubiculō iacēbat. Quīntus eī vīnum dedit.
2. Galatēa marītum vituperābat. tōta turba eam audīvit.
3. puellae suāviter cantābant. Aristō vōcēs eārum laudāvit.
4. ubi Petrō advēnit, Phormiō eum ad cubiculum dūxit.
5. Rūfus, postquam epistulam accēpit, eam lēgit.
6. Plancus, ubi templō appropinquāvimus, dē eō garrīre coepit.
7. carmina spectātōrēs dēlectābant. omnēs ea magnō cum gaudiō audiēbant.
8. locum optimum nōvimus unde pompam spectāre possumus. servus eum servat.

astrologus victor

astrologus, quī in vīllā Barbillī habitābat, erat vir ingeniī prāvī.
astrologus et Petrō inimīcī erant. astrologus Syrius, medicus
Graecus erat. Petrō artem medicīnae in urbe diū exercuerat. multī
Alexandrīnī, quōs Petrō sānāverat, artem eius laudābant.

astrologus tamen in vīllā Barbillī habitābat, Petrō in urbe   5
Alexandrīā. facile igitur erat astrologō Barbillum vīsitāre. ad
cubiculum, in quō dominus aeger iacēbat, saepe veniēbat. ubi
Petrō aberat, astrologus in aurem dominī susurrābat.

"in perīculō maximō es, domine. Petrō medicus pessimus est.
paucōs sānāvit. multōs aegrōs ad mortem mīsit. num Petrōnī   10
cōnfīdis? Petrō est vir avārissimus; nēmō est avārior quam ille.
pecūniam tuam cupit. necesse est tibi eum ē vīllā expellere."

Barbillus astrologum anxius audīvit. sed, quamquam dolor
cotīdiē ingravēscēbat, medicō etiam nunc crēdēbat. ubi medicum
expellere Barbillus nōlēbat, astrologus cōnsilium cēpit. in   15
cubiculum dominī māne irrūpit, clāmāns,

"domine! tibi nūntium optimum ferō. tē sānāre possum! dea
Īsis, quae precēs meās semper audit, noctū somnium ad mē mīsit.
in somniō per viās urbis Alexandrīae ambulābam. subitō puerum
vīdī in triviīs stantem. puer erat servus tuus, quem Aegyptiī in   20
tumultū necāvērunt. mihi dē medicāmentō exquīsītissimō
nārrāvit."

Barbillus, ubi hoc audīvit, astrologō sē tōtum trādidit. ille igitur,
postquam medicāmentum composuit, umerum dominī aperuit et
ūnxit. sed medicāmentum astrologī pessimum erat. ingravēscēbat   25
vulnus Barbillī.

vir ingeniī prāvī	*a man of evil character*
dolor	*pain*
ingravēscēbat: ingravēscere	*grow worse*
nūntium: nūntius	*news, message*
noctū	*by night*
somnium	*dream*
medicāmentō: medicāmentum	*ointment*
exquīsītissimō: exquīsītus	*special*
composuit: compōnere	*put together, mix, make up*
ūnxit: unguere	*anoint, smear*

astrologus, ubi hoc sēnsit, ē vīllā fūgit perterritus. Barbillus, dē
vītā suā dēspērāns, mē ad cubiculum arcessīvit.

"mī Quīnte," inquit, in aurem susurrāns, "nōlī lacrimāre!
moritūrus sum. id plānē intellegō. necesse est omnibus mortem   *30*
obīre. hoc ūnum ā tē postulō. fīlium meum in Britanniā quaere!
refer eī hanc epistulam! ubi Rūfum ē vīllā expulī īrātus, eī magnam
iniūriam intulī. nunc tandem veniam ā Rūfō petō."

ubi hoc audīvī, Petrōnem arcessere volēbam, sed Barbillus
obstinātus recūsābat. arcessīvī tamen illum. sed ubi advēnit,   *35*
Barbillus iam mortuus erat.

obīre	*meet*
refer: referre	*carry, deliver*
iniūriam intulī:	*do an injustice (to),*
iniūriam īnferre	*bring injury*

A letter from Alexandria,
written in Greek on papyrus in
the first century A.D.

Study the following document, and then answer the questions at the end.

testāmentum

ego Tiberium Claudium Rufum heredem meum facio. si Rufus, filius meus,
mortuus est, ego Quintum Caecilium Iucundum heredem meum facio. do, lego
Quinto Caecilio Iucundo, amico meo, praedium meum, quod prope Nilum situm est.
  Marcum et Philadelphum, servos meos, libero, quod mihi fideliter
servierunt. do, lego Marco viginti aureos, Philadelpho quindecim. Annam, quae
ornatrix uxoris meae erat, libero, quod uxori meae bene serviebat. ceteris servis,
qui in villa mea plus quam quinque annos habitaverunt, novas tunicas do.
  do, lego Helenae, filiae Aristonis et Galateae, gemmas quas a mercatore
Arabi emi. Aristoni, patri Helenae, tragoedias quas ipse mihi scripsit reddo.
Aristo amicus optimus, poeta pessimus est.

Phormioni, vilico meo, qui me adiuvit, postquam iste servus me vulneravit, libertatem do. Petroni medico, qui me sanare temptavit, quingentos aureos lego. Petro medicus optimus est, ego vir stultissimus. scelesto astrologo, qui mihi mortem intulit, neque libertatem neque quidquam aliud do. necesse est Quinto, amico meo, eum punire.

mando Quinto Caecilio Iucundo curam funeris mei. Quintum iubeo monumentum mihi ponere.

Tiberius Claudius Barbillus signavit.

testāmentum	will	mortem intulit:	bring death
hērēdem: hērēs	heir	mortem īnferre	(upon)
sī	if	quidquam aliud	anything else
dō, lēgō	I give and bequeath	mandō: mandāre	entrust
fidēliter	faithfully	fūneris: fūnus	funeral
serviērunt: servīre	serve (as a slave)	signāvit: signāre	sign, seal
plūs	more		
quīngentōs:			
quīngentī	five hundred		

Questions

1 Who is Barbillus' heir?
2 What is to happen if the heir chosen by Barbillus is dead?
3 What legacy does Barbillus leave to Quintus?
4 What instructions does Barbillus give about each of his slaves?
5 What does Barbillus leave to Helena?
6 What does he leave to Aristo?
   What is Barbillus' opinion of Aristo?
7 Barbillus mentions three people besides Quintus who took care of him when he was ill. What does he give to each of them?
8 In his will, Barbillus asks Quintus to do three things. What are they?
9 Barbillus leaves nothing to Aristo's wife. Suggest possible reasons for this.
10 Judging from this will, what sort of person do you think Barbillus was?

Practicing the Language

A Complete each sentence with the correct form of the participle. Then translate the sentence.

1 Barbillus, dē vītā (dēspērāns, dēspērantēs), Quīntum arcessīvit.
2 Quīntus lībertum in tabernā (labōrāns, labōrantem) invēnit.
3 sacerdōtēs, prō templō (stāns, stantēs), silentium poposcērunt.
4 hippopotamum (adveniēns, advenientem) nōn cōnspexī.
5 Aegyptiī per viās cucurrērunt, magnum clāmōrem (tollēns, tollentēs).
6 Clēmēns tabernāriōs ā latrōnibus (fugiēns, fugientēs) vīdit.
7 puer mortuus dēcidit, dominum (dēfendēns, dēfendentem, dēfendentēs).
8 Aristō iuvenēs versum scurrīlem (recitāns, recitantem, recitantēs) audīvit.

B Use the **is, ea, id** chart on page 170, and substitute the correct form of this pronoun for the words in boldface. You may need to check the gender of the words in the Complete Vocabulary. Then translate each sentence.

1 Phormiō Petrōnem bene nōverat. **Petrōnem** in urbe quaesīvit.
2 in dēsertīs erant bēstiae ferōcēs. Rūfus **bēstiās** agitāre solēbat.
3 astrologus medicāmentum composuit. **medicāmentum** in vulnus Barbillī collocāvit.
4 poēta versūs scurrīlēs scrīpsit. **versūs** amīcō dedit.
5 "nōlīte nāvigāre!" inquit astrologus. Barbillus Plōtīnaque **astrologō** crēdidērunt.
6 Clēmēns ōrnāmenta vitrea in tabernā vēndēbat. in templō Īsidis **ōrnāmenta** saepe cōnsecrābat.
7 Barbillus Quīntō servum dedit. Quīntus cum **servō** tabernam Clēmentis petēbat.
8 sacerdōtēs Īsidem per viās portābant. Galatēa stolam **Īsidis** laudāvit.

C Translate into English:

Narcissus

Aristō: Galatēa! fortūna nōbīs favet! iuvenis Narcissus,
              quem herī vīdimus, Helenae dōnum mīsit. dōnum,
              quod iuvenis mīsit, pretiōsissimum est. dōnum mihi
              quoque mīsit. iuvenis Narcissus Helenam nostram
              amat.   5
Galatēa: quid dīcis, asine? iuvenis, quī prope nōs stābat, fīliae
              nostrae dōnum mīsit? ēheu! marītum habeō, quī nihil
              intellegit. Narcissus humilis est. māter Narcissī est
              Aegyptia.
Aristō: fēminam, quam vituperās, nōn nōvī. sed Narcissum   10
              bene nōvī. iuvenis optimus est, quem omnēs laudant.
Galatēa: sed pater Narcissī est caupō. taberna, quam tenet,
              sordida est. vīnum, quod vēndit, pessimum est.
Aristō: tabernam patris nōn floccī faciō. Narcissus ipse
              probus et benignus est. iuvenis etiam līberālis est.   15
              dōnum, quod mihi mīsit, libellus est. (*Aristō libellum*
              īnspicere incipit.) ēheu! Narcissus poēta est. suōs
              versūs scurrīlēs mihi mīsit.
Galatēa: fortūna nōbīs favet! nunc marītus meus illī iuvenī
              Helenam dare nōn vult.   20

humilis	*low-born, of low class*
libellus	*little book*
incipit: incipere	*begin*

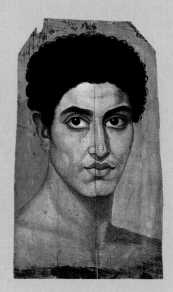

Write out the relative clauses in this
story and state the noun which each
relative clause describes.

Medicine and Science

Soon after its foundation, Alexandria became famous as a center of science and learning. The Museum and its Library, which were set up and financed by the Greek rulers of Egypt, attracted intelligent scholars from all over the Greek world, both to learn and to teach. They quickly began to make discoveries in all the sciences, including medicine. A good beginning had already been made in medicine by the Greek Hippocrates, who had attempted to remove magic

A seal stone carved with a picture of a doctor examining a patient, supervised by the god of healing, Aesculapius (left).

and superstition from the treatment of disease by observing his patients' symptoms carefully and trying to discover their causes. Hippocrates, who lived on the island of Cos in the fifth century B.C. and wrote 53 books on medical topics, is rightly regarded as the founder of medical science. He and his followers pledged themselves to high standards of ethical conduct in the famous Hippocratic Oath. Part of it reads as follows:

Into whatever houses I enter, I will go into them for the benefit of the sick, and I will abstain from every voluntary act of mischief and corruption. Whatever in my professional practice I see or hear, which should not be spoken to others, I will not divulge.

Alexandrian doctors were particularly expert about the inside of the body. This clay model of the intestines and models of other body parts were dedicated to the gods by patients at a healing shrine in Italy.

However, Hippocrates and his Greek followers usually investigated only the surface of the body and not its interior, because the Greeks felt the idea of dissecting a body was disagreeable and perhaps wicked. The Egyptians, with a different attitude to the body, had gained a limited knowledge of anatomy from the dissection necessary for their ancient custom of mummifying corpses. Alexandria was therefore a good place for studying anatomy. In the third century B.C. Herophilus, the most famous Alexandrian anatomist, performed the first recorded public dissection on a human corpse. He gave a detailed description of the brain, and explained the differences between tendons and nerves, and arteries and veins. He even described the optic nerve and the eye, including the retina. He also measured the frequency of the pulse and used this to diagnose fever. Like earlier doctors, he laid great stress on the importance of hygiene, diet, exercise, and bathing.

In addition to general advice of this kind, an experienced doctor of the first century A.D. would treat minor ailments with medicine which he prepared himself. The juice of the wild poppy, which contains opium, was used to relieve pain. Unwashed sheep's wool, containing lanolin, was often applied to wounds and swellings to soothe the irritation. Many prescriptions, however, would have been useless. For example, one account of the treatment of chilblains begins: "In the first place the chilblains are to be bathed thoroughly with boiled turnips..." Any benefit felt by the patient would be due not to the turnips, but to the heat of the turnips or the patient's own belief that the treatment would be effective.

Some prescriptions are rather alarming, such as this for severe toothache: "When a tooth decays, there is no great need to remove it, but if the pain compels its removal, a peppercorn or an ivy berry should be inserted into the cavity of the tooth, which will then split and fall out in bits."

Minor surgery was regularly practiced: "Tonsils are covered by a thin layer of skin. If they become hardened after inflammation, they should be scratched round with a finger

A set of medical instruments carved on the walls of an Egyptian temple about 25 years after Quintus' visit to Alexandria. In the third row, notice the scales for weighing medicines, and the forceps (see page 179). The upside-down cups at the bottom left were used to draw off blood (see page 178).

The bronze cup was heated and its mouth was applied to a patch of skin whose surface had been cut or crushed; as the air in the cup cooled, blood was gently sucked out.

and drawn out. If they cannot be drawn out in this way they should be gripped with a hook and cut out with a scalpel. The hollow should then be swilled out with vinegar and the wound smeared with something to check the blood."

Fractures and wounds presented greater problems. Nevertheless, doctors were able to make incisions, tie veins and arteries, reset broken bones with splints, and stitch up wounds. Difficult or very delicate operations were sometimes attempted, such as operations on the eye to relieve cataracts. Amputation of limbs was undertaken only as a last resort.

Like Petro in the story on pages 164–165, Greek doctors insisted on high standards of cleanliness to reduce the risk of infection. Although the Romans made few advances over the medical knowledge they adopted from the Egyptians and Greeks, they did make vast improvements in the field of sanitation. Aqueducts, sewers, latrines, and public baths all contributed to the public health. The Romans even organized a medical service for their army. Although the quality of medical treatment in the ancient world would naturally vary considerably from one doctor to another, it is probably true that the standards of the best doctors were not improved upon in western Europe until about a hundred and fifty years ago.

The Museum was also famous for the study of mathematics. Euclid, who worked at Alexandria in the third century B.C., wrote a book known as the *Elements*, in which he summarized all previous knowledge of geometry; it continued to be used as a school textbook almost down to the present day. In applying the mathematical knowledge to the world around them, the Greeks at Alexandria reached some very accurate conclusions. For example, Eratosthenes calculated that the circumference of the Earth was 24,662 miles (39,459 km); this is remarkably close to the true figure of 24,860 miles (40,008 km).

Astronomy, which had begun in Babylonia and ancient Egypt, was developed further at Alexandria. There the first attempts were made to calculate the distances between the Earth and the Sun, and between the Earth and the Moon. The idea was also put forward that the Earth was round, rotated on its axis, and, with the other planets, circled the Sun. After the end of the western Roman Empire in the fifth century A.D., this

Above left: *A Roman doctor had a wide range of instruments at his disposal.*
Above right top: *A saw for cutting through bone.* Above right bottom: *A stamp for labeling cakes of eye ointment and a plaster cast of the impressions of the four sides.*

idea was forgotten until Copernicus rediscovered it in the 1500s. It is remarkable that Alexandrian astronomers devised their theories and made their calculations without the aid of telescopes or other accurate instruments.

The pseudo-science of astrology was developed by the Chaldeans, a priestly caste from Babylonia, as early as 3000 B.C. The Chaldeans, like the **astrologus** in our stories, believed that the positions and movements of the Sun, Moon, and planets affected or represented events on Earth and that observers of these astronomical bodies could therefore forecast earthly happenings. This pseudo-science spread to Egypt where even some Alexandrian astronomers, such as Hipparchus and Ptolemy, believed in it. By the time of our stories, astrology had believers in every level of Roman society.

The scholars at Alexandria also designed a wide range of engineering devices. Hero of Alexandria, for example, made the first recorded waterclock. He also invented the first steam turbine, in the form of a toy, in which a hollow ball was mounted on two brackets on the lid of a vessel of boiling water. One bracket was hollow and conducted steam from the vessel into the ball. The steam escaped from the ball by means of two bent pipes, thus creating a force which made the ball spin around. He also made a hollow altar, where, when a fire was lit, hot air streamed through four bent pipes to make puppets dance.

Gears, levers, pulleys, pumps, screws, siphons, springs, and valves were widely used throughout the Mediterranean world from the third century on. However, the Alexandrians and Romans did not take advantage of their scientific discoveries to build complicated and

Eratosthenes discovered that at Syene (modern Aswan, Egypt) the sun was directly overhead at noon on the day of the summer solstice so that a vertical stick cast no shadow. At the same time in Alexandria a vertical stick did cast a shadow. Eratosthenes measured the length of the shadow. From this he could calculate the angle A between the sun's rays and the stick. Since the sun's rays are parallel, by simple geometry, angle B is the same size as angle A. Knowing angle B and the distance between Syene and Alexandria, he was able to calculate the circumference of the earth.

Diagram of Eratosthenes' experiment

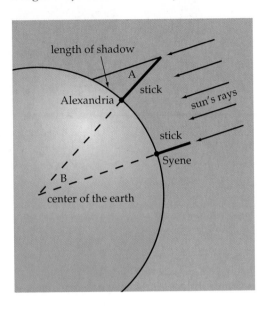

powerful machines for use in industry. Perhaps they felt they had no need for such machines, as they had a large workforce of slaves and free men available; perhaps they regarded trade and manufacturing as less dignified than scientific research and investigation; or perhaps they were prevented from developing industrial machinery by their lack of technical skills, such as the ability to make large metal containers and hold them together with screws and welds. Whatever the reason, some of the discoveries made by the Alexandrians were not put to industrial use until many centuries later.

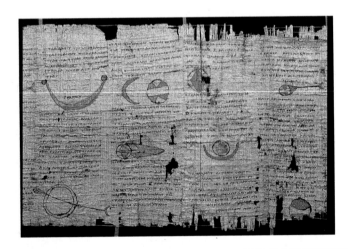

Part of a papyrus treatise on astronomy, written in Greek at Alexandria in the 2nd century B.C.

180 *Stage 20*

Word Study

A Give a derivative from the Latin words below to match each of the definitions.

domus   lūna   novem   persuādēre   relinquere   vulnus

1 to abandon or to give up
2 devoted to the home and household affairs
3 to use reasoning to cause someone to do something
4 originally the ninth month in the Roman calendar
5 insanity or utter foolishness
6 able to be wounded

B Match each word to its antonym (opposite).

1 pessimus   a vīta
2 adīre   b benignus
3 mors   c optimus
4 crūdēlis   d stultus
5 doctus   e discēdere

C Match the definitions to the nouns.

1 dereliction   a enticement or attraction
2 desperation   b embarrassment or humiliation
3 indoctrination   c a setting free
4 liberation   d the teaching of principles or beliefs
5 mortification   e an abandoning or a forsaking
6 temptation   f recklessness resulting from having
                       little or no hope

Hero's steam turbine.

Stage 20
Vocabulary Checklist

adeō, adīre, adiī	go up to, approach
arcessō, arcessere, arcessīvī	summon, send for
ars, artis, f.	art
auris, auris, f.	ear
collocō, collocāre, collocāvī	place, put
crūdēlis, crūdēlis, crūdēle	cruel
dēnique	at last, finally
dēspērō, dēspērāre, dēspērāvī	despair
doctus, docta, doctum	learned, clever
domus, domūs, f.	home
īnferō, īnferre, intulī	bring in, bring on
irrumpō, irrumpere, irrūpī	burst in
lātus, lāta, lātum	wide
līberō, līberāre, līberāvī	free, set free
lūna, lūnae, f.	moon
mors, mortis, f.	death
oculus, oculī, m.	eye
persuādeō, persuādēre, persuāsī (+ DAT)	persuade
pessimus, pessima, pessimum	very bad, worst
precēs, precum, f. pl.	prayers
relinquō, relinquere, relīquī	leave
remedium, remediī, n.	cure
sermō, sermōnis, m.	conversation
sīcut	like
tam	so
temptō, temptāre, temptāvī	try
vulnus, vulneris, n.	wound

ūnus, ūna, ūnum	one	octō	eight
duo, duae, duo	two	novem	nine
trēs, trēs, tria	three	decem	ten
quattuor	four	vīgintī	twenty
quīnque	five	trīgintā	thirty
sex	six	quadrāgintā	forty
septem	seven	quīnquāgintā	fifty

LANGUAGE INFORMATION

Contents

Part One: About the Language

Nouns

A

	first declension	*second declension*			*third declension*
gender	f.	m.	m.	n.	m.
SINGULAR					
nominative and *vocative*	puella	servus (*voc.* serve)	faber	templum	leō
genitive	puellae	servī	fabrī	templī	leōnis
dative	puellae	servō	fabrō	templō	leōnī
accusative	puellam	servum	fabrum	templum	leōnem
ablative	puellā	servō	fabrō	templō	leōne
PLURAL					
nominative and *vocative*	puellae	servī	fabrī	templa	leōnēs
genitive	puellārum	servōrum	fabrōrum	templōrum	leōnum
dative	puellīs	servīs	fabrīs	templīs	leōnibus
accusative	puellās	servōs	fabrōs	templa	leōnēs
ablative	puellīs	servīs	fabrīs	templīs	leōnibus

B For all declensions except the 2nd, the vocative singular is the same as the nominative singular. This is also true for 2nd declension neuter nouns (e.g. **templum**) and 2nd declension nouns ending in **-r** (e.g. **puer**, **vir**). 2nd declension nouns ending in **-us** form their vocative like **servus** (e.g. **domine**, **Marce**). 2nd declension nouns ending in **-ius** drop the ending completely in the vocative (e.g. **fīlī**, **Salvī**).

C 1st declension nouns like **puella** and **via** are usually feminine. 2nd declension nouns are usually either masculine like **servus**, or neuter like **templum**. 3rd declension nouns may be either masculine like **leō**, or

f.	m.f.	n.	n.	fourth declension m.	fifth declension f.	gender
						SINGULAR
vōx	cīvis	nōmen	mare	portus	rēs	*nominative* and *vocative*
vōcis	cīvis	nōminis	maris	portūs	reī	*genitive*
vōcī	cīvī	nōminī	marī	portuī	reī	*dative*
vōcem	cīvem	nōmen	mare	portum	rem	*accusative*
vōce	cīve	nōmine	marī	portū	rē	*ablative*
						PLURAL
vōcēs	cīvēs	nōmina	maria	portūs	rēs	*nominative* and *vocative*
vōcum	cīvium	nōminum	marium	portuum	rērum	*genitive*
vōcibus	cīvibus	nōminibus	maribus	portibus	rēbus	*dative*
vōcēs	cīvēs	nōmina	maria	portūs	rēs	*accusative*
vōcibus	cīvibus	nōminibus	maribus	portibus	rēbus	*ablative*

feminine like **vōx**, or neuter like **nōmen**.
4th declension nouns like **portus** are usually masculine.
5th declension nouns like **rēs** are usually feminine.

D Translate each sentence, then change the words in boldface from the singular to the plural, and translate again. Notice that in these examples two words in each sentence have to be changed.

For example: **agricola** in fundō **labōrābat**.
                 *The **farmer** was **working** on the farm.*
This becomes: **agricolae** in fundō **labōrābant**.
                 *The **farmers** were **working** on the farm.*

1 **servus** ferrum ē terrā **effodiēbat**.

2 **faber** ad āream celeriter **currēbat**.

3 **rēs erat perīculōsa**.

4 **centuriō** fūrem ferōciter **pulsābat**.

5 **tumultus** plūrimōs Alexandrīnōs **terrēbat**.

6 **domina** coquum in culīnā **exspectābat**.

7 **flūmen** prope praedium Barbillī **fluēbat**.

8 **hospes** cibum **gustābat**.

9 **sonitus** fēminārum Graecārum iuvenēs **vexābat**.

10 **custōs** servōs **spectābat**.

E Translate the following sentences, then change their meaning by turning each nominative into an accusative, *and* each accusative into a nominative, and then translate again.

> For example: dominus ancillās salūtāvit.
> *The master greeted the slave-girls.*
> This becomes: ancillae dominum salūtāvērunt.
> *The slave-girls greeted the master.*

Notice that in some sentences, as in the example above, you will have to change the verb from singular to plural or from plural to singular.

1 puerī leōnēs audīvērunt.

2 Belimicus ursam cōnspexit.

3 barbarī mīlitēs necāvērunt.

4 rēx cīvēs laudāvit.

5 agmen Salvium impedīvit.

6 fēminae mercātōrem vīsitāvērunt.

7 mātrōnam pictor spectāvit.

8 Rōmānōs Britannī interfēcērunt.

9 plaustrum amphorās cēlāvit.

10 imperātor mīlitēs honōrāvit.

F Translate the following sentences, which contain examples of the dative case. Be careful to distinguish between singular and plural forms.

1 imperātor lībertīs et cīvibus spectāculum dedit.

2 Salvius vīlicō et agricolae canem ostendit.

3 puer iuvenibus et senī rem nārrāvit.

4 ancillae mercātōrī et mīlitibus triclīnium parāvērunt.

5 coquus dominō et amīcīs respondit.

6 nūntius cīvī et nautae crēdēbat.

7 tabernāriī impetuī operārum resistere nōn poterant.

8 medicus prāvus rēgī prīncipibusque mortem intulit.

9 Belimicus, gubernātor Cantiacus, saxīs appropinquāvit.

10 quis huic aedificiō praeest?

G In Latin, dative forms often appear with verbs of "giving," "showing," and "telling" (e.g. above, **dedit**, **ostendit**, and **nārrāvit**). What other kinds of verbs with the dative are illustrated in the sentences above?

H Translate the following sentences which contain examples of the ablative case.

1 vīlla Barbillī longē ā portū abest.

2 fēlēs sub mēnsā sedēbat.

3 prō officīnā Eutychī stābant quattuor servī ingentēs.

4 mercātor Arabs sōlus erat in dēsertīs, sine aquā, sine servīs.

5 Holcōnius dē hīs rēbus nihil cūrāvit.

6 Rūfilla ē cubiculō currit, lacrimāns. in vīllā rūsticā sine amīcīs habitāre nōn vult.

7 aquila ex effigiē ēvolāvit.

8 flōrēs dē manibus ancillae cecidērunt.

I Translate the following sentences which contain examples of the genitive case.

1 puer ad tabernam Clēmentis cucurrit.

2 spectātōrēs clāmābant, sed rēx clāmōrēs spectātōrum nōn audīvit.

3 iuvenis vōcem fēminae laudāvit.

4 Quīntus, quī prope nāvem stābat, vōcēs nautārum audīvit.

5 Īsis erat dea Aegyptia. sacerdōtēs ad templum deae cotīdiē ībant.

6 magna multitūdō mīlitum in viā nōbīs obstābat.

7 in vīllā amīcī meī saepe cēnābam.

8 clāmōrēs puerōrum senem vexābant.

9 prīncipēs ad aulam rēgis quam celerrimē contendērunt.

10 umerus fabrī erat sordidus.

11 mīlitēs quī appropinquābant vōcēs cīvium audīre poterant.

12 praesidium exercitūs recūsāre nōlumus.

13 servus īram cīvium sentiēbat.

14 omnium diērum hic est optimus.

15 spectātōrēs fabrum effigiēī laudāvērunt.

J The following sentences include examples of the cases in the noun tables on pages 186–187. Translate the sentences and then write down the case and number of the nouns in boldface.

1 mercātōrēs Alexandrīnī **nāvēs** spectābant.

2 Clēmēns dōnum pretiōsum **deae** obtulit.

3 **tabernāriī**, operīs resistite!

4 domina stolās novās **ancillīs** dedit.

5 hasta caput **mīlitis** percussit.

6 puerum necāvērunt **Aegyptiī**.

7 Augustus illud **templum** aedificāvit.

8 vōcēs **prīncipum** in aulā audīvimus.

9 "**mī fīlī**," inquit pater, "nōlī ad Graeciam nāvigāre!"

10 spectātōrēs, quī in lītore stābant, **certāmen** nāvāle spectābant.

11 puellae rosās in **manibus** tenēbant.

12 Cogidubnus dē **sonitū mīrābilī** audīvit.

13 **nōmina** deōrum scīmus.

14 hospitēs **pōcula** sustulērunt.

15 vīlicus in **horreum** contendit.

K Using the table of nouns on pages 186–187, complete these sentences by filling in the endings, and then translate.
For example:
mercātor in viā stābat. amīcī mercātor ... salūtāvērunt.
mercātor in viā stābat. amīcī **mercātōrem** salūtāvērunt.
A merchant was standing in the street. The friends greeted the merchant.

1 puella stolam habēbat. stola puell... erat splendidissima.

2 servus leōn... in silvā vīdit. leō dormiēbat.

3 puellae tabernam intrāvērunt. mercātor puell... multās stolās ostendit.

4 cīvēs rēgem laudāvērunt, quod rēx cīv... magnum spectāculum dederat.

5 multī cīvēs in casīs habitābant. casae cīv... erant sordidae.

6 puer perterritus ad templum cucurrit et iānuam templ... pulsāvit.

7 rē ..., quī in aulā sedēbat, tubam audīvit.

8 Salvius puer..., quī amphorās portābant, vehementer vituperāvit.

9 "quam raucī," inquit Galatēa, "sunt sonit... tubārum!"

10 Rūfus, postquam ē Graeciā discessit, in exercit... Rōmānō mīlitābat.

11 vitriāriī ōllās per tōtum di... faciēbant.

12 pavīment..., quod Marcia lavābat, erat nitidum.

13 Quīntus, postquam vīllās in Campāniā vēndidit, multa itiner... faciēbat.

Adjectives

A An adjective changes its endings to agree with the noun it describes in three ways: case, number, and gender.

B Most adjectives in Latin belong either to the 1st and 2nd declension or to the 3rd declension. The adjective **bonus** "good" is one that belongs to the 1st and 2nd declension:

	SINGULAR			PLURAL		
	masculine	*feminine*	*neuter*	*masculine*	*feminine*	*neuter*
nominative and *vocative*	bonus (*voc.* bone)	bona	bonum	bonī	bonae	bona
genitive	bonī	bonae	bonī	bonōrum	bonārum	bonōrum
dative	bonō	bonae	bonō	bonīs	bonīs	bonīs
accusative	bonum	bonam	bonum	bonōs	bonās	bona
ablative	bonō	bonā	bonō	bonīs	bonīs	bonīs

Compare the endings of **bonus** with those of the 1st and 2nd declension nouns **servus**, **puella**, and **templum** listed on page 186.

C The adjective **fortis** "brave" is one that belongs to the 3rd declension:

	SINGULAR			PLURAL		
	masculine	*feminine*	*neuter*	*masculine*	*feminine*	*neuter*
nominative and *vocative*	fortis	fortis	forte	fortēs	fortēs	fortia
genitive	fortis	fortis	fortis	fortium	fortium	fortium
dative	fortī	fortī	fortī	fortibus	fortibus	fortibus
accusative	fortem	fortem	forte	fortēs	fortēs	fortia
ablative	fortī	fortī	fortī	fortibus	fortibus	fortibus

Compare the endings of **fortis** with those of the 3rd declension nouns **vōx**, **cīvis** and **mare** listed on page 187.

D With the help of sections B and C, find the correct form of **bonus** or **fortis** to agree with the noun in boldface, and then translate the sentences.

1 mercātor **fīliam** ..... laudāvit. (bonus)

2 rēx **mīlitēs** ..... salūtāvit. (fortis)

3 **hominēs** ..... dīligenter labōrābant. (bonus)

4 scrībe librum dē ..... **rēbus**! (bonus)

5 **fēmina** ..... hostī restitit. (fortis)

6 dominus **puerīs** ..... praemium dedit. (fortis)

7 fabrī effigiem **imperātōris** ..... fēcērunt. (bonus)

8 prīnceps **cīvium** ..... est vulnerātus. (fortis)

9 pater **uxōrī** ..... pecūniam lēgāvit. (bonus)

10 Quīntus **cōnsilia** ..... cēpit. (bonus)

Comparison of Adjectives

A Most adjectives have a positive, a comparative, and a superlative degree (form). Study the formation and the meaning for each of the following:

positive	comparative	superlative
longus (*gen.* longī) *long*	longior *longer*	longissimus *very long, longest*
pulcher (*gen.* pulchrī) *beautiful*	pulchrior *more beautiful*	pulcherrimus *very beautiful, most beautiful*
fortis (*gen.* fortis) *brave*	fortior *braver*	fortissimus *very brave, bravest*
ferōx (*gen.* ferōcis) *fierce*	ferōcior *more fierce*	ferōcissimus *very fierce, fiercest*
facilis (*gen.* facilis) *easy*	facilior *easier*	facillimus *very easy, easiest*

B Like the positive degree, the comparative and superlative forms change their endings to indicate case, number, and gender. (Note that the endings of the comparative adjective are like those of **leō** (masculine and feminine) and **nōmen** (neuter).

nominative: leō **saevissimus** intrāvit.
*A **very fierce** lion entered.*

accusative: leōnem **saevissimum** interfēcī.
*I killed a **very fierce** lion.*

singular: Dumnorix est **callidior** quam Belimicus.
*Dumnorix is **cleverer** than Belimicus.*

plural: Rēgnēnsēs sunt **callidiōrēs** quam Cantiacī.
*The Regnenses are **cleverer** than the Cantiaci.*

masculine: dominus meus est **īrātissimus**.
*My master is **very angry**.*

feminine: uxor mea est **īrātissima**.
*My wife is **very angry**.*

C Some important adjectives form their comparatives and superlatives in an irregular way:

positive	comparative	superlative
bonus	melior	optimus
good	*better*	*very good, best*
malus	peior	pessimus
bad	*worse*	*very bad, worst*
magnus	maior	maximus
big	*bigger*	*very big, biggest*
parvus	minor	minimus
small	*smaller*	*very small, smallest*
multus	plūs	plūrimus
much	*more*	*very much, most*
multī	plūrēs	plūrimī
many	*more*	*very many, most*

D Further examples:

1 leō erat maior quam Herculēs.
2 Clēmēns plūrēs amīcōs quam Eutychus habēbat.
3 Aristō erat poēta melior quam Barbillus.
4 Quīntus numquam nāvēs minōrēs vīderat.

E Translate each sentence, then change the adjective in boldface into the superlative form, and translate again.

For example: ātrium **magnum** erat.
*The hall was **big**.*
This becomes: ātrium **maximum** erat.
*The hall was **very big**.*

1 vīlicus puerōs **bonōs** laudāvit.
2 **multī** cīvēs in flammīs periērunt.
3 Quīntus servīs **malīs** lībertātem nōn dedit.
4 Herculēs erat **magnus**, et **magnum** fūstem habēbat.
5 prīmō flammae erant **parvae**.

F The Latin word **quam** may be written with a positive adjective, a comparative adjective, and a superlative adverb. Study these examples:

> **quam pulchra** est puella!
> *How beautiful the girl is!*

> vōs Rōmānī estis **Graeciōrēs quam** nōs Graecī.
> *You Romans are **more Greek than** we Greeks.*

> Pompēiānī ad amphitheātrum **quam celerrimē** contendērunt.
> *The Pompeians hurried **as quickly as possible** to the amphitheater.*

Translate the following sentences which contain these three uses of **quam**.

1 necesse est mihi cubiculum quam pūrissimum facere.

2 quam ēlegāns est cubiculum!

3 cubiculum tuum ēlegantius est quam tablīnum meum.

4 quam plūrimī Alexandrīnī pompam splendidam Īsidis spectāre volēbant.

5 ego sum senior quam frāter meus.

6 ego ex urbe quam celerrimē discēdō.

G Translate the first sentence of each pair. Complete the second sentence with the comparative and superlative of the adjective given in parentheses at the end of the sentence. Use the first sentence as a guide. Then translate.

1 canis est stultissimus; canem stultiōrem numquam vīdī. (stultus)
  Volūbilis est . . . . . ; servum . . . . . numquam vīdī. (laetus)

2 frāter meus est sapientior quam tū; sapientissimus est. (sapiēns)
  Bregāns est . . . . . quam Loquāx; . . . . . est. (īnsolēns)

3 mīlitēs sunt fortiōrēs quam cīvēs; fortissimī sunt. (fortis)
  servī sunt . . . . . quam lībertī; . . . . . sunt. (trīstis)

4 Melissa vōcem suāvissimam habēbat; vōcem suāviōrem numquam audīvī. (suāvis)
  Caecilius servum . . . . . habēbat; servum . . . . . numquam vīdī. (malus)

Pronouns I:
ego, tū, nōs, vōs, sē

A A pronoun is a word which takes the place of a noun.

B Study the forms of the following personal pronouns.

	First person		Second person	
	singular (I)	*plural (we)*	*singular (you)*	*plural (you)*
nominative	ego	nōs	tū	vōs
genitive	meī	nostrum	tuī	vestrum
dative	mihi	nōbīs	tibi	vōbīs
accusative	mē	nōs	tē	vōs
ablative	mē	nōbīs	tē	vōbīs

domina **tē** laudāvit.
*The mistress praised **you**.*

senex **mihi** illum equum dedit.
*The old man gave that horse **to me**.*

nōs Rōmānī sumus mīlitēs.
We Romans are soldiers.

dominus **vōs** īnspicere vult.
*The master wants to inspect **you**.*

C Study the forms of the reflexive pronoun, **sē**. Because a reflexive pronoun refers back to the subject, there is no nominative case. It has the same forms for both singular and plural.

	singular and plural
nominative	(no forms)
genitive	suī
dative	sibi
accusative	sē
ablative	sē

Dumnorix in ursam **sē** coniēcit.
*Dumnorix hurled **himself** at the bear.*

servī in ōrdinēs longōs **sē** īnstrūxērunt.
*The slaves drew **themselves** up in long lines.*

rēgīna **sē** interfēcit.   mercātor **sibi** vīllam ēmit.
*The queen killed **herself**.   The merchant bought the house for **himself**.*

D Note how Latin uses **cum** with these pronouns.

Salvius **mēcum** ambulābat. Rūfilla **tēcum** sedēbat.
Salvius was walking with me. *Rufilla was sitting with you.*

rēx **nōbīscum** cēnābat. iuvenēs **vōbīscum** pugnābant?
The king was dining with us. *Were the young men fighting with you?*

Belimicus **sēcum** cōgitābat.
Belimicus thought to himself.

Compare this with the usual Latin way of saying *with*:

rēx **cum Salviō** ambulābat.
The king was walking with Salvius.

mīlitēs **cum iuvenibus** pugnābant.
The soldiers were fighting with the young men.

E Further examples:

1 ego tibi pecūniam dedī.

2 rēx nōs ad aulam invītāvit.

3 Cogidubnus nōbīscum sedēbat.

4 cūr mē vituperās?

5 Galatēa Aristōnem castīgāvit, sē laudāvit.

6 necesse est vōbīs mēcum venīre.

7 vōs Quīntō crēditis, sed Salvius mihi crēdit.

8 tē pūnīre possum, quod ego sum dominus.

9 fābulam dē vōbīs nārrant.

10 prīncipēs sermōnēs inter sē habēbant.

Pronouns II:
Relative Pronoun quī

A Study the various forms of the relative pronoun **quī**, which is placed at the start of a relative clause and means "who," "which," etc.:

	SINGULAR			PLURAL		
	masculine	*feminine*	*neuter*	*masculine*	*feminine*	*neuter*
nominative	quī	quae	quod	quī	quae	quae
genitive	cuius	cuius	cuius	quōrum	quārum	quōrum
dative	cui	cui	cui	quibus	quibus	quibus
accusative	quem	quam	quod	quōs	quās	quae
ablative	quō	quā	quō	quibus	quibus	quibus

ursa, **quam** Quīntus vulnerāvit, nunc mortua est.
*The bear **which** Quintus wounded is now dead.*

ubi est templum, **quod** Augustus Caesar aedificāvit?
*Where is the temple **which** Augustus Caesar built?*

in mediō ātriō stābant mīlitēs, **quī** rēgem custōdiēbant.
*In the middle of the hall stood the soldiers, **who** were guarding the king.*

The noun described by a relative clause is known as the *antecedent* of the relative pronoun. For example, in the first Latin sentence above, **ursa** is the antecedent of **quam**.

B Translate the following sentences.

1 flōrēs, quī in hortō erant, rēgem dēlectāvērunt.

2 puer, quem Aegyptiī interfēcērunt, Quīntum fortiter dēfendēbat.

3 fabrī, quōs rēx ex Ītaliā arcessīverat, effigiem Claudiī fēcērunt.

4 cubiculum, quod Quīntus intrāvit, ēlegantissimum erat.

5 aula, in quā Cogidubnus habitābat, erat prope mare.

In each sentence pick out the antecedent and the relative pronoun.

Pronouns III:
Demonstratives hic, ille, is

A **hic**, **ille**, and **is** can be used as both pronouns and adjectives.

B Study the following forms of the demonstrative **hic** meaning "this" (plural "these"):

	SINGULAR			PLURAL		
	masculine	*feminine*	*neuter*	*masculine*	*feminine*	*neuter*
nominative	hic	haec	hoc	hī	hae	haec
genitive	huius	huius	huius	hōrum	hārum	hōrum
dative	huic	huic	huic	hīs	hīs	hīs
accusative	hunc	hanc	hoc	hōs	hās	haec
ablative	hōc	hāc	hōc	hīs	hīs	hīs

hae stolae sunt sordidae! quis **hoc** fēcit?
These dresses are dirty! *Who did this?*

C Study the following forms of the demonstrative **ille** meaning "that" (plural "those"):

	SINGULAR			PLURAL		
	masculine	*feminine*	*neuter*	*masculine*	*feminine*	*neuter*
nominative	ille	illa	illud	illī	illae	illa
genitive	illīus	illīus	illīus	illōrum	illārum	illōrum
dative	illī	illī	illī	illīs	illīs	illīs
accusative	illum	illam	illud	illōs	illās	illa
ablative	illō	illā	illō	illīs	illīs	illīs

illa taberna nunc est mea. spectā **illud**!
That shop is now mine. *Look at that!*

D Study the following forms of **is**, **ea**, **id** meaning "he," "she," "it" (plural "they"):

	SINGULAR			PLURAL		
	masculine	*feminine*	*neuter*	*masculine*	*feminine*	*neuter*
nominative	is	ea	id	eī	eae	ea
genitive	eius	eius	eius	eōrum	eārum	eōrum
dative	eī	eī	eī	eīs	eīs	eīs
accusative	eum	eam	id	eōs	eās	ea
ablative	eō	eā	eō	eīs	eīs	eīs

iuvenēs **eam** laudāvērunt.
The young men praised her.

ego ad vīllam **eius** contendī.
I hurried to his house.

dominus **eī** praemium dedit.
The master gave a reward to him.

senex cum **eīs** pugnāvit.
The old man fought with them.

E The various forms of **hic** and **ille** can also be used to mean "he," "she," "it," or "they."

ille tamen nōn erat perterritus.
He, however, was not terrified.

nēmō **hunc** in urbe vīdit.
No one saw him in the city.

F The following sentences include the different pronouns described on pages 197–201. Translate the sentences.

1 postquam senex hoc dīxit, Barbillus eum laudāvit.

2 in palaestrā erant multī āthlētae, quī sē exercēbant.

3 quamquam puellae prope mē stābant, eās vidēre nōn poteram.

4 illud est vīnum, quod Cogidubnus ex Ītaliā importāvit.

5 simulac mercātōrēs advēnērunt, Clēmēns eīs pecūniam trādidit.

6 dā mihi illum fūstem!

7 Vārica Bregantī plaustra dēmōnstrāvit. Bregāns illa ēmōvit.

8 mīlitēs, quōs imperātor mīserat, nōbīscum sedēbant.

9 remedia, quae astrologus composuit, erant pessima.

10 Barbillus hās statuās sibi ēmit.

11 rēgīna, quae tē honōrāvit, nōs castīgāvit.

12 simulac latrō hanc tabernam intrāvit, vōcem eius audīvī.

Verbs

A

first conjugation	second conjugation	third conjugation	third "-iō" conjugation	fourth conjugation

PRESENT INFINITIVE

to carry	*to teach*	*to drag*	*to take*	*to hear*
portāre	docēre	trahere	capere	audīre

PRESENT TENSE

I carry, you carry, etc.	*I teach, you teach, etc.*	*I drag, you drag, etc.*	*I take, you take, etc.*	*I hear, you hear, etc.*
portō	doceō	trahō	capiō	audiō
portās	docēs	trahis	capis	audīs
portat	docet	trahit	capit	audit
portāmus	docēmus	trahimus	capimus	audīmus
portātis	docētis	trahitis	capitis	audītis
portant	docent	trahunt	capiunt	audiunt

IMPERFECT TENSE

I was carrying, etc.	*I was teaching, etc.*	*I was dragging, etc.*	*I was taking, etc.*	*I was hearing, etc.*
portābam	docēbam	trahēbam	capiēbam	audiēbam
portābās	docēbās	trahēbās	capiēbās	audiēbās
portābat	docēbat	trahēbat	capiēbat	audiēbat
portābāmus	docēbāmus	trahēbāmus	capiēbāmus	audiēbāmus
portābātis	docēbātis	trahēbātis	capiēbātis	audiēbātis
portābant	docēbant	trahēbant	capiēbant	audiēbant

PERFECT TENSE

I (have) carried, etc.	*I (have) taught, etc.*	*I (have) dragged, etc.*	*I (have) taken, etc.*	*I (have) heard, etc.*
portāvī	docuī	trāxī	cēpī	audīvī
portāvistī	docuistī	trāxistī	cēpistī	audīvistī
portāvit	docuit	trāxit	cēpit	audīvit
portāvimus	docuimus	trāximus	cēpimus	audīvimus
portāvistis	docuistis	trāxistis	cēpistis	audīvistis
portāvērunt	docuērunt	trāxērunt	cēpērunt	audīvērunt

PLUPERFECT TENSE

I had carried, etc.	*I had taught, etc.*	*I had dragged, etc.*	*I had taken, etc.*	*I had heard, etc.*
portāveram	docueram	trāxeram	cēperam	audīveram
portāverās	docuerās	trāxerās	cēperās	audīverās
portāverat	docuerat	trāxerat	cēperat	audīverat
portāverāmus	docuerāmus	trāxerāmus	cēperāmus	audīverāmus
portāverātis	docuerātis	trāxerātis	cēperātis	audīverātis
portāverant	docuerant	trāxerant	cēperant	audīverant

IMPERATIVE

carry!	*teach!*	*drag!*	*take!*	*hear!*
portā	docē	trahe	cape	audī
portāte	docēte	trahite	capite	audīte

PRESENT ACTIVE PARTICIPLE

carrying	*teaching*	*dragging*	*taking*	*hearing*
portāns	docēns	trahēns	capiēns	audiēns

B Translate the following examples:

1 portāvī; audīvī; portābam; audiēbam.

2 portābant; docēbant; portāvimus; trāximus.

3 trahēbās; capiēbāmus; audiēbātis; audiēbam.

4 portāvistī; audīvistī; audīvistis; cēpistī.

5 docuerās; audīverās; audīverātis; trāxerātis.

6 capiēbat; cēperat; audīverat; audiēbat.

7 portātis; docēbātis; trāxistis; audīverātis.

8 docueram; portābam; cēperam; trahēbam.

9 trahō; cēpī; audiēbam; portāveram.

10 portāmus; audiēbāmus; cēpimus; docuerāmus.

C In Section A, find the Latin words for:

I was carrying; I was dragging; you (singular) were hearing; you (plural) were taking.

What would be the Latin for the following?

we carried; we heard; we took; we taught; you (plural) had heard; they taught; they dragged; you (plural) dragged.

D Translate the following examples, then change them from the singular to the plural, so that they mean "we . . . . ." instead of "I . . . . .," and translate again.

traho; audīvī; docēbam; labōrābam; faciēbam; scrīpsī; iubeō; īnspiciō.
(Remember that **īnspiciō** is third conjugation "-iō.")

E Translate the following examples, then change them to mean "you (sing.) . . . . ." instead of "they . . . . .," and translate again.

nāvigāvērunt; scrīpsērunt; īnspiciunt; terrent; vēndēbant; faciunt; complēverant.

F Translate the following examples, then change them from the *perfect* to the *pluperfect* tense, and then translate again.

portāvimus; trāxī; audīvērunt; fēcistī; docuit; laudāvistis; cēpimus; intellēxistī.

Persons and Endings

A The forms of the verb which indicate "I," "you" (singular), and "he" (or "she" or "it") are known as *1st*, *2nd*, and *3rd person singular*.

The forms which indicate "we," "you" (plural), and "they" are known as the *1st*, *2nd*, and *3rd person plural*.

The following chart summarizes the Latin personal endings and the English translations which are used to indicate the different persons:

	Latin Personal Endings PRESENT IMPERFECT PLUPERFECT	PERFECT	English
1st person singular	-ō or -m	-ī	*I*
2nd person singular	-s	-istī	*you*
3rd person singular	-t	-it	*he, she, it*
1st person plural	-mus	-imus	*we*
2nd person plural	-tis	-istis	*you*
3rd person plural	-nt	-ērunt	*they*

So a word like **trāxerant** can be either translated (*they had dragged*) or described (3rd person plural pluperfect). Two further examples, **portāvī** and **docent**, are described and translated as follows:

portāvī	1st person singular perfect	*I carried*
docent	3rd person plural present	*they teach*

B Describe and translate the following examples:

trāxī; audīs; portābāmus; docuerant; ambulāvistī; dīxerat.

C Translate these further examples.

1	discēdit	discessit	discesserat
2	currit	cucurrit	cucurrerat
3	potest	potuit	potuerat
4	facit	fēcit	fēcerat
5	dat	dedit	dederat
6	est	fuit	fuerat

Irregular Verbs

A

PRESENT INFINITIVE

to be	*to be able*	*to want*	*to go*	*to bring*
esse	posse	velle	īre	ferre

PRESENT TENSE

I am,	*I am able,*	*I want,*	*I go,*	*I bring,*
you are,	*you are able,*	*you want,*	*you go,*	*you bring,*
etc.	*etc.*	*etc.*	*etc.*	*etc.*
sum	possum	volō	eō	ferō
es	potes	vīs	īs	fers
est	potest	vult	it	fert
sumus	possumus	volumus	īmus	ferimus
estis	potestis	vultis	ītis	fertis
sunt	possunt	volunt	eunt	ferunt

IMPERFECT TENSE

I was,	*I was able,*	*I was*	*I was going,*	*I was*
etc.	*etc.*	*wanting, etc.*	*etc.*	*bringing, etc.*
eram	poteram	volēbam	ībam	ferēbam
erās	poterās	volēbās	ībās	ferēbās
erat	poterat	volēbat	ībat	ferēbat
erāmus	poterāmus	volēbāmus	ībāmus	ferēbāmus
erātis	poterātis	volēbātis	ībātis	ferēbātis
erant	poterant	volēbant	ībant	ferēbant

PERFECT TENSE

I was	*I was able*	*I (have)*	*I have gone,*	*I (have)*
(have been),	*(have been*	*wanted,*	*I went,*	*brought,*
etc.	*able), etc.*	*etc.*	*etc.*	*etc.*
fuī	potuī	voluī	iī	tulī
fuistī	potuistī	voluistī	iistī	tulistī
fuit	potuit	voluit	iit	tulit
fuimus	potuimus	voluimus	iimus	tulimus
fuistis	potuistis	voluistis	iistis	tulistis
fuērunt	potuērunt	voluērunt	iērunt	tulērunt

PLUPERFECT TENSE

I had been, etc.	*I had been able, etc.*	*I had wanted, etc.*	*I had gone, etc.*	*I had brought, etc.*
fueram	potueram	volueram	ieram	tuleram
fuerās	potuerās	voluerās	ierās	tulerās
fuerāt	potuerat	voluerat	ierat	tulerat
fuerāmus	potuerāmus	voluerāmus	ierāmus	tulerāmus
fuerātis	potuerātis	voluerātis	ierātis	tulerātis
fuerant	potuerant	voluerant	ierant	tulerant

Note: **tulī**, the perfect tense of **ferō**, is very different from the present tense. Compare this kind of difference with *I went* and *I go* in English.

B The negative forms for the present tense for **volō** *I want* are formed in an irregular way. Compare the forms of **volō** *I want* with those of **nōlō** *I do not want*:

I want, you want, etc.	*I do not want, you do not want, etc.*
volō	nōlō
vīs	nōn vīs
vult	nōn vult
volumus	nōlumus
vultis	nōn vultis
volunt	nōlunt

In all other tenses, **nōlō** follows the same pattern as **volō**.

For example, **volēbam, nōlēbam**.

C The verbs **adsum** *I am present* and **absum** *I am absent* are formed by adding **ad** and **ab** to the forms of **sum**.

I am, *you are, etc.*	*I am present,* *you are present, etc.*	*I am absent,* *you are absent, etc.*
sum	adsum	absum
es	ades	abes
est	adest	abest
sumus	adsumus	absumus
estis	adestis	abestis
sunt	adsunt	absunt

D Translate the following examples:

ferunt; es; potes; aderātis; ībat; erāmus; poteram; fert; nōn vultis; eunt; tulit; sumus; ferēbant; vīs; absunt; nōlēbāmus; potuerātis; fuit.

E Translate the following into Latin:

he wants; to bring; I have gone; they did want; we are absent; she has been able; you (singular) are present; you (plural) have been; she used to be; we had brought.

Verbs with the Dative

A You have met a number of verbs which are often used with a noun in the dative case. For example:

> mercātōrēs **Holcōniō** favēbant.
> *The merchants gave their support **to Holconius**.*
> or *The merchants supported Holconius.*

> turba **nōbīs** obstat.
> *The crowd is an obstacle **to us**.*
> or *The crowd is obstructing us.*

> Clēmēns **operīs** resistēbat.
> *Clemens put up a resistance **to the thugs**.*
> or *Clemens resisted the thugs.*

B Further examples:

1 Barbillus Quīntō cōnfīdēbat.

2 mīlitibus resistere nōn potuimus.

3 tandem fīlius mātrī persuāsit.

4 sacerdōtēs lentē templō appropinquāvērunt.

C Complete the following sentences with the right word and then translate.

1 fortūna semper eī (cūrat, favet).

2 servus invītus Belimicō (audiēbat, pārēbat).

3 magna multitūdō nōs (impediēbat, obstābat).

4 tabernāriī laetī Clēmentī iam (adiuvant, crēdunt).

5 Quīntus vīllam Barbillī (appropinquāvit, intrāvit).

6 taberna Barbillī Clēmentem maximē (dēlectāvit, placuit).

Word Order

A The word order in the following sentences is very common.

   1 Rēgnēnsēs clāmābant.   *The Regnenses were shouting.*

   2 dominus amīcum salūtāvit.   *The master greeted his friend.*

   3 cēnam parābat.   *S/he was preparing dinner.*

   4 māter fīliō dōnum quaerēbat. *The mother was searching for a gift for her son.*

   5 mercātōrī pecūniam reddidit. *S/he returned the money to the merchant.*

B The following sentence patterns are also found.

   1 discum petēbat āthlēta.   *The athlete was looking for the discus.*

   2 nautās Belimicus vituperābat. *Belimicus was cursing the sailors.*

   3 lacrimābant ancillae.   *The slave girls were crying.*

Further examples:

   1 amphoram portābat vīlicus.

   2 fēminās dominus spectābat.

   3 surrēxērunt prīncipēs.

   4 leōnem gladiātor interfēcit.

   5 mē dēcēpistī.

   6 gladiātōrēs laudāvit nūntius.

   7 mīlitibus cibum parāvī.

   8 rēgem cīvēs vīdērunt.

C The following examples are slightly different.

   Rēgnēnsēs erant laetī, Cantiacī miserī.
   The Regnenses were happy, the Cantiaci were miserable.

   Britannī cibum laudāvērunt, Rōmānī vīnum.
   The Britons praised the food, the Romans praised the wine.

sacerdōs templum, poēta tabernam quaerēbat.
The priest was looking for a temple, the poet was looking for an inn.

Further examples:
1 ūnus servus est fūr, cēterī innocentēs.
2 Cantiacī Belimicum spectābant, Rēgnēnsēs Dumnorigem.
3 Clēmēns attonitus, Quīntus īrātus erat.
4 mercātor stolās, caupō vīnum vēndēbat.
5 nōs pompam, iuvenēs Helenam spectābant.

D Note the position of **autem**, **enim**, **igitur**, and **tamen** in the following sentences.

Clēmēns numquam hominēs ingentiōrēs quam illōs
Aegyptiōs vīderat. eōs **autem** nōn timēbat.
Clemens had never seen huger men than those Egyptians.
However, he was not afraid of them.

apud Barbillum diū manēbam, negōtium eius administrāns.
Barbillus **enim** mihi sōlī cōnfīdēbat.
I stayed a long time with Barbillus, handling his business. For
Barbillus trusted only me.

Salvius fundum īnspicere voluit. Vārica **igitur** eum per agrōs
et aedificia dūxit.
Salvius wanted to inspect the farm. Varica, therefore, led him
through the fields and buildings.

Belimicus **tamen**, quī saxa ignōrābat, cursum rēctum tenēbat.
However, Belimicus, who did not know about the rocks, held a
straight course.

E Further examples:
1 puer Aegyptius Quīntum dē viā perīculōsā monuit. Quīntus
tamen Clēmentem vīsitāre volēbat.
2 in viā vitreāriōrum Eutychus et operae Clēmentem terrēre
temptābant. eum autem nōn terruērunt.
3 Cogidubnus Claudium quotannīs honōrat. rēx igitur multōs
prīncipēs ad aulam invītāvit.
4 Diogenēs nōbīs fūstēs trādidit. Aegyptiī enim casam
oppugnābant.

Subordinate Conjunctions: postquam, quamquam, etc.

A Study the following examples.

  1 Salvius, postquam fundum īnspexit, ad vīllam revēnit.
After Salvius inspected the farm, he returned to the house.

  2 Pompēius, quamquam invītus erat, custōdēs interfēcit.
Although Pompeius was unwilling, he killed the guards.

  3 simulac Salvius signum dedit, puer ē triclīniō contendit.
As soon as Salvius gave the signal, the boy hurried out of the dining room.

  4 ubi Salvius revēnit īrātus, Bregāns fūgit.
When Salvius came back angry, Bregans fled.

  5 Clēmēns, quod operae appropinquābant, amīcōs arcessīvit.
Because the thugs were approaching, Clemens summoned his friends.

postquam, **quamquam**, **simulac** (**simulatque**), **ubi**, and **quod** are subordinate conjunctions which introduce subordinate clauses. Subordinate clauses, unlike main clauses, cannot stand on their own as complete sentences.

Compare the Latin word order with the natural English word order in sentences 1, 2, and 5.

B Further examples:

  1 senex, quamquam uxor pompam vidēre volēbat, ex urbe discessit.

  2 amīcī, simulac tabernam vīdērunt dīreptam, ad Clēmentem cucurrērunt.

  3 iuvenēs, ubi Helenam cōnspexērunt, appropinquāvērunt.

  4 simulatque nāvem vīdit, Quīntus exclāmāvit.

  5 Salvius, quamquam servī dīligenter labōrābant, nōn erat contentus.

  6 tabernārius tabernam vēndere vult, quod operae pecūniam extorquent.

7 nūntius, postquam cīvibus spectāculum nūntiāvit, ad tabernam festīnāvit.

8 Quīntus, quod amīcus Barbillus ad vēnātiōnem īre volēbat, in vīllā eius manēre nōn potuit.

C Complete each sentence with the most suitable group of words from the box below, and then translate. Use each group of words once only.

> ubi saxō appropinquant
> quamquam ancilla dīligenter labōrābat
> simulac sacerdōtēs ē cellā templī prōcessērunt
> postquam hospitī cubiculum ostendit
> ubi iuvenēs laetī ad theātrum contendērunt
> quod turbam īnfestam audīre poterat

1 ....., domina nōn erat contenta.

2 necesse est nautīs, ..., cursum tenēre rēctum.

3 puer timēbat ē casā exīre, ...

4 ....., tacuērunt omnēs.

5 māter, ..., cibum in culīnā gustāvit.

6 ....., senex in tablīnō manēbat occupātus.

Part Two: Complete Vocabulary

The Complete Vocabulary for Unit 2 includes only those words which appear in the stories and notes for this Unit.

A Nouns are listed in the following way:
the nominative case, e.g. **servus** (*slave*);
the genitive case, e.g. **servī** (*of a slave*);
the gender of the noun (m. = masculine, f. = feminine, n. = neuter).

So, if the following forms are given:
pāx, pācis, f.   *peace*
pāx means *peace*, **pācis** means *of peace*, and the word is feminine.

B The genitive case indicates the declension to which a noun belongs.
puellae	1st declension
servī	2nd declension
leōnis	3rd declension
portūs	4th declension
reī	5th declension

C Find the meaning and the declension number for each of the following.
1 seges
2 effigiēs
3 scapha
4 tumultus
5 umerus

D Find the meaning and the gender for each of the following words, some of which are in the nominative case and some in the genitive.
1 taurus	4 manūs	7 tempestātis
2 hastae	5 diēī	8 praediī
3 flūminis	6 dolor	9 impetus

E Give the gender and the declension number for each of the following words.
1 fundus; fūnus; lectus; lītus; situs; sonitus; ventus; vulnus.
2 comes; clādēs; diēs; mīles; pēs; fēlēs.

3 epistula; horrea; pompa; pretia.
4 caupō; cōnsiliō; ōrdō.
5 dignitās; grātiās.
6 dōnī; effigiēī; impetuī.
7 faber; frāter; iter; puer.
8 flōs; iocōs; sacerdōs.
9 āctōrum; lūdōrum.
10 prīncipum; auxilium; cīvium; signum.
11 sanguis; sellīs.

F Adjectives are listed in the following way:
the masculine, feminine, and neuter forms of the nominative singular,
e.g. **bonus**, **bona**, **bonum**; **fortis**, **fortis**, **forte**. Sometimes the genitive
singular of 3rd declension adjectives (which is always the same for all
genders) is added to show the stem, e.g. **ferōx**, **ferōx**, **ferōx**, *gen.*
ferōcis.

G Verbs are usually listed by their principal parts.

parō, **parāre**, **parāvī**   *prepare*

The first part listed (**parō**) is the 1st person singular of the present
tense (*I prepare*).
The second part (**parāre**) is the present infinitive (*to prepare*).
The third part (**parāvī**) is the 1st person singular of the perfect tense
(*I prepared*).

So, if the following forms are given:
āmittō, **āmittere**, **āmīsī**   *lose*
āmittō means *I lose*, **āmittere** means *to lose*, **āmīsī** means *I lost*.

H The present infinitive indicates the conjugation to which a verb
belongs.
parāre	1st conjugation
docēre	2nd conjugation
trahere	3rd conjugation
audīre	4th conjugation

I Give the meaning for each of the following.
1 susurrō; susurrāre; susurrāvī.
2 agō; agere; ēgī.
3 tetigī; mīsī; quaesīvī; sustulī; āfuī.
4 haereō; impedīre; importāvī; vibrāre; interfēcī.

J Give the conjugation number and the meaning for each of the following.
  1 rapiō; dēsiliō; inveniō; accipiō.
  2 nāvigō; dēfendō; emō; rogō.
  3 relinquere; rīdēre; movēre; cōnsūmere.

K All words which are given in the **Vocabulary Checklists** for Stages 1–20 are marked with an asterisk (*).

a

* ā, ab (+ ABL) *from; by*
* abeō, abīre, abiī *go away*
  abiciō, abicere, abiēcī *throw away*
* absum, abesse, āfuī *be gone, be absent, be away*
  accidō, accidere, accidī *happen*
* accipiō, accipere, accēpī *accept, take in, receive*
  accurrēns, accurrēns, accurrēns, *gen.* accurrentis *running up*
  accūsō, accūsāre, accūsāvī *accuse*
  acētum, acētī, n. *vinegar*
  ācriter *keenly, fiercely*
  āctor, āctōris, m. *actor*
* ad (+ ACC) *to*
* adeō, adīre, adiī *approach, go up to*
  adeō *so much, so greatly*
  adhibeō, adhibēre, adhibuī *use, apply*
    precēs adhibēre *offer prayers*
  adiuvō, adiuvāre, adiūvī *help*
  administrāns, administrāns, administrāns, *gen.* administrantis *managing*
  administrō, administrāre, administrāvī *manage*
  admittō, admittere, admīsī *admit, let in*
  adōrō, adōrāre, adōrāvī *worship*
* adsum, adesse, adfuī *be here, be present*
* adveniō, advenīre, advēnī *arrive*
* aedificium, aedificiī, n. *building*
* aedificō, aedificāre, aedificāvī *build*
* aeger, aegra, aegrum *sick, ill*
  Aegyptius, Aegyptia, Aegyptium *Egyptian*
  Aegyptus, Aegyptī, f. *Egypt*
  aēneus, aēnea, aēneum *made of bronze*
  aequus, aequa, aequum *fair*
  Aethiopes, Aethiopum, m.f.pl. *Ethiopians*
  afflīgō, afflīgere, afflīxī *afflict, hurt*
  ager, agrī, m. *field*
  agilis, agilis, agile *nimble, agile*
  agitāns, agitāns, agitāns, *gen.* agitantis *chasing, hunting*
* agitō, agitāre, agitāvī *chase, hunt*
* agmen, agminis, n. *column (of people), procession*
* agnōscō, agnōscere, agnōvī *recognize*

agnus, agnī, m. *lamb*
* agō, agere, ēgī *do, act*
  age! *come on!*
  fābulam agere *act in a play*
* grātiās agere *thank, give thanks*
* negōtium agere *do business, work*
  quid agis? *how are you?*
* agricola, agricolae, m. *farmer*
  āla, ālae, f. *wing*
  Alexandrīnus, Alexandrīna, Alexandrīnum *Alexandrian*
  aliquandō *sometimes*
* aliquid *something*
* alius, alia, aliud *other, another, else*
* alter, altera, alterum *the other, the second*
  altus, alta, altum *deep*
    in altum *onto the deep, towards the open sea*
* ambulō, ambulāre, ambulāvī *walk*
  amīca, amīcae, f. *friend*
  amīcē *in a friendly way*
* amīcus, amīcī, m. *friend*
* āmittō, āmittere, āmīsī *lose*
* amō, amāre, amāvī *love, like*
  amphora, amphorae, f. *wine-jar*
  amulētum, amulētī, n. *amulet, lucky charm*
* ancilla, ancillae, f. *slave-girl, slave-woman*
  animal, animālis, n. *animal*
* animus, animī, m. *spirit, soul*
    animum recipere *recover consciousness*
  annus, annī, m. *year*
  anteā *before*
  antīquus, antīqua, antīquum *old, ancient*
* ānulus, ānulī, m. *ring*
  anus, anūs, f. *old woman*
  anxius, anxia, anxium *anxious*
  aperiō, aperīre, aperuī *open*
  appāreō, appārēre, appāruī *appear*
* appropinquō, appropinquāre, appropinquāvī (+ DAT) *approach, come near to*
* apud (+ ACC) *among, at the house of*
* aqua, aquae, f. *water*
  aquila, aquilae, f. *eagle*
* āra, ārae, f. *altar*
  Arabs, Arabs, Arabs, *gen.* Arabis *Arabian*

arānea, arāneae, f.   *spider's web, cobweb*
arātor, arātōris, m.   *plowman*
arca, arcae, f.   *strong-box, chest*
* arcessō, arcessere, arcessīvī   *summon, send for*
architectus, architectī, m.   *builder, architect*
ardeō, ardēre, arsī   *burn, be on fire*
ārea, āreae, f.   *courtyard*
arēna, arēnae, f.   *arena*
argenteus, argentea, argenteum   *made of silver*
armārium, armāriī, n.   *chest, cupboard*
* ars, artis, f.   *art, skill*
ascendō, ascendere, ascendī   *climb, rise*
asinus, asinī, m.   *ass, donkey*
assiduē   *continually*
astrologus, astrologī, m.   *astrologer*
Athēnae, Athēnārum, f.pl.   *Athens*
Athēniēnsis, Athēniēnsis, Athēniēnse   *Athenian*
āthlēta, āthlētae, m.   *athlete*
* ātrium, ātriī, n.   *atrium, reception hall*
* attonitus, attonita, attonitum   *astonished*
audāx, audāx, audāx, *gen.* audācis   *bold, daring*
* audeō, audēre   *dare*
* audiō, audīre, audīvī   *hear, listen to*
* aula, aulae, f.   *palace*
aurātus, aurāta, aurātum   *gilded, gold-plated*
aureus, aurea, aureum   *golden, made of gold*
aureus, aureī, m.   *gold coin, gold piece*
* auris, auris, f.   *ear*
autem   *however, but*
* auxilium, auxiliī, n.   *help*
avārus, avāra, avārum   *miserly, stingy*
* avārus, avārī, m.   *miser*
avidus, avida, avidum   *eager*

b

bālō, bālāre, bālāvī   *bleat*
barbarus, barbarī, m.   *barbarian*
* bene   *well*
benignitās, benignitātis, f.   *kindness*
* benignus, benigna, benignum   *kind*
bēstia, bēstiae, f.   *wild animal, beast*
* bibō, bibere, bibī   *drink*

* bonus, bona, bonum   *good*
Britannī, Britannōrum, m.pl.   *Britons*
Britannia, Britanniae, f.   *Britain*
Britannicus, Britannica, Britannicum   *British*
Brundisium, Brundisiī, n.   *Brindisi (a port on the Adriatic Sea)*

c

cachinnāns, cachinnāns, cachinnāns, *gen.* cachinnantis   *laughing, cackling*
cachinnō, cachinnāre, cachinnāvī   *laugh, cackle, roar with laughter*
cachinnus, cachinnī, m.   *laughter*
cadō, cadere, cecidī   *fall*
* caedō, caedere, cecīdī   *kill*
caelum, caelī, n.   *sky*
caerimōnia, caerimōniae, f.   *ceremony*
caeruleus, caerulea, caeruleum   *blue*
caesus, caesa, caesum   *killed*
calcō, calcāre, calcāvī   *step on*
caldārium, caldāriī, n.   *hot room (at the baths)*
* callidus, callida, callidum   *clever, smart*
candēlābrum, candēlābrī, n.   *lamp-stand, candelabrum*
candidātus, candidātī, m.   *candidate*
* canis, canis, m.   *dog*
canistrum, canistrī, n.   *basket*
cantāns, cantāns, cantāns, *gen.* cantantis   *singing, chanting*
* cantō, cantāre, cantāvī   *sing, chant*
capillī, capillōrum, m.pl.   *hair*
* capiō, capere, cēpī   *take, catch, capture*
   cōnsilium capere   *make a plan, have an idea*
captus, capta, captum   *taken, caught, captured*
* caput, capitis, n.   *head*
carmen, carminis, n.   *song*
carnifex, carnificis, m.   *executioner*
* cārus, cāra, cārum   *dear*
casa, casae, f.   *small house, cottage*
* castīgō, castīgāre, castīgāvī   *scold, nag*
caudex, caudicis, m.   *blockhead, idiot*
caupō, caupōnis, m.   *innkeeper*
cautē   *cautiously*
cecidī SEE cadō
cecīdī SEE caedō

cēdō, cēdere, cessī *give in, yield*
* celebrō, celebrāre, celebrāvī *celebrate*
* celeriter *quickly, fast*
    celerius *faster*
    celerrimē *very quickly*
    quam celerrimē *as quickly as possible*
  cella, cellae, f. *sanctuary*
  cellārius, cellāriī, m. *(house) steward*
  cēlō, cēlāre, cēlāvī *hide*
* cēna, cēnae, f. *dinner*
* cēnō, cēnāre, cēnāvī *eat dinner, dine*
  centum *a hundred*
* centuriō, centuriōnis, m. *centurion*
* cēpī SEE capiō
* cēra, cērae, f. *wax, wax tablet*
  cērātus, cērāta, cērātum *wax, made of wax*
  certāmen, certāminis, n. *struggle, contest*
    certāmen nāvāle *boat race*
  certō, certāre, certāvī *compete*
  certus, certa, certum *certain, infallible*
* cessī SEE cēdō
* cēterī, cēterae, cētera *the others, the rest*
  Chaldaeī, Chaldaeōrum, m.pl. *Chaldeans*
* cibus, cibī, m. *food*
* cinis, cineris, m. *ash*
  circum (+ ACC) *around*
* circumspectō, circumspectāre, circumspectāvī *look around*
  circumveniō, circumvenīre, circumvēnī, *surround*
  citharoedus, citharoedī, m. *cithara player*
* cīvis, cīvis, m.f. *citizen*
  clādēs, clādis, f. *disaster*
  clam *secretly, in private*
  clāmāns, clāmāns, clāmāns, *gen.* clāmantis *shouting*
* clāmō, clāmāre, clāmāvī *shout*
* clāmor, clāmōris, m. *shout, uproar, racket*
  claudicō, claudicāre, claudicāvī *be lame*
* claudō, claudere, clausī *shut, close, block*
* coepī *I began*
* cōgitō, cōgitāre, cōgitāvī *think, consider*
* cognōscō, cognōscere, cognōvī *find out, get to know*
  collēctus, collēcta, collēctum *gathered, assembled*

collēgium, collēgiī, n. *guild, association of craftsmen*
colligō, colligere, collēgī *gather, collect, assemble*
* collocō, collocāre, collocāvī *place, put*
  colōnia, colōniae, f. *town (settled by Roman army veterans)*
  columba, columbae, f. *dove, pigeon*
  comes, comitis, m.f. *comrade, companion*
  cōmis, cōmis, cōme *polite, courteous, friendly*
  cōmiter *politely, courteously*
  commemorō, commemorāre, commemorāvī *talk about*
* commodus, commoda, commodum *convenient*
  commōtus, commōta, commōtum *moved, upset, affected, alarmed, excited, distressed*
* comparō, comparāre, comparāvī *obtain*
  competītor, competītōris, m. *competitor*
* compleō, complēre, complēvī *fill*
  compōnō, compōnere, composuī *put together, arrange, mix, make up*
  condūcō, condūcere, condūxī *hire*
  cōnfectus, cōnfecta, cōnfectum *finished*
* cōnficiō, cōnficere, cōnfēcī *finish*
    rem cōnficere *finish the job*
  cōnfīdō, cōnfīdere (+ DAT) *trust*
  coniciō, conicere, coniēcī *hurl, throw*
  coniungō, coniungere, coniūnxī *join*
    sē coniungere *join*
* coniūrātiō, coniūrātiōnis, f. *plot, conspiracy*
  coniūrō, coniūrāre, coniūrāvī *plot, conspire*
  cōnscendō, cōnscendere, cōnscendī *embark on, go on board*
  cōnscius, cōnsciī, m. *accomplice*
  cōnsecrō, cōnsecrāre, cōnsecrāvī *dedicate*
* cōnsentiō, cōnsentīre, cōnsēnsī *agree*
  cōnserō, cōnserere, cōnseruī *stitch*
  cōnsīdō, cōnsīdere, cōnsēdī *sit down*
* cōnsilium, cōnsiliī, n. *plan, idea*
    cōnsilium capere *make a plan, have an idea*
* cōnsistō, cōnsistere, cōnstitī *stand one's ground, stand firm*

* cōnspiciō, cōnspicere, cōnspexī *catch sight of*
* cōnsūmō, cōnsūmere, cōnsūmpsī *eat*
* contendō, contendere, contendī *hurry*
  contentiō, contentiōnis, f. *argument*
* contentus, contenta, contentum *satisfied*
  contrā (+ ACC) *against*
  contrōversia, contrōversiae, f. *debate*
* conveniō, convenīre, convēnī *come together, gather, meet*
  convertō, convertere, convertī *turn*
    sē convertere *turn*
* coquō, coquere, coxī *cook*
* coquus, coquī, m. *cook*
  corōna, corōnae, f. *garland, wreath, crown*
* cotīdiē *every day*
* crēdō, crēdere, crēdidī (+ DAT) *trust, believe, have faith in*
  crīnēs, crīnium, m.pl. *hair*
  croceus, crocea, croceum *yellow*
  crocodīlus, crocodīlī, m. *crocodile*
* crūdēlis, crūdēlis, crūdēle *cruel*
* cubiculum, cubiculī, n. *bedroom*
* cucurrī SEE currō
  culīna, culīnae, f. *kitchen*
* cum (+ ABL) *with*
  cumulus, cumulī, m. *pile*
* cupiō, cupere, cupīvī *want*
* cūr? *why?*
  cūra, cūrae, f. *care*
* cūrō, cūrāre, cūrāvī *take care of, supervise*
    nihil cūrō *I don't care*
  currēns, currēns, currēns, gen. currentis *running*
* currō, currere, cucurrī *run*
  cursus, cursūs, m. *course*
* custōdiō, custōdīre, custōdīvī *guard*
* custōs, custōdis, m. *guard*
  cutis, cutis, f. *skin*

d

* dare SEE dō
* dē (+ ABL) *from, down from; about*
* dea, deae, f. *goddess*
* dēbeō, dēbēre, dēbuī *owe, ought, should, must*
* decem *ten*

* dēcidō, dēcidere, dēcidī *fall down*
  dēcipiō, dēcipere, dēcēpī *deceive, trick*
* decōrus, decōra, decōrum *right, proper*
* dedī SEE dō
  dēfendō, dēfendere, dēfendī *defend*
  dēiciō, dēicere, dēiēcī *throw down, throw*
* deinde *then*
* dēlectō, dēlectāre, dēlectāvī *delight, please*
* dēleō, dēlēre, dēlēvī *destroy*
  dēliciae, dēliciārum, f.pl. *darling*
  dēligātus, dēligāta, dēligātum *tied up, moored*
  dēligō, dēligāre, dēligāvī *bind, tie, tie up*
* dēmōnstrō, dēmōnstrāre, dēmōnstrāvī *point out, show*
  dēnārius, dēnāriī, m. *a denarius (small coin worth four sesterces)*
* dēnique *at last, finally*
  dēns, dentis, m. *tooth, tusk*
* dēnsus, dēnsa, dēnsum *thick*
  dēpellō, dēpellere, dēpulī *drive off*
  dēplōrāns, dēplōrāns, dēplōrāns, gen. dēplōrantis *complaining about*
  dēplōrō, dēplōrāre, dēplōrāvī *complain about*
  dēpōnō, dēpōnere, dēposuī *put down, take off*
* dērīdeō, dērīdēre, dērīsī *mock, make fun of*
  dēscendēns, dēscendēns, dēscendēns, gen. dēscendentis *coming down*
  dēscendō, dēscendere, dēscendī *come down*
  dēserō, dēserere, dēseruī *desert*
  dēsertus, dēserta, dēsertum *deserted*
    in dēsertīs *in the desert*
  dēsiliō, dēsilīre, dēsiluī *jump down*
  dēspērāns, dēspērāns, dēspērāns, gen. dēspērantis *despairing*
* dēspērō, dēspērāre, dēspērāvī *despair*
  dēstringō, dēstringere, dēstrīnxī *draw (a sword), pull out*
* deus [deī, dī (nom. pl.)], m. *god*
    prō dī immortālēs! *heavens above!*
  dexter, dextra, dextrum *right*
    ad dextram *to the right*
* dīcō, dīcere, dīxī *say*
  dictō, dictāre, dictāvī *dictate*

* diēs, diēī, m. *day*

    diēs fēstus, diēī fēstī, m. *festival, holiday*

* diēs nātālis, diēī nātālis, m. *birthday*

* difficilis, difficilis, difficile *difficult*

    dignitās, dignitātis, f. *dignity*

* dīligenter *carefully, hard*

* dīmittō, dīmittere, dīmīsī *send away, dismiss*

    dīreptus, dīrepta, dīreptum *torn apart, ransacked*

    dīrigō, dīrigere, dīrēxī *steer*

    dīripiō, dīripere, dīripuī *tear apart, ransack*

    dīrus, dīra, dīrum *dreadful, awful*

* discēdō, discēdere, discessī *depart, leave*

    dissecō, dissecāre, dissecuī *cut up*

    dissectus, dissecta, dissectum *cut up, dismembered*

* diū *for a long time*

    diūtius *any longer, for too long*

    dīves, dīves, dīves, *gen.* dīvitis *rich*

* dīxī SEE dīcō

* dō, dare, dedī *give*

    poenās dare *pay the penalty, be punished*

    doceō, docēre, docuī *teach*

* doctus, docta, doctum *educated, learned, skillful*

    dolor, dolōris, m. *pain*

* domina, dominae, f. *lady (of the house), mistress*

* dominus, dominī, m. *master (of the house)*

* domus, domūs, f. *home*

    domī *at home*

    domum redīre *return home*

* dōnum, dōnī, n. *present, gift*

    dormiēns, dormiēns, dormiēns, *gen.* dormientis *sleeping*

* dormiō, dormīre, dormīvī *sleep*

    dubitō, dubitāre, dubitāvī *be doubtful, hesitate*

    dubium, dubiī, n. *doubt*

    ducentī, ducentae, ducenta *two hundred*

* dūcō, dūcere, dūxī *lead*

* dulcis, dulcis, dulce *sweet*

    mī dulcissime! *my very dear friend!*

* duo, duae, duo *two*

    dūrus, dūra, dūrum *harsh, hard*

e

* ē, ex (+ ABL) *from, out of*

* eam *her*

* eās *them*

    eburneus, eburnea, eburneum *ivory*

* ecce! *see! look!*

* effigiēs, effigiēī, f. *image, statue*

    effluō, effluere, efflūxī *pour out, flow out*

    effodiō, effodere, effōdī *dig*

    effringō, effringere, effrēgī *break down*

* effugiō, effugere, effūgī *escape*

    effundō, effundere, effūdī *pour out*

* ēgī SEE agō

* ego, meī *I, me*

    mēcum *with me*

    ehem! *well, well!*

* ēheu! *alas! oh dear!*

* eī *to him, to her, to it*

* eīs *to them, for them*

* eius *his, her, its*

    ēlegāns, ēlegāns, ēlegāns, *gen.* ēlegantis *elegant*

    ēligō, ēligere, ēlēgī *choose*

    ēlūdō, ēlūdere, ēlūsī *slip past*

* ēmittō, ēmittere, ēmīsī *throw, send out*

* emō, emere, ēmī *buy*

    ēmoveō, ēmovēre, ēmōvī *move, clear away*

    enim *for*

* eō, īre, iī *go*

* eōs *them*

* epistula, epistulae, f. *letter*

    eques, *gen.* equitis, m. *horseman*

    equitō, equitāre, equitāvī *ride (a horse)*

* equus, equī, m. *horse*

* eram SEE sum

    ērubēscēns, ērubēscēns, ērubēscēns, *gen.* ērubēscentis *blushing*

    ērubēscō, ērubēscere, ērubuī *blush*

    ērumpō, ērumpere, ērūpī *break away*

* est SEE sum

* et *and*

* etiam *even, also*

* euge! *hurrah!*

* eum *him*

    ēvellēns, ēvellēns, ēvellēns, *gen.* ēvellentis *wrenching off*

    ēvertō, ēvertere, ēvertī *overturn*

    ēvolō, ēvolāre, ēvolāvī *fly out*

ēvulsus, ēvulsa, ēvulsum *wrenched off*
* ex, ē (+ ABL) *from, out of*
* exanimātus, exanimāta, exanimātum *unconscious*
* excitō, excitāre, excitāvī *arouse, wake up*
exclāmāns, exclāmāns, exclāmāns, *gen.* exclāmantis *exclaiming, shouting*
* exclāmō, exclāmāre, exclāmāvī *exclaim, shout*
* exeō, exīre, exiī *go out*
* exerceō, exercēre, exercuī *exercise*
exercitus, exercitūs, m. *army*
expellō, expellere, expulī *throw out*
explōrātor, explōrātōris, m. *scout, spy*
exquīsītus, exquīsīta, exquīsītum *special*
exspectātus, exspectāta, exspectātum *welcome*
* exspectō, exspectāre, exspectāvī *wait for*
extendō, extendere, extendī *stretch out*
extorqueō, extorquēre, extorsī *extort*
extrā (+ ACC) *outside*
extrahō, extrahere, extrāxī *pull out, take out*

f

* faber, fabrī, m. *craftsman*
* fābula, fābulae, f. *play, story*
*   fābulam agere *act in a play*
* facile *easily*
* facilis, facilis, facile *easy*
* faciō, facere, fēcī *make, do*
    floccī nōn faciō *I don't give a hoot about*
    impetum facere *charge, make an attack*
* familiāris, familiāris, m. *relative, relation*
familiāriter *closely, intimately*
fascia, fasciae, f. *bandage*
* faveō, favēre, fāvī (+ DAT) *favor, support*
fax, facis, f. *torch*
* fēcī SEE faciō
fēlēs, fēlis, f. *cat*
* fēmina, fēminae, f. *woman*
fenestra, fenestrae, f. *window*
* ferō, ferre, tulī *bring, carry*
    graviter ferre *take badly*
* ferōciter *fiercely*
* ferōx, ferōx, ferōx, *gen.* ferōcis *fierce, ferocious*
ferrum, ferrī, n. *iron*

fervēns, fervēns, fervēns, *gen.* ferventis *boiling*
* fessus, fessa, fessum *tired*
* festīnō, festīnāre, festīnāvī *hurry*
fēstus, fēsta, fēstum *festive, holiday*
    diēs fēstus, diēī fēstī, m. *festival, holiday*
* fidēlis, fidēlis, fidēle *faithful, loyal*
fidēliter *faithfully, loyally*
* fīlia, fīliae, f. *daughter*
* fīlius, fīliī, m. *son*
fīō *I become*
firmē *firmly*
* flamma, flammae, f. *flame*
floccī nōn faciō *I don't give a hoot about*
* flōs, flōris, m. *flower*
flūmen, flūminis, n. *river*
* fluō, fluere, flūxī *flow*
foedus, foeda, foedum *foul, horrible*
fōns, fontis, m. *fountain*
forceps, forcipis, m. *doctor's tongs, forceps*
* fortasse *perhaps*
* forte *by chance*
* fortis, fortis, forte *brave, strong*
* fortiter *bravely*
fortitūdō, fortitūdinis, f. *courage*
fortūna, fortūnae, f. *fortune, luck*
fortūnātus, fortūnāta, fortūnātum *lucky*
* forum, forī, n. *forum, business center*
fossa, fossae, f. *ditch*
* frāctus, frācta, frāctum *broken*
frangēns, frangēns, frangēns, *gen.* frangentis *breaking*
* frangō, frangere, frēgī *break*
* frāter, frātris, m. *brother*
frequentō, frequentāre, frequentāvī *crowd, fill*
frūmentum, frūmentī, n. *grain*
* frūstrā *in vain*
* fugiō, fugere, fūgī *run away, flee (from)*
* fuī SEE sum
fulgēns, fulgēns, fulgēns, *gen.* fulgentis *shining, glittering*
fulgeō, fulgēre, fulsī *shine, glitter*
fundō, fundere, fūdī *pour*
* fundus, fundī, m. *farm*
fūnebris, fūnebris, fūnebre *funereal, of a funeral*
    lūdī fūnebrēs *funeral games*

fūnus, fūneris, n. *funeral*
* fūr, fūris, m. *thief*
furēns, furēns, furēns, *gen.* furentis
     furious, in a rage
fūstis, fūstis, m. *club, stick*

g

garriēns, garriēns, garriēns, *gen.*
     garrientis *chattering, gossiping*
garriō, garrīre, garrīvī *chatter, gossip*
garum, garī, n. *sauce*
geminī, geminōrum, m.pl. *twins*
gemitus, gemitūs, m. *groan*
gemma, gemmae, f. *jewel, gem*
* gēns, gentis, f. *family; tribe*
Germānicus, Germānica, Germānicum
     German
gerō, gerere, gessī *wear*
gladiātor, gladiātōris, m. *gladiator*
* gladius, gladiī, m. *sword*
Graecia, Graeciae, f. *Greece*
Graecus, Graeca, Graecum *Greek*
grātiae, grātiārum, f.pl. *thanks*
*   grātiās agere *thank, give thanks*
gravis, gravis, grave *heavy*
* graviter *seriously*
     graviter ferre *take badly*
gubernātor, gubernātōris, m. *helmsman*
* gustō, gustāre, gustāvī *taste*

h

* habeō, habēre, habuī *have*
* habitō, habitāre, habitāvī *live*
* hāc *this*
* hae *these*
* haec *this*
haedus, haedī, m. *young goat, kid*
* haereō, haerēre, haesī *stick, cling*
* hanc *this*
harundō, harundinis, f. *reed*
* hās *these*
* hasta, hastae, f. *spear*
hauriō, haurīre, hausī *drain, drink up*
hercle! *by Hercules!*
hērēs, hērēdis, m.f. *heir*
* heri *yesterday*
heus! *hey!*
* hī *these*

* hic, haec, hoc *this*
hiemō, hiemāre, hiemāvī *spend the
     winter*
hiems, hiemis, f. *winter*
hippopotamus, hippopotamī, m.
     hippopotamus
* hoc *this*
* hodiē *today*
* homō, hominis, m. *person, man*
homunculus, homunculī, m. *little man,
     pip-squeak*
honōrō, honōrāre, honōrāvī *honor*
hōra, hōrae, f. *hour*
* horreum, horreī, n. *barn, granary*
* hortus, hortī, m. *garden*
* hōs *these*
* hospes, hospitis, m. *guest, host*
* hūc *here, to this place*
humilis *low-born, of low class*
* hunc *this*

i

* iaceō, iacēre, iacuī *lie, rest*
iaciō, iacere, iēcī *throw*
iactō, iactāre, iactāvī *throw*
* iam *now, already*
* iānua, iānuae, f. *door*
* ībam SEE eō*
* ibi *there*
* id *it*
* iēcī SEE iaciō*
* igitur *therefore, and so*
* ignāvus, ignāva, ignāvum *cowardly,
     lazy*
ignōrō, ignōrāre, ignōrāvī *not know
     about*
* iī SEE eō*
* ille, illa, illud *that, he, she, it*
illinc *from there*
* illūc *there, to that place*
immemor, immemor, immemor, *gen.*
     immemoris *forgetful*
immortālis, immortālis, immortāle
     immortal
     prō dī immortālēs! *heavens above!*
immōtus, immōta, immōtum *still,
     motionless*
impavidus, impavida, impavidum
     fearless

*impediō, impedīre, impedīvī *delay, hinder*

impellō, impellere, impulī *carry, push, force*

* imperātor, imperātōris, m. *emperor*

* imperium, imperiī, n. *empire*

* impetus, impetūs, m. *attack*
    impetum facere *charge, make an attack*

impiger, impigra, impigrum *lively, energetic*

impleō, implēre, implēvī *fill*

importō, importāre, importāvī *import*

* in (+ ABL) *in, on*

* in (+ ACC) *into, onto*

incēdō, incēdere, incessī *march, stride*

incendēns, incendēns, incendēns, gen.
    incendentis *burning, setting fire to*

incendō, incendere, incendī *burn, set fire to*

* incidō, incidere, incidī *fall*

incipiō, incipere, incēpī *begin*

* incitō, incitāre, incitāvī *urge on, encourage*

incolumis, incolumis, incolume *safe*

incurrō, incurrere, incurrī *run onto, collide*

inēlegāns, inēlegāns, inēlegāns, gen.
    inēlegantis *unattractive*

* īnfāns, īnfantis, m. *baby, child*

īnfēlīx, īnfēlīx, īnfēlīx, gen. īnfēlīcis *unlucky*

īnfēnsus, īnfēnsa, īnfēnsum *hostile, enraged*

* īnferō, īnferre, intulī *bring in, bring on*
    iniūriam īnferre *do an injustice, bring injury*
    mortem īnferre (+ DAT) *bring death (upon)*
    vim īnferre *use force, violence*

īnfestus, īnfesta, īnfestum *hostile, dangerous*

īnfirmus, īnfirma, īnfirmum *weak*

īnflō, īnflāre, īnflāvī *blow*

ingenium, ingeniī, n. *character*

* ingēns, ingēns, ingēns, gen. ingentis *huge*

ingravēscō, ingravēscere *grow worse*

iniciō, inicere, iniēcī *throw in*

* inimīcus, inimīcī, m. *enemy*

iniūria, iniūriae, f. *injustice, injury*
    iniūriam īnferre *do an injustice, bring injury*

iniūstē *unfairly*

innocēns, innocēns, innocēns, gen.
    innocentis *innocent*

* inquit *says, said*

īnsānus, īnsāna, īnsānum *insane, crazy*

īnsidiae, īnsidiārum, f.pl. *trap, ambush*

īnsiliō, īnsilīre, īnsiluī *jump onto, jump into*

īnsolēns, īnsolēns, īnsolēns, gen.
    īnsolentis *rude, insolent*

* īnspiciō, īnspicere, īnspexī *look at, inspect, examine*

īnstrūctus, īnstrūcta, īnstrūctum *drawn up*

īnstruō, īnstruere, īnstrūxī *draw up*
    sē īnstruere *draw oneself up*

* īnsula, īnsulae, f. *island*

* intellegō, intellegere, intellēxī *understand*
    rem intellegere *understand the truth*

* intentē *intently*

intentus, intenta, intentum *intent*

* inter (+ ACC) *among, between*
    inter sē *among themselves, with each other*

intereā *meanwhile*

* interficiō, interficere, interfēcī *kill*

interpellō, interpellāre, interpellāvī *interrupt*

interrogō, interrogāre, interrogāvī *question*

* intrō, intrāre, intrāvī *enter*

* intulī SEE īnferō

inūtilis, inūtilis, inūtile *useless*

invādō, invādere, invāsī *invade*

* inveniō, invenīre, invēnī *find*

invicem *in turn*

* invītō, invītāre, invītāvī *invite*

* invītus, invīta, invītum *unwilling, reluctant*

iocus, iocī, m. *joke*

* ipse, ipsa, ipsum *himself, herself, itself*

* īrātus, īrāta, īrātum *angry*

* īre SEE eō

* irrumpō, irrumpere, irrūpī *burst in*

* is, ea, id *he, she, it, this, that*

Īsiacī, Īsiacōrum, m.pl. *followers of Isis*

Īsis, Īsidis, f.   *Isis (Great Mother goddess of Egypt)*
* iste, ista, istud   *that*
* ita   *in this way*
* ita vērō   *yes*
Ītalia, Ītaliae, f.   *Italy*
Ītalicus, Ītalica, Ītalicum   *Italian*
* itaque   *and so*
* iter, itineris, n.   *journey, trip, progress*
* iterum   *again*
iubeō, iubēre, iussī   *order*
Iūdaeī, Iūdaeōrum, m.pl.   *Jews*
* iūdex, iūdicis, m.   *judge*
* iuvenis, iuvenis, m.   *young man*

l

* labōrō, labōrāre, labōrāvī   *work*
lacrima, lacrimae, f.   *tear*
   lacrimīs sē trādere   *burst into tears*
lacrimāns, lacrimāns, lacrimāns, *gen.* lacrimantis   *crying, weeping*
* lacrimō, lacrimāre, lacrimāvī   *cry, weep*
laedō, laedere, laesī   *harm*
* laetus, laeta, laetum   *happy*
languidus, languida, languidum   *weak, feeble*
lapis, lapidis, m.   *stone*
lateō, latēre, latuī   *lie hidden*
lātrō, lātrāre, lātrāvī   *bark*
latrō, latrōnis, m.   *robber*
* lātus, lāta, lātum   *wide*
* laudō, laudāre, laudāvī   *praise*
* lavō, lavāre, lāvī   *wash*
* lectus, lectī, m.   *couch, bed*
legiō, legiōnis, f.   *legion*
lēgō, lēgāre, lēgāvī   *bequeath*
* legō, legere, lēgī   *read*
lēniter   *gently*
* lentē   *slowly*
* leō, leōnis, m.   *lion*
levis, levis, leve   *changeable, inconsistent*
libellus, libellī, m.   *little book*
* libenter   *gladly*
* liber, librī, m.   *book*
* līberālis, līberālis, līberāle   *generous*
līberī, līberōrum, m.pl.   *children*
* līberō, līberāre, līberāvī   *free, set free*
lībertās, lībertātis, f.   *freedom*
* lībertus, lībertī, m.   *freedman, ex-slave*

lībō, lībāre, lībāvī   *pour an offering*
līmōsus, līmōsa, līmōsum   *muddy*
liquō, liquāre, liquāvī   *melt*
* lītus, lītoris, n.   *seashore, shore*
* locus, locī, m.   *place*
Londinium, Londiniī, n.   *London*
longē   *far, a long way*
longus, longa, longum   *long*
loquāx, loquāx, loquāx, *gen.* loquācis   *talkative*
lucrum, lucrī, n.   *profit*
lūdus, lūdī, m.   *game*
   lūdī fūnebrēs   *funeral games*
* lūna, lūnae, f.   *moon*

m

madidus, madida, madidum   *soaked through, drenched*
magicus, magica, magicum   *magic*
   versus magicus, versūs magicī, m.   *magic spell*
magis   *more*
   multō magis   *much more*
magister, magistrī, m.   *foreman*
magnificus, magnifica, magnificum   *splendid, magnificent*
* magnus, magna, magnum   *big, large, great*
maior, maior, maius, *gen.* maiōris   *bigger, larger, greater*
mālus, mālī, m.   *mast*
* māne   *in the morning*
* maneō, manēre, mānsī   *remain, stay*
mānsuētus, mānsuēta, mānsuētum   *tame*
* manus, manūs, f.   *hand*
* mare, maris, n.   *sea*
* marītus, marītī, m.   *husband*
marmoreus, marmorea, marmoreum   *made of marble*
* māter, mātris, f.   *mother*
mātrōna, mātrōnae, f.   *lady*
maximē   *most of all, very much*
* maximus, maxima, maximum   *very big, very large, very great*
* mē SEE ego
medicāmentum, medicāmentī, n.   *ointment, salve*
medicīna, medicīnae, f.   *medicine*

medicus, medicī, m. *doctor*
* medius, media, medium *middle*
  mel, mellis, n. *honey*
* melior *better*
    melius est *it would be better*
* mendāx, mendācis, m. *liar*
* mēnsa, mēnsae, f. *table*
  mēnsis, mēnsis, m. *month*
* mercātor, mercātōris, m. *merchant*
  merx, mercis, f. *goods, merchandise*
  mēta, mētae, f. *turning point*
  metallum, metallī, n. *a mine*
* meus, mea, meum *my, mine*
    mī dulcissime! *my very dear friend!*
    mī Salvī! *my dear Salvius!*
* mihi SEE ego
* mīles, mīlitis, m. *soldier*
  mīlitō, mīlitāre, mīlitāvī *be a soldier*
* minimē! *no!*
  minor, minor, minus *smaller*
* mīrābilis, mīrābilis, mīrābile *marvelous,*
    strange, wonderful
  mīrāculum, mīrāculī, n. *miracle*
* miser, misera, miserum *miserable,*
    wretched, sad
    o mē miserum! *oh wretched me!*
  miserrimus, miserrima, miserrimum
    very sad
* mittō, mittere, mīsī *send*
  modicus, modica, modicum *ordinary,*
    little
  molestus, molesta, molestum
    troublesome
  moneō, monēre, monuī *warn, advise*
* mōns, montis, m. *mountain*
  mōnstrum, mōnstrī, n. *monster*
  monumentum, monumentī, n.
    monument
  moritūrus, moritūra, moritūrum *going*
    to die
* mors, mortis, f. *death*
    mortem īnferre (+ DAT) *bring death*
    (upon)
* mortuus, mortua, mortuum *dead*
  moveō, movēre, mōvī *move*
* mox *soon*
  mulceō, mulcēre, mulsī *pet, pat*
* multitūdō, multitūdinis, f. *crowd*
* multus, multa, multum ` *much*
*   multī, multae, multa *many*

  multō magis *much more*
* mūrus, mūrī, m. *wall*
  mūs, mūris, m.f. *mouse*
  mystēria, mystēriōrum, n.pl. *mysteries,*
    secret worship

n

* nam *for*
* nārrō, nārrāre, nārrāvī *tell, relate*
    rem nārrāre *tell the story*
  natō, natāre, natāvī *swim*
  nātūra, nātūrae, f. *nature*
  naufragium, naufragiī, n. *shipwreck*
  naufragus, naufragī, m. *shipwrecked*
    sailor
* nauta, nautae, m. *sailor*
* nāvigō, nāvigāre, nāvigāvī *sail*
* nāvis, nāvis, f. *ship*
* necesse *necessary*
* necō, necāre, necāvī *kill*
  nefāstus, nefāsta, nefāstum *terrible*
* neglegēns, neglegēns, neglegēns, *gen.*
    neglegentis *careless*
* negōtium, negōtiī, n. *business*
*   negōtium agere *do business, work*
* nēmō *no one, nobody*
  neque … neque *neither … nor*
  nīdus, nīdī, m. *nest*
  niger, nigra, nigrum *black*
* nihil *nothing*
    nihil cūrō *I don't care*
  Nīlus, Nīlī, m. *the river Nile*
  nitidus, nitida, nitidum *gleaming,*
    brilliant
  niveus, nivea, niveum *snow-white*
* nōbilis, nōbilis, nōbile *noble, of noble*
    birth
* nōbīs SEE nōs
  nocēns, nocēns, nocēns, *gen.* nocentis
    guilty
  noceō, nocēre, nocuī (+ DAT) *hurt*
  noctū *by night*
* nōlō, nōlle, nōluī *not want, be*
    unwilling, refuse
    nōlī *do not, don't*
  nōmen, nōminis, n. *name*
    nōmine *named, by name*
* nōn *not*
* nōnne? *surely?*

nōnnūllī, nōnnūllae, nōnnūlla *some, several*

* nōs *we, us*

  nōbīscum *with us*

* noster, nostra, nostrum *our*

* nōtus, nōta, nōtum *well-known, famous*

* novem *nine*

* nōvī *I know*

* novus, nova, novum *new*

* nox, noctis, f. *night*

* nūbēs, nūbis, f. *cloud*

* nūllus, nūlla, nūllum *not any, no*

* num? *surely … not?*

* numerō, numerāre, numerāvī *count*

  numerus, numerī, m. *number*

* numquam *never*

* nunc *now*

* nūntiō, nūntiāre, nūntiāvī *announce*

* nūntius, nūntiī, m. *messenger, message, news*

  nūper *recently*

  nūptiae, nūptiārum, f.pl. *wedding*

o

  obdormiō, obdormīre, obdormīvī *fall asleep*

  obeō, obīre, obiī *meet*

  obruō, obruere, obruī *overwhelm*

  obstinātus, obstināta, obstinātum *stubborn*

* obstō, obstāre, obstitī (+ DAT) *obstruct, block the way*

* obtulī SEE offerō

  occupātus, occupāta, occupātum *busy*

* octō *eight*

* oculus, oculī, m. *eye*

  offendō, offendere, offendī *displease*

* offerō, offerre, obtulī *offer*

  officīna, officīnae, f. *workshop*

* ōlim *once, some time ago*

  ōlla, ōllae, f. *vase*

  omittō, omittere, omīsī *drop*

* omnis, omnis, omne *all*

  omnēs *everyone*

  • omnia *everything*

  operae, operārum, f. pl. *hired thugs*

  opportūnē *just at the right time*

  oppugnō, oppugnāre, oppugnāvī *attack*

* optimē *very well*

* optimus, optima, optimum *very good, excellent, best*

* ōrdō, ōrdinis, m. *row, line*

  ōrnāmentum, ōrnāmentī, n. *ornament*

  ōrnātrīx, ōrnātrīcis, f. *hairdresser*

  ōrnātus, ōrnāta, ōrnātum *decorated, elaborately furnished*

  ōrnō, ōrnāre, ōrnāvī *decorate*

  ōsculum, ōsculī, n. *kiss*

* ostendō, ostendere, ostendī *show*

  ostrea, ostreae, f. *oyster*

  ōtiōsus, ōtiōsa, ōtiōsum *at leisure, with time off, idle, on vacation*

  ōvum, ōvī, n. *egg*

p

* paene *nearly, almost*

  palaestra, palaestrae, f. *palaestra, exercise ground*

  palūs, palūdis, f. *marsh, swamp*

* parātus, parāta, parātum *ready, prepared*

  parēns, parentis, m.f. *parent*

  pāreō, pārēre, pāruī (+ DAT) *obey*

* parō, parāre, parāvī *prepare*

* pars, partis, f. *part*

  in prīmā parte *in the forefront*

* parvus, parva, parvum *small*

* pater, patris, m. *father*

  patera, paterae, f. *bowl*

* paucī, paucae, pauca *few, a few*

  paulātim *gradually*

* paulīsper *for a short time*

  paulum, paulī, n. *little, a little*

  pavīmentum, pavīmentī, n. *floor*

* pāx, pācis, f. *peace*

* pecūnia, pecūniae, f. *money*

  pendeō, pendēre, pependī *hang*

* per (+ ACC) *through, along*

  percutiō, percutere, percussī *strike*

* pereō, perīre, periī *die, perish*

  perīculōsus, perīculōsa, perīculōsum *dangerous*

* perīculum, perīculī, n. *danger*

  perītē *skillfully*

  perītia, perītiae, f. *skill*

  perītus, perīta, perītum *skillful*

* persuādeō, persuādēre, persuāsī (+ DAT) *persuade*

perterritus, perterrita, perterritum
    terrified

* pervenio, pervenire, perveni   *reach,*
    arrive at
* pes, pedis, m.   *foot, paw*
* pessimus, pessima, pessimum   *very bad,*
    worst
* pestis, pestis, f.   *pest, rascal*
* peto, petere, petivi   *head for, attack; seek,*
    beg for, ask for
pharus, phari, m.   *lighthouse*
philosophus, philosophi, m.   *philosopher*
pica, picae, f.   *magpie*
pictor, pictoris, m.   *painter, artist*
pictura, picturae, f.   *painting, picture*
pila, pilae, f.   *ball*
pingo, pingere, pinxi   *paint*
pius, pia, pium   *respectful to the gods*
* placeo, placere, placui (+ DAT)   *please,*
    suit
placidus, placida, placidum   *calm,*
    peaceful
plane   *clearly*
* plaudo, plaudere, plausi   *applaud, clap*
* plaustrum, plaustri, n.   *wagon, cart*
plenus, plena, plenum   *full*
pluit, pluere, pluit   *rain*
* plurimus, plurima, plurimum   *very*
    much, most
* plurimi, plurimae, plurima   *very*
    many
plus, pluris, n.   *more*
* poculum, poculi, n.   *cup (often for wine)*
poena, poenae, f.   *punishment*
    poenas dare   *pay the penalty, be*
    punished
* poeta, poetae, m.   *poet*
pompa, pompae, f.   *procession*
Pompeianus, Pompeiana, Pompeianum
    Pompeian
* pono, ponere, posui   *put, place, put up*
pontifex, pontificis, m.   *high priest*
* porta, portae, f.   *gate*
portans, portans, portans, *gen.* portantis
    carrying
* porto, portare, portavi   *carry*
* portus, portus, m.   *harbor*
* posco, poscere, poposci   *demand, ask for*
possideo, possidere, possedi   *possess*
* possum, posse, potui   *can, be able*

* post (+ ACC)   *after, behind*
* postea   *afterwards*
* postquam   *after, when*
* postremo   *finally, lastly*
* postridie   *(on) the next day*
* postulo, postulare, postulavi   *demand*
* posui SEE pono
* potui SEE possum
praeceps, praeceps, praeceps, *gen.*
    praecipitis   *straight for, headlong*
praecursor, praecursoris, m.   *forerunner*
praedium, praedii, n.   *estate*
praemium, praemii, n.   *profit, prize,*
    reward
praeruptus, praerupta, praeruptum
    steep
* praesidium, praesidii, n.   *protection*
* praesum, praeesse, praefui (+ DAT)   *be in*
    charge of
praetereo, praeterire, praeterii   *go past*
pravus, prava, pravum   *evil*
* preces, precum, f.pl.   *prayers*
    preces adhibere   *offer prayers*
premo, premere, pressi   *push*
pretiosus, pretiosa, pretiosum
    expensive, precious
pretium, pretii, n.   *price*
primo   *first*
* primus, prima, primum   *first*
    in prima parte   *in the forefront*
* princeps, principis, m.   *chief, chieftain*
prior   *first, in front*
* pro (+ ABL)   *in front of*
    pro di immortales!   *heavens above!*
probus, proba, probum   *honest*
* procedo, procedere, processi   *advance,*
    proceed
procul   *far off*
procumbo, procumbere, procubui   *fall*
    down
* promitto, promittere, promisi   *promise*
* prope (+ ACC)   *near*
prosilio, prosilire, prosilui   *leap forward*
provideo, providere, providi   *foresee*
proximus, proxima, proximum   *nearest*
psittacus, psittaci, m.   *parrot*
* puella, puellae, f.   *girl*
* puer, pueri, m.   *boy*
pugil, pugilis, m.   *boxer*
pugio, pugionis, m.   *dagger*

* pugna, pugnae, f. *fight*
  pugnāns, pugnāns, pugnāns, *gen.*
      pugnantis *fighting*
* pugnō, pugnāre, pugnāvī *fight*
* pulcher, pulchra, pulchrum *beautiful*
* pulsō, pulsāre, pulsāvī *hit, knock on,*
      whack, punch
  pūmiliō, pūmiliōnis, m.f. *dwarf*
* pūniō, pūnīre, pūnīvī *punish*
  puppis, puppis, f. *stern*
  pūrus, pūra, pūrum *clean, spotless*
  putō, putāre, putāvī *think, consider*

q

* quā *whom*
* quadrāgintā *forty*
* quae *who, which*
  quaerēns, quaerēns, quaerēns, *gen.*
      quaerentis *searching for, looking for*
* quaerō, quaerere, quaesīvī *search for,*
      look for, inquire
* quam (1) *how*
* quam (2) *than*
      quam celerrimē *as quickly as possible*
* quam (3) *whom, which*
* quamquam *although*
  quārtus, quārta, quārtum *fourth*
* quās *whom, which*
* quattuor *four*
* -que *and*
* quem *whom, which*
* quī, quae, quod *who, which*
* quid? *what?*
      quid agis? *how are you?*
      quid vīs? *what do you want?*
  quīdam, quaedam, quoddam *one, a*
      certain
  quidquam *anything*
  quiēscō, quiēscere, quiēvī *rest*
  quiētus, quiēta, quiētum *quiet*
  quīndecim *fifteen*
  quīngentī, quīngentae, quingenta *five*
      hundred
* quīnquāgintā *fifty*
* quīnque *five*
* quis? *who?*
* quō? (1) *where? where to?*
* quō (2) *whom*
  quō modō? *how?*

* quod (1) *because*
* quod (2) *which*
* quondam *one day, once*
* quoque *also, too*
* quōs *whom, which*
  quot? *how many?*
  quotannīs *every year*

r

  rādō, rādere, rāsī *scratch, scrape*
* rapiō, rapere, rapuī *seize, grab*
  rārō *rarely*
  raucus, rauca, raucum *harsh*
  recidō, recidere, reccidī *fall back*
* recipiō, recipere, recēpī *recover, take back*
      sē recipere *recover*
  recitāns, recitāns, recitāns, *gen.* recitantis
      reciting
  recitō, recitāre, recitāvī *recite*
  rēctā *directly, straight*
  rēctus, rēcta, rēctum *straight*
  recumbēns, recumbēns, recumbēns, *gen.*
      recumbentis *lying down, reclining*
* recumbō, recumbere, recubuī *lie down,*
      recline
* recūsō, recūsāre, recūsāvī *refuse*
* reddō, reddere, reddidī *give back*
* redeō, redīre, rediī *return, go back, come*
      back
      domum redīre *return home*
  referō, referre, rettulī *carry, deliver*
  reficiō, reficere, refēcī *repair*
  rēgīna, rēgīnae, f. *queen*
  regiō, regiōnis, f. *region*
* relinquō, relinquere, relīquī *leave*
* remedium, remediī, n. *cure*
  rēmus, rēmī, m. *oar*
  renovō, renovāre, renovāvī *restore*
  reportō, reportāre, reportāvī *carry back*
* rēs, reī, f. *thing, affair*
      rem cōnficere *finish the job*
      rem intellegere *understand the truth*
      rem nārrāre *tell the story*
      rēs rūstica *the farming*
* resistō, resistere, restitī (+ DAT) *resist*
* respondeō, respondēre, respondī *reply*
  respōnsum, respōnsī, n. *answer*
* retineō, retinēre, retinuī *keep, hold back*
  retrahō, retrahere, retrāxī *drag back*

* reveniō, revenīre, revēnī *come back, return*
* rēx, rēgis, m. *king*
rhētor, rhētoris, m. *teacher*
* rīdeō, rīdēre, rīsī *laugh, smile*
rīpa, rīpae, f. *river bank*
rōbustus, rōbusta, rōbustum *strong*
* rogō, rogāre, rogāvī *ask*
rogus, rogī, m. *pyre*
Rōmānus, Rōmāna, Rōmānum *Roman*
rosa, rosae, f. *rose*
rota, rotae, f. *wheel*
rudēns, rudentis, m. *cable, rope*
* ruō, ruere, ruī *rush*
rūsticus, rūstica, rūsticum *country, in the country*
    rēs rūstica *the farming*

s

saccus, saccī, m. *bag, purse*
* sacer, sacra, sacrum *sacred*
* sacerdōs, sacerdōtis, m. *priest*
sacrificium, sacrificiī, n. *offering, sacrifice*
sacrificō, sacrificāre, sacrificāvī *sacrifice*
* saepe *often*
* saeviō, saevīre, saeviī *be in a rage*
saevus, saeva, saevum *savage*
saltātrīx, saltātrīcis, f. *dancing-girl*
saltō, saltāre, saltāvī *dance*
* salūtō, salūtāre, salūtāvī *greet*
* salvē! *hello!*
sānē *obviously*
* sanguis, sanguinis, m. *blood*
sānō, sānāre, sānāvī *heal, cure*
sapiēns, sapiēns, sapiēns, *gen.* sapientis *wise*
* satis *enough*
* saxum, saxī, n. *rock*
scapha, scaphae, f. *small boat*
scelestus, scelesta, scelestum *wicked*
scēptrum, scēptrī, n. *scepter*
scindō, scindere, scidī *tear, tear up*
scio, scīre, scīvī *know*
scōpae, scōpārum, f.pl. *broom*
* scrībō, scrībere, scrīpsī *write*
scrīptor, scrīptōris, m. *writer, sign-writer*
scurrīlis, scurrīlis, scurrīle *obscene, dirty*

* sē *himself, herself, themselves*
    sēcum *with him, with her, with them*
secō, secāre, secuī *cut*
* secundus, secunda, secundum *second*
    ventus secundus *favorable wind, following wind*
sēcūrus, sēcūra, sēcūrum *without a care*
* sed *but*
sedēns, sedēns, sedēns, *gen.* sedentis *sitting*
* sedeō, sedēre, sēdī *sit*
seges, segetis, f. *crop, harvest*
sella, sellae, f. *chair*
sēmirutus, sēmiruta, sēmirutum *half-collapsed*
* semper *always*
* senātor, senātōris, m. *senator*
* senex, senis, m. *old man*
* sententia, sententiae, f. *opinion*
* sentiō, sentīre, sēnsī *feel, notice*
* septem *seven*
sēricus, sērica, sēricum *silk*
* sermō, sermōnis, m. *conversation*
serviō, servīre, servīvī (and serviī) *serve (as a slave)*
* servō, servāre, servāvī *save, protect*
* servus, servī, m. *slave*
* sex *six*
sī *if*
* sibi *to him (self), to her (self), to them (selves)*
* sīcut *like*
signātor, signātōris, m. *witness*
signō, signāre, signāvī *sign, seal*
* signum, signī, n. *sign, seal, signal*
silentium, silentiī, n. *silence*
* silva, silvae, f. *woods, forest*
* simulac, simulatque *as soon as*
* sine (+ ABL) *without*
sistrum, sistrī, n. *sistrum, sacred rattle*
situs, sita, situm *situated*
situs, sitūs, m. *position, site*
sōl, sōlis, m. *sun*
* soleō, solēre *be accustomed, usually*
sollemniter *solemnly*
sollicitūdō, sollicitūdinis, f. *anxiety*
* sollicitus, sollicita, sollicitum *worried, anxious*
sōlum *only*

* sōlus, sōla, sōlum *alone, lonely, only, on one's own*
  solūtus, solūta, solūtum *untied, cast off*
  solvō, solvere, solvī *untie, cast off*
  somnium, somniī, n. *dream*
* sonitus, sonitūs, m. *sound*
  sonō, sonāre, sonuī *sound*
  sonus, sonī, m. *sound*
  sordidus, sordida, sordidum *dirty*
  spargō, spargere, sparsī *scatter*
  sparsus, sparsa, sparsum *scattered*
* spectāculum, spectāculī, n. *show, spectacle*
  spectātor, spectātōris, m. *spectator*
* spectō, spectāre, spectāvī *look at, watch*
  splendidus, splendida, splendidum *splendid*
  spongia, spongiae, f. *sponge*
  stāns, stāns, stāns, gen. stantis *standing*
* statim *at once*
  statua, statuae, f. *statue*
  stilus, stilī, m. *pen, stick*
* stō, stāre, stetī *stand*
  stola, stolae, f. *(long) dress*
  studeō, studēre, studuī (+ DAT) *study*
  stultē *stupidly, foolishly*
* stultus, stulta, stultum *stupid, foolish*
  suāvis, suāvis, suāve *sweet*
  suāviter *sweetly*
  sub (+ ABL) *under*
* subitō *suddenly*
  sūdō, sūdāre, sūdāvī *sweat*
  sufficiō, sufficere, suffēcī *be enough*
* sum, esse, fuī *be*
  summergō, summergere, summersī *sink, dip*
  summersus, summersa, summersum *sunk*
* summus, summa, summum *highest, greatest, top*
  superbus, superba, superbum *arrogant, proud*
* superō, superāre, superāvī *overcome, overpower, overtake*
* supersum, superesse, superfuī *survive*
  supplicium, suppliciī, n. *death penalty*
  surdus, surda, surdum *deaf*
* surgō, surgere, surrēxī *get up, stand up, rise*

suscipiō, suscipere, suscēpī *undertake, take on*
* sustulī SEE tollō
  susurrāns, susurrāns, susurrāns, gen. susurrantis *whispering, mumbling*
  susurrō, susurrāre, susurrāvī *whisper, mumble*
* suus, sua, suum *his (own), her (own), their (own)*
  Syrī, Syrōrum, m.pl. *Syrians*
  Syrius, Syria, Syrium *Syrian*

t

* taberna, tabernae, f. *store, shop, inn*
  tabernārius, tabernāriī, m. *store-owner, storekeeper, shopkeeper*
  tablīnum, tablīnī, n. *study*
* taceō, tacēre, tacuī *be silent, be quiet*
    tacē! *shut up! be quiet!*
* tacitē *quietly, silently*
  tacitus, tacita, tacitum *quiet, silent, in silence*
* tam *so*
* tamen *however*
* tandem *at last*
  tangō, tangere, tetigī *touch*
  tantus, tanta, tantum *so great, such a great*
  tardus, tarda, tardum *late*
  taurus, taurī, m. *bull*
* tē SEE tū
  tempestās, tempestātis, f. *storm*
* templum, templī, n. *temple*
* temptō, temptāre, temptāvī *try*
  tenēns, tenēns, tenēns, gen. tenentis *holding, owning*
* teneō, tenēre, tenuī *hold, own*
  tepidārium, tepidāriī, n. *warm room (at the baths)*
  tergeō, tergēre, tersī *wipe*
  tergum, tergī, n. *back*
    ā tergō *from behind, in the rear*
* terra, terrae, f. *ground, land*
* terreō, terrēre, terruī *frighten*
  terribilis, terribilis, terribile *terrible*
* tertius, tertia, tertium *third*
  testāmentum, testāmentī, n. *will*
  theātrum, theātrī, n. *theater*
  thermae, thermārum, f. pl. *the baths*

* tibi SEE tū
tībīcen, tībīcinis, m.   *pipe player*
* timeō, timēre, timuī   *be afraid, fear*
timidus, timida, timidum   *fearful, frightened*
* toga, togae, f.   *toga*
* tollō, tollere, sustulī   *raise, lift up, hold up*
* tot   *so many*
* tōtus, tōta, tōtum   *whole*
tractō, tractāre, tractāvī   *handle*
* trādō, trādere, trādidī   *hand over*
lacrimīs sē trādere   *burst into tears*
tragoedia, tragoediae, f.   *tragedy*
* trahō, trahere, trāxī   *drag*
tranquillitās, tranquillitātis, f.   *calmness, serenity*
trānseō, trānsīre, trānsiī   *cross*
trānsfīgō, trānsfīgere, trānsfīxī   *pierce*
* trēs, trēs, tria   *three*
* triclīnium, triclīniī, n.   *dining-room*
* trīgintā   *thirty*
tripodes, tripodum, m.pl. (acc. pl.: tripodas)   *tripods*
trīstis, trīstis, trīste   *sad*
trivium, triviī, n.   *crossroads*
trūdō, trūdere, trūsī   *push, shove*
* tū, tuī   *you (singular)*
tēcum   *with you (singular)*
* tuba, tubae, f.   *trumpet*
tubicen, tubicinis, m.   *trumpeter*
* tulī SEE ferō
* tum   *then*
tumultus, tumultūs, m.   *riot*
* tunica, tunicae, f.   *tunic*
* turba, turbae, f.   *crowd*
turbulentus, turbulenta, turbulentum   *rowdy, disorderly*
tūtus, tūta, tūtum   *safe*
tūtius est   *it would be safer*
* tuus, tua, tuum   *your, yours*

u

* ubi   *where, when*
ultor, ultōris, m.   *avenger*
* umbra, umbrae, f.   *ghost, shadow*
* umerus, umerī, m.   *shoulder*
* unda, undae, f.   *wave*
unde   *from where*
unguentum, unguentī, n.   *perfume*

unguis, unguis, m.   *claw*
unguō, unguere, ūnxī   *anoint, smear*
* ūnus, ūna, ūnum   *one*
urbānus, urbāna, urbānum   *fashionable, sophisticated*
* urbs, urbis, f.   *city*
urna, urnae, f.   *bucket, jar, jug*
ursa, ursae, f.   *bear*
ut   *as*
* ūtilis, ūtilis, ūtile   *useful*
* uxor, uxōris, f.   *wife*

v

* valdē   *very much, very*
* valē   *good-by*
valvae, valvārum, f.pl.   *doors*
varius, varia, varium   *different*
* vehementer   *violently, loudly*
vehō, vehere, vēxī   *carry*
* vēnātiō, vēnātiōnis, f.   *hunt*
* vēndō, vēndere, vēndidī   *sell*
venia, veniae, f.   *mercy, forgiveness*
* veniō, venīre, vēnī   *come*
ventus, ventī, m.   *wind*
ventus secundus   *a favorable wind*
vēr, vēris, n.   *spring*
* verberō, verberāre, verberāvī   *strike, beat*
verrō, verrere   *sweep*
versus, versūs, m.   *verse, line of poetry*
versus magicus, versūs magicī, m.   *magic spell*
* vertō, vertere, vertī   *turn*
sē vertere   *turn around*
vērus, vēra, vērum   *true, real*
vestiō, vestīre, vestīvī   *dress*
* vexō, vexāre, vexāvī   *annoy*
* via, viae, f.   *street*
vibrō, vibrāre, vibrāvī   *wave, brandish*
vīcīnus, vīcīna, vīcīnum   *neighboring, nearby*
victima, victimae, f.   *victim*
victor, victōris, m.   *victor, winner*
vīcus, vīcī, m.   *village*
* videō, vidēre, vīdī   *see*
* vīgintī   *twenty*
vīlicus, vīlicī, m.   *overseer, manager*
vīlis, vīlis, vīle   *cheap*
* vīlla, vīllae, f.   *villa, (large) house*
* vincō, vincere, vīcī   *win, be victorious*

vindex, vindicis, m. *champion, defender*
vindicō, vindicāre, vindicāvī *avenge*
* vīnum, vīnī, n. *wine*
* vir, virī, m. *man*
  virga, virgae, f. *rod, stick*
  vīs, f. *force, violence*
    vim īnferre *use force, violence*
* vīs SEE volō
  vīsitō, vīsitāre, vīsitāvī *visit*
* vīta, vītae, f. *life*
  vītō, vītāre, vītāvī *avoid*
  vitreārius, vitreāriī, m. *glassmaker*
  vitreus, vitrea, vitreum *glass, made of*
    glass
  vitrum, vitrī, n. *glass*
* vituperō, vituperāre, vituperāvī *find*
    fault with, tell off, curse
* vīvō, vīvere, vīxī *live, be alive*
* vix *hardly, scarcely, with difficulty*
* vōbīs SEE vōs
* vocō, vocāre, vocāvī *call*
* volō, velle, voluī *want*
    quid vīs? *what do you want?*
* vōs *you (plural)*
    vōbīscum *with you (plural)*
* vōx, vōcis, f. *voice*
  vulnerātus, vulnerāta, vulnerātum
    wounded
* vulnerō, vulnerāre, vulnerāvī *wound,*
    injure
* vulnus, vulneris, n. *wound*
* vult SEE volō

Z

  zōna, zōnae, f. *belt*

Index of Cultural Topics

The page references are for illustrations and for the Cultural Background sections at the ends of the Stages.

Index of Grammatical Topics

Time Chart

Date	Alexandria and Britain	Rome and Italy
B.C. c. 2500	Salisbury Plain inhabited	
c. 2200–1300	Stonehenge built	
c. 1900	Tin first used in Britain	
c. 1450	Wessex invaded from Europe	
c. 900	Celts move into Britain	
c. 750	Plow introduced into Britain	Rome founded (traditional date) 753
post 500	Maiden Castle, Iron Age fort in Britain	Kings expelled and Republic begins, 509
		Duodecim Tabulae, 450
4th C	Hill forts used by Celts	Gauls capture Rome, 390
331	Alexandria founded	
311–285	Ptolemy Soter, first Greek ruler in Egypt	Rome controls Italy/Punic Wars, 300–200
280	Ptolemy II builds Pharos	Hannibal crosses the Alps, 218
c. 250	Septuagint (translation of Bible), Alexandria	Rome expands outside Italy, 200–100
post 240	Eratosthenes, scientist/librarian	Gracchi and agrarian reforms, 133–123
		Cicero, Roman orator (106–43)
55–54	Julius Caesar invades Britain	
48–47	Julius Caesar in Alexandria	Julius Caesar assassinated, 44
41–42	Marc Antony and Cleopatra in Alexandria	Augustus becomes emperor, 27
31	Egypt becomes a Roman province	Vergil, author of the *Aeneid*, 70–19
13	Obelisks re-erected before Caesareum	
A.D. 1st C	Alexandrians use monsoon pattern to India	Tiberius becomes emperor, 14
60	Boudica leads Iceni revolt	Nero emperor, 54–68
		Great Fire at Rome/Christians blamed, 64
		Vespasian emperor, 69–79
c. 75	Fishbourne Palace begun	Colosseum begun, c. 72
78–84	Agricola governor in Britain	Titus emperor, 79–81
c. 80	Salvius arrives in Britain	Vesuvius erupts, 79
2nd C	Galen studies in Alexandria	Tacitus, historian, c. 56–117
		Domitian emperor, 81–96
c. 200		Trajan emperor, 98–117
296	Origen, Christian scholar in Alexandria	Hadrian emperor, 117–138
328	Diocletian besieges Alexandria	Septimius Severus dies in Britain, 211
391	Athanasius, bishop in Alexandria	Constantine tolerates Christianity, 313
c. 400	Serapeum and Daughter Library destroyed	Bible translated into Latin, c. 385
410	Hypatia, woman philosopher in Alexandria	Alaric the Goth sacks Rome, 410
	Rome refuses Britain help against Saxons	Last Roman Emperor deposed, 476

World History	World Culture	Date
Babylonian/Sumerian Civilizations		B.C. c. 3000
Pharaohs in Egypt		c. 3000–332
Indo-European migrations, c. 2100	Maize cultivation, American SW	c. 2000
Hammurabi's Legal Code, c. 1750	Epic of Gilgamesh	post 2000
Minoan Civilization at its height, c. 1500	Rig-Veda verses (Hinduism) collected	c. 1500
Israelite exodus from Egypt, c. 1250	Development of Hinduism	c. 1450
Israel and Judah split, c. 922	Phoenician alphabet adapted by Greeks	c. 1000–800
Kush/Meroe Kingdom expands	*Iliad* and *Odyssey*	c. 800
	First Olympic Games	776
Solon, Athenian lawgiver, 594	Buddha	c. 563–483
	Confucius	551–479
Persia invades Egypt and Greece, c. 525–400	Golden Age of Greece	500–400
	Death of Socrates	399
Conquests of Alexander the Great		335–323
	Museum founded in Alexandria	290
Great Wall of China built		c. 221
Judas Maccabaeus regains Jerusalem	Feast of Hanukkah inaugurated	165
	Adena Serpent Mound, Ohio	2nd C
		106–43
Julius Caesar in Gaul, 58–49	Canal locks exist in China	50
	Glass blowing begins in Sidon	post 50
Cleopatra commits suicide		30
Herod rebuilds the Temple, Jerusalem		c. 20
Roman boundary at Danube, 15	Birth of Jesus	c. 4
	Crucifixion of Jesus	A.D. c. 29
Britain becomes a Roman province, 43	St. Peter in Rome	42–67
	St. Paul's missionary journeys	45–67
	Camel introduced into the Sahara	1st C
		64
Sack of Jerusalem and the Temple		70
Roman control extends to Scotland		77–85
	Paper invented in China	c. 100
		c. 56–117
	Construction at Teotihuacán begins	c. 100
Roman Empire at its greatest extent		98–117
Hadrian's Wall in Britain		122–127
"High Kings" of Ireland		c. 200–1022
Byzantium renamed Constantinople, 330	Golden Age of Guptan Civilization, India	c. 320–540
	Last ancient Olympic Games	393
Mayan Civilization		c. 300–1200
Byzantine Empire expands		518

Date	Alexandria and Britain	Rome and Italy
? 537	Death of King Arthur	Gregory the Great, Pope, 590–604
9th–10th C	Saxon forts against the Vikings	Period of turmoil in Italy, 800–1100
c. 900	Alfred drives Danes from England	Republic of St. Mark, Venice, 850
973	Cairo replaces Alexandria as capital	
1189–1199	Richard the Lionheart	
12th C	Robin Hood legends circulated	Independent government in Rome, 1143–1455
1258	Salisbury Cathedral finished	Marco Polo travels to the East, 1271–1295
1346	Battle of Crecy, cannon first used	Dante, poet, 1265–1321
1348	Black Death begins	Renaissance begins in Italy, c. 1400
1485	Henry VII, first Tudor king	Botticelli, painter, 1445–1510
1509–1547	Henry VIII	
1517	Ottomans conquer Egypt	Titian, painter, 1489–1576
		Rebuilding of St. Peter's begins, 1506
		Michelangelo starts Sistine Chapel ceiling, 1508
1558–1603	Elizabeth I	Rome sacked by German/Spanish troops, 1527
1577–1580	Drake circumnavigates the globe	Spain controls much of Italy, 1530–1796
1588	Defeat of Spanish Armada	
1603	James I, first Stuart king	
1649	Charles I executed	Galileo invents the telescope, 1610
1649–1659	Cromwellian Protectorate	Bernini, architect and sculptor, 1598–1680
1660	Restoration of Charles II	
1675	Wren begins St. Paul's Cathedral	
1760–1820	George III	
1789	Wilberforce moves to end slave trade	
1795–1821	John Keats, poet	
1796	Smallpox vaccination in England	Napoleon enters Italy, 1796
1798	Napoleon invades Alexandria	Verdi, composer, 1813–1901
1798	Nelson defeats French at the Nile	
1807	Mohammed Ali develops Alexandria	
1833	Factory Act limits child labor in Britain	Mazzini, Garibaldi, Cavour, active 1846–1861
1837–1901	Victoria, queen	Victor Emmanuel II, United Italy, 1861
1844	Railways begin in Britain	
1863–1933	Cavafy, Alexandrian poet	
1869	Suez Canal opened	
1882	British occupation of Egypt	Marconi invents wireless telegraphy, 1896
1911	N. Mafouz born, Nobel winner	
1924	Egypt declares independence	Mussolini controls Italy, 1922–1945
1940	Churchill Prime Minister	
1944	Arab League starts in Alexandria	Italy a Republic, 1946

World History	World Culture	Date
	Birth of Mohammed	570
Charlemagne crowned, 800	Arabs adopt Indian numerals	c. 771
Vikings reach America, c. 1000	*1001 Nights* collected in Iraq	ante 942
Norman invasion of England, 1066	*Tale of Genji*, Japan	1010
First Crusade, 1096	Ife-Benin art, Nigeria	1100–1600
Magna Carta, 1215	Classic Pueblo Cliff dwellings	1050–1300
Genghis Khan, 1162–1227	Al-Idrisi, Arab geographer	1100–1166
Mali Empire expands, 1235	Arabs use black (gun) powder in a gun	1304
Joan of Arc dies, 1431	Chaucer's *Canterbury Tales*	ante 1400
Inca Empire expands, 1438	Gutenberg Bible printed	1456
Turks capture Constantinople, 1453	Building at Zimbabwe	c. 15th C–c. 1750
Moors driven from Spain, 1492	Vasco da Gama sails to India	1497–1498
Columbus arrives in America, 1492		
	Martin Luther writes 95 Theses	1517
Cortez conquers Mexico		1519–1522
Mogul Dynasty established	Magellan names Pacific Ocean	1520
French settlements in Canada, 1534	Copernicus publishes heliocentric theory	1543
	Shakespeare	1564–1616
Burmese Empire at a peak	Muskets first used in Japan	c. 1580
Continuing Dutch activity in the East	Cervantes publishes *Don Quixote*	1605
Pilgrims land at Plymouth Rock, 1620	Taj Mahal begun	1632
Manchu Dynasty, China, 1644–1912	Palace of Versailles begun	1661
Peter the Great rules Russia, 1682–1725	Newton discovers the Law of Gravity	1682
	J. S. Bach, composer	1685–1750
Industrial Revolution begins, c. 1760	Mozart, composer, 1756–1791	c. 1760
US Declaration of Independence	Quakers refuse to own slaves	1776
French Revolution begins	Washington, US President	1789
Napoleon defeated at Waterloo	Bolivar continues struggle, S. America	1815
Mexico becomes a Republic, 1824	S. B. Anthony, women's rights advocate	1820–1906
American Civil War, 1861–1865	Communist manifesto	1848
Lincoln's *Emancipation Proclamation*		1863
Canada becomes a Dominion	French Impressionism begins	1867
Serfdom abolished in Russia, 1861	Mahatma Gandhi	1869–1948
Cetewayo, King of the Zulus, 1872	Edison invents phonograph	1877
	First modern Olympic Games	1896
First World War, 1914–1918	Model T Ford constructed	1909
Bolshevik Revolution in Russia, 1918	Bohr theory of the atom	1913
	US Constitution gives women the vote	1920
Second World War		1939–1945
United Nations Charter		1945

Acknowledgments

Thanks are due to the following for permission to reproduce photographs:

p. 1, Grahame Soffe; p. 5 *l*, p. 17 *r*, Cambridge University Museum of Archaeology and Anthropology; p. 5 *r*, by permission of the National Museum of Wales; p. 10 *l*, p. 38, St Albans Museums; p. 17 *l*, p. 18 *br*, p. 19 *b*/p. 23 *r 2nd from t*, p. 23 *br*, p. 25, p. 46 *tr, cr*, p. 48 *l*, p. 49, p. 91, p. 96 *l*, p. 99 *c*, p. 108 *l*, p. 119 *all*, p. 133, p. 134 *tl*, p. 137/p. 157 *l*, p. 155 *c*, p. 161/p. 176 *t*, p. 172, p. 175, p. 176 *b*, p. 178, p. 179 *tr, br*, © The British Museum; p. 17 *c*, p. 26, Institute of Archaeology, University of Oxford; p. 20, p. 50, Colchester Museums; p. 21, Cambridge University Committee for Aerial Photography; p. 23 *r 2nd from b*/p. 84, p. 71, p. 76, p. 83, p. 85 *tc, bl*, p. 86 *cr, b*, p. 87 *r*, p. 90, Fishbourne Roman Palace/Sussex Archaeological Society; p. 27, p. 33, p. 179 *l*, Courtesy of the Museum of London; p. 45 *t*, Dr Simon James; p. 45 *c, b*, © Estate of Alan Sorrell/English Heritage Photographic Library; p. 46 *b*, Dr PJ Reynolds/Butser Ancient Farm; p. 48 *r*, Courtesy of the Yorkshire Museum; p. 65, Bob Croxford/Atmosphere; p. 68 *t, br*, Francesca Radcliffe; p. 68 *bl*, Society of Antiquaries of London; p. 69, The Saxifrage Society; p. 70, Dorset County Museum; p. 79, John Deakin; p. 99 *r*, p. 140 *l*, Don Flear; p. 101, p. 107 *b*, p. 110 *t, bl*, Stéphane Compoint/Corbis Sygma; p. 103, © IFAO/Alain Leclerc; p. 104, p. 107 *tl, tr*, Jean-Claude Golvin, *Le Phare d'Alexandrie*, coll. Découvertes Gallimard, © Editions Gallimard Jeunesse; p. 108 *r*, GoJourney.com; p. 109, The Estate of Carl Sagan; p. 112, Centre d'Etudes Alexandrines; p. 115 *r*, © Photo RMN/Richard Lambert; p. 123, p. 127 *b*, p. 128, p. 129, p. 130 *l*, p. 131 *t*, The Corning Museum of Glass, Corning, NY; p. 134 *br*, The National Gallery, London; p. 141, Württembergisches Landesmuseum, Stuttgart; p. 153, p. 158 *tr*, Rex Features Limited; p. 155 *br*, Michael Holford; p. 158 *tl*, The Metropolitan Museum of Art, Gift of Edward S. Harkness, 1917 (17.9.1) Photograph © 1992 The Metropolitan Museum of Art; p. 158 *b*, Scala; p. 180, © Photo RMN/H Lewandowski/Musée du Louvre.

Other photography by Roger Dalladay. Thanks are due to the following for permission to reproduce photographs:

p. 6, Dr Gerald Brodribb/Beauport Park; p. 10 *r*, p. 140 *r*, p. 169, Bardo Museum, Tunis; p. 18 *l*/p. 23 *tr*, p. 18 *tr*/p. 23 *tl*, p. 23 *bl*/p. 68 *inset*, p. 85 *tr*, p. 111, p. 132 *bl*, p. 150, p. 151, p. 154 *l*, p. 156, p. 157 *r*, p. 183, Museo Archeologico Nazionale, Naples; p. 19 *r*, Musei Capitolini, Rome; p. 22 *br*, p. 37, p. 41, p. 99 *l*, p. 105, p. 115 *l*, p. 127 *t*, p. 130 *r*, p. 134 *b 2nd from r*, p. 154 *r*, p. 155 *bl*, The British Museum; p. 31, p. 67 *r*, p. 74, Rheinisches Landesmuseum, Trier; p. 67 *l*, Sousse Museum; p. 77, Villa Romana del Casale, Piazza Armerina; p. 85 *tl, br*, p. 86 *tl, tr, cl, b*, p. 87 *l*, p. 88 *all*, Fishbourne Roman Palace/Sussex Archaeological Society; p. 118, p. 136, Museo Nazionale Romano, Rome; p. 134 *t 2nd from l, t 2nd from r, tr*, Musée du Louvre, Paris; p. 134 *b 2nd from l*, Pushkin Museum, Moscow; p. 146, National Archaeological Museum of Sperlonga; p. 164, Monumenti, Musei e Gallerie Pontificie, Vatican City.

Every effort has been made to reach copyright holders. The publishers would be glad to hear from anyone whose rights they have unknowingly infringed.